MAKING THIS BOOK

Books contain multitudes. Mattering Press is keen to render more visible the otherwise invisible processes and people that make our books. Our gratitude goes to our readers, for books are nothing without them and our supporters for helping us to keep our commons open. We thank the editors and contributors, and the reviewers Jamie Lorimer and Ann H. Kelly. Further, we thank Tilly O'Neill, Monique Horstmann and Steven Lovatt for the copy-editing; Jennifer Tomomitsu for the manuscript formatting; Tetragon Publishing for the type-setting and design; Julien McHardy for the cover design; Will Roscoe for our website and for maintaining our books online; Anna Dowrick for caring for the book's promotion and for its community of readers and contributors; and Uli Beisel and Michaela Spencer who acted as the production editors for this book.

WITH
MICROBES

EDITED BY
CHARLOTTE BRIVES,
MATTHÄUS REST
AND **SALLA SARIOLA**

 Mattering Press

First edition published by Mattering Press, Manchester.

Copyright © Charlotte Brives, Matthäus Rest and Salla Sariola, chapters by respective authors, 2021.

Cover photo: A variety of soil bacteria colonies growing on agar in a Petri dish. Oksana Lastochkina, 2015, CC BY-SA 4.0.

Cover design © Julien McHardy, 2021.

Freely available online at https://www.matteringpress.org/books/with-microbes

ISBN: 978-1-912729-18-0 (pbk)
ISBN: 978-1-912729-19-7 (pdf)
ISBN: 978-1-912729-20-3 (ebk)
ISBN: 978-1-912729-21-0 (html)
DOI: http://doi.org/10.28938/9781912729180

Mattering Press has made every effort to contact copyright holders and will be glad to rectify, in future editions, any errors or omissions brought to our notice.

CONTENTS

III: IDENTIFYING

LIST OF FIGURES

ACKNOWLEDGEMENTS

THE IDEA FOR THIS COLLECTION GREW OUT OF A CONFERENCE PANEL IN Graz, Austria in May 2018. At a street café next to the Kunsthaus, we decided that it was time to edit a volume of ethnographic encounters with microbes. In October, we sent out a first call for abstracts to twenty colleagues. We met again in March 2019 in Berlin, Germany to write a proposal for Mattering Press. We felt this would be the right publisher for our project and we were delighted when we learned of the positive feedback from two external reviewers in August. In the meantime, Salla had secured funding for a workshop with the contributors, and she kept telling stories about the research station that the University of Helsinki maintained at a place called Kilpisjärvi, in the north of Finland beyond the Arctic Circle. Why not go there in the dead of the winter, we thought. So, in January 2020, 18 people made their way through the polar night. Of course, we were hoping for northern lights, but the moon was strong and the clouds heavy, so instead we got a metre of snow and had to cancel our plan to climb Saana, the fell that dominates the landscape. But we had an open fireplace and a sauna by the frozen lake. Here, we decided to write the introduction for this book together.

As editors, we are persuaded by the open access model that Mattering Press is based on, which enables open access without compromising peer review and quality. We want *With Microbes* to be available and accessible to colleagues in the global South in institutions without institutional funds to buy books or subscribe to journals. The field of the social study of microbes is new, characterised by STS scholars, anthropologists, geographers, historians, philosophers and sociologists working in and on interdisciplinary projects in collaboration with life scientists, biomedical researchers, microbiologists, etc., often in dispersed siloes. We hope that publishing open access will serve the function of reaching out to these scholars, forge new collaborative relations and help them to think their own work on microbes through ours. We want to promote open access also as a value in and of itself, working against the corporatisation of academic publishing and instead contributing to the strengthening and advancement of the various open science movements.

Publishing an edited volume open access is a question of funding. Therefore, we would like to acknowledge the support of the Finnish Academy (316941), the Finnish Cultural Foundation (0116947-3), the French National Research Agency (ANR-18-CE36-0001), the Kone Foundation (201906614 & 201802186), the Region Nouvelle-Aquitaine (2018-1R40218) and the Werner Siemens-Stiftung.

The work of editing this book was split equally between the three editors, and the order of our names on the cover follows the conventions of the alphabet. None of us could have done this work alone and we deeply believe that the sum of this book is more than its parts. So, finally, we three want to thank each other for staying together in this process throughout the year 2020.

CONTRIBUTORS

SALLY ATKINSON is a social anthropologist working on the intersections of technoscience in everyday human and more-than-human life. Branching out into medical anthropology and science and technology studies, Sally is interested in how relations in technoscientific practice, in fields as diverse as neurodegenerative disease, aging and industrial bioproduction, co-construct socio-cultural understanding of living matters. Daughter of a cheesemaker, Sally is acutely aware of how her life has been continually shaped by living with microbes.

SABINE BIEDERMANN is a Berlin-based anthropologist and a member of the *Laboratory: Anthropology of Environment | Human Relations*. Her research interests comprise the social anthropology of science and technology, medical anthropology, human-environment relations, multispecies ethnography and posthumanism. Her current research deals with the question of how the human microbiome is enacted in everyday practices, focusing on human-microbial collaborations towards health and wellbeing.

CHARLOTTE BRIVES is an anthropologist of science and biomedicine at the CNRS in France. She has been working on human-microbe relationships since her thesis, which focused on biologists-*Saccharomyces cerevisiae* relations in a laboratory. She then worked on clinical trials on HIV therapies in sub-Saharan Africa before her transformative encounter with bacteriophage viruses. For the past four years, she has been developing interdisciplinary projects with biologists, microbial ecologists and physicians to work on the potentialities and creative powers of these companion species.

ANDREA BUTCHER is a postdoctoral researcher at the University of Helsinki. Her expertise lies broadly in the anthropology of development, applying STS-inspired approaches to questions of climate, environment and health in low-resource settings. Her previous research focused on political questions of climate, development and spirituality in the Himalayas. She began studying human-microbial relations in the context of international development in 2017 and has worked on projects examining antimicrobial resistance drivers in Bangladesh and West Africa.

JOSE A. CAÑADA is a postdoctoral researcher at the University of Helsinki, Faculty of Social Sciences. Having earned a PhD from the University of Helsinki in 2018, his career has especially focused on studying knowledge production and material practices associated with socio-technical controversies, working on topics such as pandemic preparedness and response, biobanking and the development of water infrastructures. He is currently involved in the SoSAMiRe project, where he studies issues related to AMR global policy-making and national implementation in West Africa.

DENIS CHARTIER is an environmental geographer and artist, professor at the University of Paris, member of The Laboratory of Social Dynamics and Spatial Reconstruction (LADYSS). He has been working for 20 years to identify responses to ecological disasters at different scales. He also tries, by mixing art and science, and by engaging in a dialogue with numerous allies such as microbes, to build tools for the reappropriation of capacities to think, feel and act in the Capitalocene.

A.C. DAVIDSON works at the intersections of social and environmental justice within queer and feminist theory. Alongside working as a lecturer in human geography at the University of Huddersfield, they work with community groups on climate action and unlearning racism. Their latest article, 'Radical Mobilities', was published in Progress in Human Geography in 2020.

MARK ERICKSON is reader in sociology, and director of doctoral studies at the University of Brighton, UK. He is a sociologist with research interests in sociology of science and technology, cultural studies of science and technology, social theory and social research methods and methodology. His most recent book is *Science, Culture and Society: Understanding Science in the 21st Century* (Polity 2015).

JOSHUA EVANS is senior researcher and leader of the Novel Fermentations Research Group, part of the Novo Nordisk Foundation Center for Biosustainability at the Danish Technical University. For his PhD in Geography and the Environment at Oxford he investigated how Copenhagen's culinary innovators and their microbial counterparts shape each other through the pursuit of novel flavours in fermentation. His doctoral research is built on prior work at Nordic Food Lab, a former non-profit institute for open-source research on flavour and food diversity.

NICOLAS FORTANÉ is a sociologist working at the French Research Institute for Food, Agriculture and Environment (INRAE). His research engages with microbes in different ways: how animal health is enacted through veterinary practices and knowledge, policy instruments and market structures. Thanks to the amazing people he met via this book project he recently developed a strong personal interest in microbial life and is now experimenting a lot with (delicious) sourdough bread recipes.

RIINA HANNULA is living in a multispecies tribe creating a practice of more-than-human care with earth-others such as goats, peacocks, soil, plants, microbes, bunnies, chickens, insects and cats. Their thinking-with happens in different mediums from audio and video essays to live situations. They are a Master of Arts in media studies and a PhD student in the Microbial Lives: Practices of New Human-Microbial Cultures project at the University of Helsinki, Finland.

KATRIINA HUTTUNEN is a PhD candidate in sociology at the University of Helsinki. She holds an MA in development studies, and her current research focuses on a Nordic-based vaccine trial conducted in West Africa. Katriina is interested in the multiple relationalities of the trial context and in the ways in which various phenomena, such as scientific knowledge production, travel and humanitarian helping are entangled.

VEERA KINNUNEN is a social scientist working on a threshold of more-than-human sociology, environmental humanities and feminist ethics. Her research interests cover the material culture of everyday life, dwelling, and ways of living with waste. Kinnunen is a senior lecturer of sociology at the University of Lapland, Finland. In her spare time, Kinnunen experiments with her microbial companions in bokashi and kombucha jars, and dreams of a garden of her own.

MARINE LEGRAND, environmental anthropologist, currently works as a 'research and knowledge sharing' fellow at the LEESU (Environment, Water & Urban Systems Lab), Ecole des Ponts Paris Tech. She explores social practices associated with the ecologisation of land-use planning, from landscape design to sanitation. She has a passion for the cycles and rhythms of the living the atomic and the organic, and the many ways post-industrial societies deal with their own shit.

OONA LEINOVIRTANEN is an artist and MA in social sciences. Her methods are corporeal and based on improvisation. She does not want to know too much. At the moment, she works with movement, sculptural installation, video and writing. She loves microbes in between and everywhere. She needs freedom and challenges. Her dream is to live outdoors and move less in an upright position. Ecological values are most important for her.

GERMAIN MEULEMANS is an anthropologist at CNRS in France. He is interested in how soil and the multiple forms of life that inhabit it become recognised as social and political actors in their own right (rather than simply as a resource or developable land) in the worlds of soil ecology, critical urban gardening and community projects aimed at reducing soil erosion. He conducts ethnographic fieldwork in France and the US.

JOHANNA NURMI is a university teacher at the Department of Social Research, University of Turku. Her research focuses on health-related expertise and its contestations concerning vaccines, complementary and alternative medicine (CAM), nutrition and microbes.

ELINA OINAS is professor in sociology at the Swedish School of Social Science at the University of Helsinki, Finland. Her research deals with shifting knowledge practices, power, gender, feminisms, development/transformation, health, and embodiment in different organisations, contexts and collaborations in Finland, Benin, Ethiopia and South Africa. She has been interested in how social sciences engage with human body fluids and microbes since the 1990s, with empirical work on menstruation, HIV, and most recently diarrhoea.

EMMA RANSOM-JONES is a microbiologist who currently works as a postdoctoral research officer at the University of Huddersfield. Her research focuses on the characterisation of probiotics and their effects on human health. She also works on research projects that identify the impact of humanity on the environment and measure the effectiveness of interventions to mitigate this damage.

MATTHÄUS REST works on the relations between the economy, the environment, science and time, mostly with peasant communities in the Alps and the Himalayas. He is interested in unbuilt infrastructures, the temporalities of fermentation and the future of agriculture. Currently based at the Max Planck Institute for Evolutionary Anthropology in Leipzig, he is working with a group of biomolecular archaeologists who trace the deep history of dairying through the DNA of modern and ancient microbes.

SALLA SARIOLA is a sociologist of science and medicine at the University of Helsinki. Her current research concerns the social study of microbes that includes fermentation, composting and making enquiries into the changing scientific practices concerning microbiota and antimicrobial resistance. Her research has included clinical trials, mistrust, community engagement, HIV activism, and bioethics in Sri Lanka, India, Benin and Kenya, at the intersections of feminist and queer theory, medical anthropology, global health and science and technology studies.

ANDIE THOMPSON thinks microbes are amazing and has a specific interest in AMR and metagenomic technologies. She is a PhD candidate in anthropology and STS at the University of Amsterdam and a member of the FutureHealth project, a team studying interventions designed in the pursuit of a sustainable and healthy collective future. Her current research involves following epigenetic studies of toxic stress and maternal health in Portland, Oregon.

VISHNU VARDHANI RAJAN – body philosopher. Vishnu ferments, agitates, and pickles e v e r y t h i n g. They use materials from the body as starter cultures to perform fermentation. They recommend human hair to make soy sauce, and chilies and ant-hill mud to make yogurts. Vish brings back to Helsinki compressed air, rocks, mud and water, especially from Hyderabad-India. A bringing together of two articulations of home, a movement from geo-politics to geo-poethics.

CATHERINE WILL works on the sociology of science and technology at the University of Sussex, studying how to account for inequality in efforts to mobilise against antimicrobial resistance. The project has been a wonderful introduction to bacteria that live with humans through the eyes of scientists, clinicians and patients struggling with recurrent, persistent and resistant infections, and writing this piece with Mark Erickson gave a chance to debate how to foreground microbes in the social science.

INTRODUCING *WITH MICROBES*: FROM WITNESSING TO WITHNESSING

The Kilpisjärvi Collective

IN JANUARY 2020, 15 SOCIAL SCIENTISTS AND THREE ARTISTS MET AT A biological research station in Kilpisjärvi, Lapland, northern Finland. We spent a week rigorously discussing a set of chapter drafts for this book and experimenting with possibilities of working and writing with microbes. The remote location by a frozen lake, surrounded by snow-covered hills with mythical relevance to Sámi culture, the magical polar nights, the scarcity of daylight and the warmth of the fireplace all contributed to an organic and fluid cohabitation and collaboration. Intensive reading and commenting were complemented by material, corporeal engagements with microbial worlds. Engaging with microbes was not only – and cannot only be – textual. Through movement explorations with slime mould and vagus nerve yoga, culturing bacteria in bread and ginger beer and making cheese, and an artistic performance 'Labracadabra' that included three bioartists collecting samples from the bodies of the participants, then culturing them in the research station's laboratory and giving tarot-style predictions from them, we drew our human selves into new connections with various kinds of microbes in ways that aimed to increase our awareness of the microbes in and around us, and possibly change our theorisation of them.

The tone of the week was set during the first night, with a slime mould exercise organised by Vishnu Vardhani, one of the bioartists attending the workshop. During a processual movement and immersion exercise, we were asked to collectively move as one, remaining aware of our environment and of our own and others' boundaries, despite having our eyes closed. A slime mould is a community of single-cell organisms with many nuclei fused together that act as one collective entity with no central operating system (Barnett 2015). The exercise required a great deal of mutual attuning, which was also central to the work during the following days and the organising and writing of this introduction together. We did not know then how much we would soon long for the presence of strangers.

It would be a mistake to use slime mould as a new metaphor for the social. While the objective of our time in Kilpisjärvi was to play with microbes, there was also a need to dislodge notions of authority, authorship and agency of the human. Epistemic experimentation was required to add further layers to knowing microbes at both an individual and a collective level. We wrote this introduction together and author it as the 'Kilpisjärvi Collective'. In doing so, we are crossing the many boundaries of authorship upheld by the writing norms of each of our disciplines; and we are developing new slime mould-inspired knowledge production practices based on what 'we' learned from engaging with microbial life forms. In Kilpisjärvi, the chapters were discussed by the group. This discussion contributed to the individual papers but also to the joint process of carving out a new niche for the social study of microbes. As such, the whole of this book is bigger than the sum of its parts.

We do not consider attuning to microbes to be the next important turn in the social studies of science (after the gene, stem cell, etc.). We agree with Stefan Helmreich (2003) that 'microbes are good to think with' – but they are also so much more than that. In this volume, we circle in on the 'with' to describe multiple microbial relationships and networks as they emerge and shift, and how various relations change their contexts in so doing. Accompanying, following, embodying these entanglements is what we decided to call 'withnessing'.

PATHOGENS AND PANDEMICS

Upon returning home, we heard the first reports of a novel respiratory disease making people ill in the Chinese city of Wuhan. This book was written during the lockdowns of 2020, at a time when the world was struggling with a pandemic caused by SARS-CoV-2. The disease itself, called Covid-19, was regularly described in the media in military terms; the virus was referred to as an enemy, and societies were said to be at war with it. Such a discourse represents a view of microbes that has dominated public health and biomedicine, and that has had strong resonance in public lives (Brives 2020). The germ theory sees microbes as causing diseases, and developments in public health during the twentieth century have enforced practices that define microbes as a quintessential enemy of health due to their detrimental effects on human and animal lives (Sariola and Gilbert 2020).

This paradigm remains strong throughout the world, as evidenced by the way it shapes regulatory tools for the prevention of epidemics, hygiene and food safety. In her analysis of raw milk cheesemakers in the US, Heather Paxson coined the term *microbiopolitics* to describe the governance of microbes. Paxson takes a cue from Foucault's (2008) notion of biopolitics, which refers to the ways in which power and biological life are intertwined in order to organise life and populations. Paxson (2008: 17) defines microbiopolitics as 'the creation of categories of microscopic biological agents; the anthropocentric evaluation of such agents; and the elaboration of appropriate human behaviours vis-a-vis microorganisms engaged in infection, inoculation, and digestion'. Biopolitics was formulated at a time when genetic medicine did not exist, and the main cause of death was infectious disease. Thus, it is not surprising that, though never explicitly articulated as such by Foucault (or Paxson), a central component of biopolitics – the production of healthy populations through public health measures – was the control of microbes.

Microbiopolitics, therefore, is not limited to artisanal cheesemakers, but can be extrapolated to the ubiquity with which the governance of microbes has penetrated various domains of modern societies. From food hygiene (Nading 2017) to the organisation of human and animal health care (Hinchliffe et al. 2016; Chan et al. 2020; Keck 2015; Sanford, Polzer, and McDonough 2016), pandemic preparedness (Lynteris and Poleykett 2018; Caduff 2012) and even architecture (Brown et al. 2019), microbes have been predominantly framed as contagious pathogens in need of control. Such an approach, termed an 'antibiotic approach to life' by Jamie Lorimer (2020), which aims to control human-microbe boundaries with antibiotics, the quintessential modern tools for governing microbes, has had dramatic outcomes for human and animal health, having led to the rise of antimicrobial resistance (AMR) (Kirchhelle 2020).

Hannah Landecker (2016) argues that antimicrobial resistance is a natural quality of microbes, but the use of antibiotics has accelerated the evolution of resistance, changing the biological qualities of microbes. Steve Hinchcliffe (2021) describes this as 'a play of forces' whereby socio-political conditions generate material (microbial) push-back. Social analyses of AMR have, for example, pointed to the ways in which antibiotics are a 'quick fix' (Denyer Willis and Chandler 2019) to control and guard against infection in the absence of health care. This applies to poorly equipped health care systems in low- and middle-income countries as well as conditions of neoliberal pharmaceuticalised healthcare characterised by individual responsibility via the use of antibiotics.

Attempts to control the circulation of microbes capable of rapid transnational reach have led to a proliferation of pandemic thinking at the global level: long before the international spread of SARS-CoV-2, in public health discourse, the next outbreak was always just around the corner (Caduff 2015; Lakoff and Collier 2008; Wald 2008). National and international infrastructures have been set up to prevent the spread of microbes, and work by scholars in sociology and international relations has drawn parallels between how nation states manage their borders against outsiders and how the body is seen to defend itself from pathogens (Brown 2019; Fishel 2017; Martin 1990). The 2000s saw an expansion in literature on preparedness against pandemics and bioterrorism that described regulatory measures such as surveillance, quarantine, separating high-risk individuals, monitoring and tracing, and rolling out global health preparedness policies (Wolf 2017; Keck and Lachenal 2019; Lakoff 2017; Cañada 2019; Caduff 2019).

While the 2020 Covid-19 pandemic reinforced these themes, the damage to health and economies is masking a more dynamic and complex notion of microbes that had been starting to take hold. An alternative definition of human-microbial relationships, taking into account the ecological dimension of diseases, has persisted throughout the twentieth century in disciplines such as microbial ecology (Anderson 2004), but in public health it was not until the early 2000s and technical developments in the field of genetic sequencing that significant changes were observed, first in the life sciences and biomedical sciences and then in the humanities and social sciences.

SYMBIONTS AND SITUATEDNESS

The early 2000s saw the development of metagenomics – the study of the genetic content of samples from complex environments that dissolves the boundaries of individual organisms and species, both materially and conceptually. Since then, this discipline has provided growing support for a story in which humans and microbes share common ecologies and maintain constitutive relationships. Work on microbiota thus provides evidence that, among other things, humans depend on microbes from a developmental, immunological, physiological and metabolic point of view (Gilbert, Sapp, and Tauber 2012). The concept of the holobiont, which accounts for this entanglement between a host and its symbionts, is thus being used more and more widely (Bosch and Miller 2016). However, in order to avoid the pre-eminence of one entity (the human) over the others (the microbes), Donna Haraway proposes to renounce the notion of host; for Haraway, a holobiont is an assemblage of symbionts (Haraway 2016). And importantly, for some ecological thinkers, viruses can also make symbiotic relations (Dupré and Guttinger 2016). Pierre-Olivier Méthot and Samuel Alizon (2014) show how pathogenicity should be viewed as a dynamic feature of an interaction between biological entities, rather than as a fixed notion.

By bringing microbes into the focus of what it means to be human, much that may have been taken for granted is brought into question. For example, the role of microbes in the human immune system has led to a reconsideration of the dichotomy between 'self' and 'non-self' that has been central to immunology for decades (Rees 2020; Martin 1990). Instead of seeing the body as a self that protects individuality against outside influence, philosopher of biology Thomas Pradeu points out that 'many foreign entities are tolerated by the body and even become major constituents of the organism, especially bacteria that have symbiotic relationships with it, such as bacteria from the gastrointestinal tract' (Pradeu 2008: 118-9, translation CB). Far from encouraging withdrawal into oneself, into genetic essentialism or a fixed conception of the boundaries of what would define us as human beings, biology tells us today that 'foreign' entities – microbes – become crucial constituents of the organism through the immune system. Furthermore, microbes' ability to share genes across species – lateral or horizontal gene transfer – questions the self-evidence of individuality at all scales. What is at stake, however, is not figuring out where the 'real' individual lies but tracing how 'what the individual is' shifts according to what it is asked to do. Social sciences have long argued that persons are distributed, non-essential, fluid and relational, but work on immunity and symbiosis demonstrates the profound implications of a relational conceptualisation for the biological notion of 'self' that Roberto Esposito (2010) and Nik Brown (2019) have argued reorganises relations with others by an emphasis on community rather than immunity.

Considering microbes as relational brings attention to the broader social relations and power structures where they are embedded. It is necessary to address the power relations that frame human-microbial relations and consider the status, legitimacy and capacities for political action of the different actors involved. Although new forms of relationships with microbes seem to be on the rise – characterised by Lorimer (2020) as a probiotic turn, where 'life is being used to manage life' – it is important not to overestimate these relationships, to recognise that they are above all 'humanist', and so to locate them within the structures of human societies. Fermentation practices, attention to our guts, alternative medicines and other 'friendly microbial practices' are not equally distributed across the globe and within societies, and therefore do not have the same meaning for everyone. It is important to recognise the socially situated dimensions of such practices, and how factors such as gender, class, race, age and culture impact, and arise within, our relations with microbes, depending on geographical and historical contexts, existing sanitation infrastructures, lifestyles, access to types of food and health care, and the environments that people live in – dynamics that Amber Benezra (2020) calls intersectional biosociality. The pandemic also cautions us about the location and relationship of the new multispecies practices with microbes in relation to the dominant framework of biosecurity and provides reasons to analyse the possible tensions and challenges that practices such as fermentation or alternative sanitation might pose to it. A new focus on microbial scales should not imply disregard of macroscopic structures and social justice.

FROM WITNESSING TO WITHNESSING: A NOTE ON METHOD

Within growing bodies of work concerned with human-microbe relationalities, both in the life sciences and social sciences, there is little sign of consensus around preferred methods or scales of enquiry. Approaches are numerous, techniques and devices are varied. Microbes, fluid and dynamic, thus remind us of the strength and fragility of knowledge, whether scientific or vernacular. Given the circular and multi-contained character of ecologically situated multispecies relationships, there is a pressing need to develop the tools and vocabulary for the social sciences and humanities to move away from a purely anthropocentric focus. How can we describe, and generatively engage, microbial multispecies relations without dichotomising nature and culture, subject and object, human and other? And how can we describe how humans and microbes compose common worlds together?

The chapters of this book document the entanglement/hybridisation between different forms of knowledge and practices regarding microbes and their circulation within multiple social worlds. They resist the urge to represent and thereby configure the object of knowledge – the microbe – as a stable entity that can be known. The traditions of knowledge practices, where the human involvement with microbes instrumentalises and objectifies the known, and where human intentionality, mastery and control are taken as given goals, are challenged and refused. The knowledge, technologies or devices that are mediating our interactions with microbes can make them either visible or invisible.

While many chapters share overlapping vocabularies, epistemologies and ontologies, these always exist also in relation to varying ways of knowing, making things visible or knowable as an object of care or concern. How things are enacted by the various entities engaged in the practice produces multiple versions of materiality (Mol 2002). Would we be speaking of 'microbes', even in relational terms, if it were not for the ever-changing microbiological techniques of making-visible, understanding, isolating and quantifying?

With Microbes examines how multiplicities of microbial life are enacted, to develop nuanced and speculative ways of talking about the kind and degree of human involvement with them rather than an assumed neutral observation. This could be described as a move from 'modest witnessing' (Haraway 1997), where the experiment establishes the facts about its target, towards 'witnessing'. Haraway draws on the writings of Shapin and Schaffer (1985) about the seventeenth-century scientist Robert Boyle to discuss the kind of modest witnessing accessible only to white, male and middle-class bodies. Only this form of modesty permitted the objective gaze required of witnessing in credible science. In contrast, the modesty of Haraway's feminist mutated Modest Witness – and the notion of *withnessing* we discuss below – is about knowledge as situated, immersed and partial.

The notion of 'withness', raised by Sally Atkinson (2021) in Kilpisjärvi and discussed collectively during the workshop discussions, is a commentary on the aspired-to neutrality of the modest witness. Withnessing becomes one way to name and bring together the otherwise diverse approaches to knowledge production taken in this volume. The epistemic orientation of withnessing – the 'knowing' – is dispersed, and non-human vitality, agency or liveliness is as much an object of curiosity as human engagement (for a similar postulation of withnessing as more-than-human co-existence, see Boscacci 2018). In many chapters of this book, the intentional human engagement with microbial processes is of interest, but it is not the central focus. By drawing on *multispecies ethnographies* (Kirksey and Helmreich 2010; Tsing 2015; Haraway 2008), we zoom in on 'contact zones where lines separating nature from culture have broken down, where encounters between Homo sapiens and other beings generate mutual ecologies and co-produced niches' (Kirksey and Helmreich 2010: 546). Here, the aim of grasping a confluence of interacting multispecies relations decentres the human, while at the same time recognising the challenges of sidestepping it.

In contrast to the ocular, cerebral and objectifying gaze of the witness, in withnessing, the relationality in any knowing process is brought to the analytical focal point. Relationality, again, means that knowing is always contingent, emergent, sensory, embodied, social, and animated by multiple, unexpected human, non-human and inhuman agencies. To understand through 'withnessing' is therefore not to claim a panacea or propound a celebratory account of knowing as necessarily possible, unproblematic, reciprocal, nor even arising out of peaceful coexistence. Even the clumsiness of the term on the tongue speaks to the inherent discomforts, the visceral violence, unevenness, and divergences in knowing as withnessing.

In the process of knowing as withnessing, the (infra)structures, knowers, tools or devices for human-microbial engagement become key sites of interest. The focus shifts from the entity to be known to the 'agential cut' (Barad 2007) of knowledge production. In her seminal work on quantum physics, Karen Barad argues that the measurement, technology, technique or surface on which the knowledge is drawn constitutes the phenomenon itself. In *With Microbes*, the microbe is sensed with widely different tools. Devices are seen as technological mediators that constitute the phenomenon itself; therefore, the site to be studied becomes one of the major choices for the ethnographer. Bruno Latour's (1993) historical work *The Pasteurization of France* was instructive in showing that a device, or a collection of devices such as the laboratory, never only constitutes the entity but also its governance. In the science and technology studies tradition that this book engages with, attention to disciplines, as well as lay knowledge, leads to a focus on practices and processes rather than outcomes only. Importantly, the chapters counter the impression that it is first and foremost the laboratory where the presence and absence, the visibilisation and invisibilisation of microbes, is enacted. Instead, the chapters offer insights into the various other sites where microbes are co-enacted, or 'withnessed': gardens and farms, kitchens and communities, environments and infrastructures.

Devices and configurations of knowledge, including disciplines, should always be understood as both constructed through relations of power and as the machinery through which power operates (Foucault 1980). The ideal of the 'knower' as a colonial, masculine, white, phallogocentric subject who controls his object, for example, is in many respects challenged in this volume. However, it is important to acknowledge the ways in which this ideal continues to 'stick' and seduce (Ahmed 2016). Similarly, an account of 'withnessing' microbes could all too readily risk focusing on microbial-human relations without situating these relations within capitalist, patriarchal and white supremacist relations of power – which condition the very possibilities and limits of these relations and how they are valued and known. The context, obligation and cosmopolitical ethos in which these shared practices take place are part of what Isabelle Stengers (2005) has called 'an ecology of practices'. In turn, microbial-human relations are enrolled to reproduce such hierarchies of value, reinforcing which (non-)humans and ways of being (in)human(e) are valued.

The chapters that understand human-microbial relations as configured through relations of power show special interest in how to attend to living materiality and to the question whether the boundary between living and non-living can be maintained as binary opposition. Power operates through these relationships not only in terms of 'interests', understood as 'political', or through discourse alone but also in terms of what forms, infrastructures and understandings of humanity, life and 'vitalness' are sustained, and which are left to die (Sharpe 2016). The chapters recognise that governance is not about power over given individuals or species, but rather about power relations within multispecies or even ecosystem-based assemblages (e.g. Agamben 1998; Povinelli 2016; Weheliye 2014; Mbembe 2019). Of the many interpretations of the meaning of 'critique' in critical analysis, Patricia Hill Collins (2019) reminds us of definitions that are vital and even lifesaving; as in 'critical care'. Critical social scientists interested in microbial sciences end up entangled with their human and non-human collaborators and the devices they operate with and cannot quite afford arrogant sceptical oppositionalism or paranoid distancing (Kirksey 2019; Irni 2017; Sedgwick 2003). Hence, we can but only be 'with microbes', an entanglement that requires situatedness, situating and reflexivity of the methodological, conceptual and ontological positionings of who and what is being drawn together and 'being with'.

THE MICROBE MULTIPLE: CHAPTER OVERVIEW

With Microbes aims to refuse the essentialisations that can arise when naming and classifying microbes, as well as the relationships between humans and microbes and among microbes of all kinds (see also Hird 2009). Dualistic analytics are simplifications of historically contingent, geographically and paradigmatically shaped human-microbial relationships. Our ethnographic observations are supported by work from within philosophy, technoscience and feminist anthropology, and the insight that postulating binary oppositions between woman and man, nature and culture, as well as human and more-than-human represent analogous moves that legitimate domination by man, culture and human (Strathern 1980; Haraway 1985; Braidotti 2006).

Nonetheless, while recent contributions to the social studies of microbes have acknowledged the multiplicities of microbes (e.g. Kirksey 2019; Lorimer 2017; Paxson 2012; Helmreich 2009; Jasarevic 2015; Kalin and Gruber 2018), the analyses of many social scientists remain dualistic. Paxson (2008: 17–8) argued that the revival of artisanal cheesemaking in the United States 'provides a window onto social and regulatory negotiations of a hyperhygienic Pasteurian social order (as forwarded by the FDA [Food and Drug Administration]) and a post-Pasteurian microbiopolitics' advocated by raw milk activists. This binary juxtaposition risks a simplifying depiction of the history of microbiology. 'Pasteurian' here might be read as a monolithic ideology concerned with seeing microbes as nothing but pathogenic threats. In a similarly dichotomous vein, Lorimer (2020) postulates a 'probiotic' turn in contrast to an antibiotic way of controlling life, and Paxson and Helmreich (2014) frame the new discourse on microbes using the notions of peril and promise.

With Microbes provides descriptions of the multiplicity, complexity, abundance and dynamism of various relationships between humans and microbes. We have organised the chapters into three sections that each highlight a particular mode of relating with microbes and of witnessing – sensing, regulating and identifying. Although this division is not arbitrary, it nevertheless, like any act of classification, cuts out and makes choices about what is put forward for each chapter. This division does not imply an unequivocal mode of relations with microbes but rather reflects the choices of each researcher to work on a given scale, and to emphasise one aspect among others of the interactions and becomings of humans with microbes.

Sensing

The first chapter section, 'sensing', collects a number of contributions that engage with the complex 'arts of noticing' (Tsing 2017) people employ in order to create products, value and meaning as they work and engage with microbes. In this section, we call attention to the series of situated and multisensory practices within which microbes are known and thus come into being (Law and Mol 2008). The chapters are positioned at the interstices of multispecies ethnography and the anthropology of the senses, and draw from diverse sources of the ethnographic tradition, which could be loosely grouped together as non-representational ethnography. As conceptualised by cultural geographer Phillip Vannini (2015), non-representational ethnography stands for making sense of the world while simultaneously considering the partiality, situatedness, contingency and creativity of that sense-making. Embodied, multi-sensory methods have proved useful for such an understanding and have been explored to sense kitchen microbiomes by Lorimer et al. (2019). As Sarah Pink (2012) summarises it, *sensory ethnography* attends to the non-verbal, kinetic and sensorial ways in which lived worlds are communicated to others. The sensory ethnography approach thus invites us to pay attention to the interplay of sight, touch, smell, hearing, taste and gestures, and the ways they are linked to skilled practices and the use of the technological mediators, such as microscopes, microphones and genome sequencing, in and through which we make sense of the microbial world. The chapters experiment with diverse ways of knowing, not only within fieldwork but also in performing, articulating and communicating our ethnographic explorations.

In 'The Deplantationocene: Listening to yeasts and rejecting the worldview of the plantation', Denis Chartier discusses the motivations and sensory repertoire of winemakers in France who have chosen to leave behind established protocols of conventional viticulture and instead produce 'natural wine', a wine without sulphur, laboratory-grown yeasts or pasteurisation. Through an exploration of the historic connections between winemaking, colonialism and the global plantation system that defines the Plantationocene (Haraway et al. 2016), Denis describes these vintners' counter-practices, embodied and sensorial, as bringing forth a Deplantationocene that subverts the ways in which industrial food production and farming create monocultures in which microbes are detached from their environments and instead involves bringing microbes, plants, geology and climate together. Importantly, listening to the sound of the yeast in the vat emerges as a central form of engagement for the winemakers.

In 'Knowing, living, and being with bokashi', Veera Kinnunen investigates a probiotic practice of fermenting kitchen waste called bokashi composting. Focussing on her autoethnographic sensual engagement with waste, interviews with other composters and online forum contributions, she argues for understanding bokashi as an embodied practice that recognises and nurtures microbial wellbeing and rejects a modern ethics of waste denial that is based on separation and rejection. Once again, smelling and touching emerge as powerful ways of knowing microbes.

In 'Oimroas: Notes on a summer alpine journey', Matthäus Rest takes us on a trip through the mountain summer pastures of the Alps where he visits artisanal cheesemakers who work with raw milk. His essay details two scales of pastoral care: how individual cheesemakers care for their starter cultures and how the state keeps the cheesemakers under surveillance. He accompanies a 'cheese consultant' on a day of dairy visits that show how he, like the cheesemakers, first and foremost relies on his senses when encountering both humans and microbes. Identifying a lack of detailed description of the sensual and physical work of cheesemaking in the anthropological literature, Rest argues for an ethnography of microbiopolitics that renders transparent specific microbes' political interventions.

Johanna Nurmi's chapter 'Building "natural" immunities: Cultivation of human-microbe relations in vaccine-refusing families' explores the ways in which vaccine-hesitant parents sense what they understand to be the effects of microbes in strengthening their children's immunity. The parents' position and practices are in opposition to the logics by which mainstream public health programmes offer childhood vaccination. Employing the term 'lay immunology', Johanna describes how parents who are critical of vaccines understand microbes and seek to regulate both their own and their children's relations with microbes in their favour in order to develop immunity 'naturally', without the techno-scientifically constructed and controlled means to build immunity with the aid of vaccines.

Regulating

The second chapter section is 'regulating'. Building on the governance of human-microbe relations, a relationship with microbes – be it antibiotic or probiotic or anything else – always involves some degree or kind of negotiation and navigation, at times more open, at times more restricted, depending on what is seen to be at stake, the underlying logic with which microbes are understood and by whom, and to what ends the regulation is implemented. The theme of regulation not only refers to the scale of governance and policies but to how, at micro and macro levels, microbes are managed at and between levels.

STS scholarship has drawn attention to the ways in which science, technology, law, policies and public participation are co-produced (Jasanoff 2004) and shape material worlds (Faulkner, Lange, and Lawless 2012). International standards regulating food safety are a pertinent example of how the circulation and trade of agricultural products are governed and standardised globally, shaping markets as well as everyday relations with microbes (Winickoff and Bushey 2010). We can already observe new kinds of relationship with microbes that are commodified or marketised: kombucha, raw-milk cheese, sourdough and natural wine are among the many products that have become trendy, their availability in the markets enhanced by intermediary actors trying to create a social demand for these products. Given the reach of international food standards and food hygiene, which act as gatekeepers to market access, it is important to question how socio-economic structures foster the development of and potential for 'alternative' approaches to microbes. Privilege, access and structures also shape the ways in which people are able to manage their bodily boundaries in relation to microbes.

At the level of regulating relations with microbes at the boundaries of environments and bodies, Katriina Huttunen, Elina Oinas and Salla Sariola's chapter 'When cultures meet: Microbes, permeable bodies, and the environment' highlights the ways in which people's everyday actions regulate the microbes that they perceive to be in the environment and that could make them sick with touristic diarrhoea, entering them at the boundaries of their bodies. The chapter analyses Finnish people who travel to West Africa as part of an *Escherichia coli* vaccine study. It shows how tourist-trial participants define microbes in multiple ways. A public health framing of microbes as pathogenic is limited, but a dualistic definition of microbes as either 'good' or 'bad' is also seen to be redundant. Katriina, Elina and Salla show that human-microbial relations would better be described on a spectrum, from antagonistic to one of friendly coexistence.

The chapters by Nicolas Fortané, Marine Legrand and Germain Meulemans, and Jose Cañada show how microbes are regulated by policies across animals, water and faeces by national and global health actors, demonstrating the sociopolitical-technical governmentality of human-microbial contact. Crucially, the chapters highlight, following Barbara Praisack and Ayo Wahlberg, that to understand regulatory frameworks, an analytical focus on policy needs to reach over and beyond policy objectives to look at the 'meanings of social conventions, political, legal, and social histories, as well as other informal practices' (Prainsack and Wahlberg 2013: 336) that shape the policies.

Marine and Germain's chapter 'Bathing in black water? The microbiopolitics of the River Seine's ecological reclamation' describes attempts in Paris to eliminate faecal pollution from the River Seine in order to make it swimmable again. The targets of the regulatory intervention to clear the waters are notably the toilets of people living on boats along the river, which are seen to leak faecal matter, a leak objectified and rendered visible by the monitoring of *E. coli* bacteria. Based on ethnographic research with boat owners and policy makers, the chapter shows the difficulties of and the resistance to setting up the many infrastructures that would be needed to implement this change. The bathing issue opens the black box of sanitation and the structural limits of a centralised system that considers the river as a diluting agent. What is for some potential gold (faeces composted into soil for growing food) is for others matter out of place (polluted water). These discrepancies are embodied in different regulatory apparatuses.

Jose Cañada's chapter 'Scalability and partial connections in tackling antimicrobial resistance in West Africa' also shows how microbial policies are socially and spatially contingent. The chapter aims to go beyond the technical description of antimicrobial resistance regulation, which Jose argues 'tends to give a static image of microbes'. In contrast, by focusing on AMR policy-making attempts in West Africa, Jose identifies a number of discursive and material processes that construct these attempts that show the challenges of scale – the macro level of global policy norms vis-a-vis local attempts to set them up. Evoking a post-scalar view of microbes, the chapter demonstrates that while in the sciences microbes are defined by their small scale, their discursive-material status is constituted across different scales of abstraction and thus cannot be separated from the global policies set in place to regulate them.

Nicholas Fortané's contribution 'Ontologies of resistance: Bacteria surveillance and the co-production of antimicrobial resistance' describes how a regulatory mechanism of microbial surveillance for animal health was set up in France. In contrast to claims that biosecurity programmes were 'a new thing' in the 1990s, the chapter shows how programmes to regulate antimicrobial resistance 'didn't emerge from nowhere'. Based on the history and development of surveillance programmes, Nicholas identifies three ontologies of surveillance, their distinctions depending on the professionals involved, the main modes of practice and how microbes were defined. Over time, these ontologies add richness to the different ways in which microbes have been defined, depending on the processes, methods and societal needs at given points in time, a theme explored in the last section of the book.

Identifying

The third and final chapter section is 'identifying'. Naming microbes, producing classifications and categories, is at the heart of knowledge production. Although the various chapters of this book address this issue to varying degrees, identification or characterisation is sometimes concomitant with the establishment of the relationship itself. In *Sorting Things Out*, Geoffrey Bowker and Susan Leigh Star remind us of the centrality of classification systems to our understanding of the world. Everything that appears as universal or standard in this world is the result of social, political and organisational negotiations, invisible and integrated into the scientific work of describing nature. 'Purely technical issues like how to name things and how to store data in fact constitute much of human interaction and much of what we come to know as natural' (Bowker and Star 2000: 326). Classifications produce units of time and space, multiple ways of relating.

To the multiple ontologies of microbes should then be added the articulation work of different epistemologies. To be truly committed to this multiplicity when it comes to microbes means 'staying with the trouble' (Haraway 2016) of different, not-fully-commensurable onto-epistemologies jostling alongside each other. These different approaches emerge particularly clearly in attitudes towards the historicity of the microbe category.

Each of the chapters in its own way stirs up relational, ontological questions at the heart of microbial social science – questions concerning, among other things, matters of scale, individuality and classification. Many, if not all, engage the conventions of biological taxonomy to describe and discuss microbial kinds as the dominant and to some degree inevitable way of ordering and thus enacting microbial life. However, these chapters do not take on these taxonomic tools uncritically but acknowledge their situatedness (Haraway 1988), engaging with both what they may illuminate and what they foreclose.

In their chapter written in the form of a Greek tragedy 'Scenes from the many lives of *Escherichia coli*: A play in three acts', Catherine Will and Mark Erickson return to the very dramaturgy of the relationship linking *Escherichia coli* to the various humans who have worked on and with it. Drawing on their own experience as well as on a large body of literature, they show how the term 'Escherichia coli' names and identifies organisms and populations that sometimes differ depending on the period or discipline by which they are classified. Who is *Escherichia coli*, anyway? It is less a question of deciding what the 'real' *Escherichia coli* would be than of situating relationships, of recognising that what makes *Escherichia coli* at a given moment is the material-semiotic relationship in which it and researchers are engaged.

A. C. Davidson's and Emma Ransom-Jones's contribution 'Micro-geographies of kombucha as methodology: A cross-cultural conversation' shows what happens when a human geographer and a microbiologist work on a common project about kombucha and record their interdisciplinary conversations. What is kombucha, and how is it understood? While Emma's student extracted the DNA of commercial kombucha in her laboratory, A. C. conducted interviews with kombucha producers, and both brewed kombucha at home. Their experimental collaboration cautions against imbuing kombucha with radical political potential: kombuchas become within particular micro-geographical conditions of production.

The constitutive character of the relationship when it comes to naming or identifying microbes is at the heart of Charlotte Brives' chapter 'Pluribiosis and the never-ending microgeohistories'. Starting from the therapeutic use of bacteriophage viruses to treat bacterial infections, Charlotte shows, by describing bacteriophage collection practices, how scientists' assignment of a name to a viral strain actually corresponds to a snapshot, at a given time, of a microgeohistory, of an ever dynamic and fluctuating relationship between bacteriophages and bacteria, and their given environments. For scientists engaged in this task, identification is not conducive, at any point of the process, to essentialisation. Rather, it is a way to engage with *pluribiosis*, with the recognition of the existence of multiple relational spectrums between entities forever in the process of becoming, constantly shaped and transformed by their interactions with other living things. Pluribiosis then allows us to envisage, with the actors of phage therapy, other ways of treating and practising infectiology.

What would happen if anthropologists themselves were to repopulate the classical theories of anthropology with microbes? What would happen if the accounts left space to name and identify the agencies of microorganisms? This is the question posed by Andrea Butcher in 'Old anthropology's acquaintance with human-microbial encounters: Interpretations and methods'. Starting from the observation that the structuralist ethnographies of Mary Douglas and Louis Dumont, although based mainly on the notions of purity and impurity, leave little room for substance and materiality, developing almost exclusively symbolic structural analyses, Andrea proposes to search for and designate hidden microbial transcripts in the available ethnographies. She then proposes reflecting on the methodological consequences of the recognition of the place and the naming of microbes in ethnographic narratives.

Engaging with human-microbe relations defies essentialisations in these relationships. Instead, microbes in this volume are multiple, abundant and dynamic, and human-microbial relationships are equally complex. Supported by work from colleagues in technoscience, philosophy and feminist anthropology, the chapters in this book introduce new concepts and methods to understand human-microbial relations and contribute to a transformation of social theory in the process.

CONTRIBUTORS

Atkinson, Sally

Brives, Charlotte

Biederman, Sabine

Cañada, Jose

Chartier, Denis

Davidson, A.C.

Evans, Joshua

Fortané, Nicolas

Kinnunen, Veera

Legrand, Marine

Oinas, Elina

Rest, Matthäus

Sariola, Salla

Thompson, Andie

Will, Catherine

REFERENCES

Agamben, G., *Homo Sacer: Sovereign Power and Bare Life* (Stanford: Stanford University Press, 1998).

Ahmed, S., *Living a Feminist Life* (Durham, NC: Duke University Press, 2016).

Anderson, W., 'Natural Histories of Infectious Disease: Ecological Vision in Twentieth-Century Biomedical Science', *Osiris*, 19 (2004), 39–61.

Barad, K., *Meeting the Universe Halfway: Quantum Physics and the Entanglement of Matter and Meaning* (Durham, NC: Duke University Press, 2007).

Barnett, H., 'Being Slime Mould', <https://heatherbarnett.co.uk/work/being-slime-mould/> [accessed 12 December 2020].

Benezra, A., 'Race in the Microbiome', *Science, Technology & Human Values*, 45.5 (2020), 877–902.

Boscacci, L., 'Wit(h)nessing', *Environmental Humanities*, 10.1 (2018), 343–7.

Bosch, T., and D. Miller, *The Holobiont Imperative: Perspectives from Early Emerging Animals* (Vienna: Springer, 2016).

Bowker, G., and S. L. Star, *Sorting Things Out: Classification and Its Consequences* (Cambridge, MA and London: MIT Press, 2000).

Braidotti, R., 'Posthuman, All Too Human: Towards a New Process Ontology', *Theory, Culture & Society*, 23 (2006), 197–208.

Brives, C., 'The Politics of Amphibiosis: The War against Viruses Will Not Take Place', <http://somatosphere.net/2020/the-politics-of-amphibiosis.html/> [accessed 12 December 2020].

Brown, N., *Immunitary Life: A Biopolitics of Immunity* (London: Palgrave Macmillan, 2019).

Brown, N., and others, 'Pathways, Practices and Architectures: Containing Antimicrobial Resistance in the Cystic Fibrosis Clinic', *Health*, 25.2 (2021), 196–213.

Caduff, C., 'Great Anticipations', in A. Kelly, F. Keck, and C. Lynteris, eds, *The Anthropology of Epidemics* (New York: Routledge, 2019), pp. 43–58.

—— *The Pandemic Perhaps: Dramatic Events in a Public Culture of Danger* (Berkeley: University of California Press, 2015).

—— 'The Semiotics of Security: Infectious Disease Research and the Biopolitics of Informational Bodies in the United States', *Cultural Anthropology: Journal of the Society for Cultural Anthropology*, 27 (2012), 333–57.

Cañada, J., 'Hybrid Threats and Preparedness Strategies: The Reconceptualization of Biological Threats and Boundaries in Global Health Emergencies', *Sociological Research Online*, 24 (2019), 93–110.

Chan, K., and others, 'Diagnostics and the Challenge of Antimicrobial Resistance: A Survey of UK Livestock Veterinarians' Perceptions and Practices', *The Veterinary Record*, 187.12 (2020), e125–e125.

Clever, I., and W. Ruberg, 'Beyond Cultural History? The Material Turn, Praxiography, and Body History', *Humanities Report*, 3 (2014), 546–66.

Collins, P., *Intersectionality as Critical Social Theory* (Durham, NC: Duke University Press, 2019).

Denyer Willis, L., and C. Chandler, 'Quick Fix for Care, Productivity, Hygiene and Inequality: Reframing the Entrenched Problem of Antibiotic Overuse', *BMJ Global Health*, 4 (2019), e001590.

Dupré, J., and S. Guttinger, 'Viruses as Living Processes', *Studies in History and Philosophy of Biological and Biomedical Sciences*, 59 (2016), 109–16.

Faulkner, A., B. Lange, and C. Lawless, 'Introduction: Material Worlds: Intersections of Law, Science, Technology, and Society', *Journal of Law and Society*, 39 (2012), 1–19.

Fishel, S., *The Microbial State: Global Thriving and the Body Politic* (Minneapolis: University of Minnesota Press, 2017).

Foucault, M., *The Birth of Biopolitics: Lectures at the Collège de France 1978-79* (Basingstoke and New York: Palgrave Macmillan, 2008).

—— *The History of Sexuality, Volume I: An Introduction* (New York: Vintage Books, 1980).

Gilbert, S., J. Sapp, and A. Tauber, 'A Symbiotic View of Life: We Have Never Been Individuals', *The Quarterly Review of Biology*, 87 (2012), 325–41.

Haraway, D., 'A Manifesto for Cyborgs: Science, Technology, and Socialist Feminism in the 1980s', *Socialist Review*, 80 (1985), 65–108.

—— *Modest-Witness@ Second-Millennium. FemaleMan (R)-Meets-OncoMouse™: Feminism and Technoscience* (New York: Routledge, 1997).

—— 'Situated Knowledges: The Science Question in Feminism and the Privilege of Partial Perspective', *Feminist Studies*, 14.3 (1988), 575–99.

—— *Staying with the Trouble: Making Kin in the Chthulucene* (Durham, NC: Duke University Press, 2016).

Haraway, D., and others, 'Anthropologists Are Talking – About the Anthropocene', *Ethnos*, 81 (2016), 535–64.

Helmreich, S., 'Trees and Seas of Information: Alien Kinship and the Biopolitics of Gene Transfer in Marine Biology and Biotechnology', *American Ethnologist*, 30 (2003), 340–58.

—— *Alien Oceans: Anthropological Voyages in Microbial Seas* (Berkeley: University of California Press, 2009).

Hinchliffe, S., and others, *Pathological Lives: Disease, Space and Biopolitics* (Malden and Oxford: Wiley Blackwell, 2016).

Hird, M., *The Origins of Sociable Life: Evolution after Science Studies* (London: Palgrave Macmillan, 2009).

Irni, K. S., 'On the Materialization of Hormone Treatment Risks: A Trans/Feminist Approach', *Body & Society*, 23 (2017), 106–31.

Jasarevic, L., 'The Thing in a Jar: Mushrooms and Ontological Speculations in Post-Yugoslavia', *Cultural Anthropology*, 30.1 (2015), 36–64.

Kalin, J., and D. Gruber, 'Gut Rhetorics: Toward Experiments in Living with Microbiota', *Rhetoric of Health & Medicine*, 1.3 (2018), 269–95.

Keck, F., 'Liberating Sick Birds: Poststructuralist Perspectives on the Biopolitics of Avian Influenza', *Cultural Anthropology*, 30 (2015), 224–35.

Keck, F., and G. Lachenal, 'Simulations of Epidemics: Techniques of Global Health and Neo-Liberal Government', in A. Kelly, F. Keck, and C. Lynteris, eds, *The Anthropology of Epidemics* (New York: Routledge, 2019), pp. 25–42.

Kirchhelle, C., *Pyrrhic Progress: The History of Antibiotics in Anglo-American Food Production* (New Brunswick: Rutgers University Press, 2020).

Kirksey, E., 'Queer Love, Gender Bending Bacteria, and Life after the Anthropocene', *Theory, Culture & Society*, 36 (2019), 197–219.

Kirksey, E., and S. Helmreich, 'The Emergence of Multispecies Ethnography', *Cultural Anthropology*, 25 (2010), 545–76.

Lakoff, A., *Unprepared: Global Health in a Time of Emergency* (Berkeley: University of California Press, 2017).

Lakoff, A., and S. Collier, *Biosecurity Interventions: Global Health and Security in Question* (New York: Columbia University Press, 2008).

Landecker, H., 'Antibiotic Resistance and the Biology of History', *Body & Society*, 22 (2016), 19–52.

Latour, B., *The Pasteurization of France* (Cambridge, MA: Harvard University Press, 1993).

Law, J., and A. Mol, 'Globalisation in Practice: On the Politics of Boiling Pigswill', *Geoforum*, 39 (2008), 133–43.

Lorimer, J., 'Probiotic Environmentalities: Rewilding with Wolves and Worms', *Theory, Culture & Society*, 34 (2017), 27–48.

—— *The Probiotic Planet: Using Life to Manage Life* (Minneapolis: University of Minnesota Press, 2020).

Lorimer, J., and others, 'Making the Microbiome Public: Participatory Experiments with DNA Sequencing in Domestic Kitchens', *Transactions of the Institute of British Geographers*, 44.3 (2019), 524–41.

Lynteris, C., and B. Poleykett, 'The Anthropology of Epidemic Control: Technologies and Materialities', *Medical Anthropology*, 37 (2018), 433–41.

Martin, E., 'Toward an Anthropology of Immunology: The Body as Nation State', *Medical Anthropology Quarterly*, 4 (1990), 410–26.

Mbembe, A., *Necropolitics* (Durham, NC: Duke University Press, 2019).

Méthot, P.-O., and S. Alizon, 'What Is a Pathogen? Toward a Process View of Host-Parasite Interactions', *Virulence*, 5 (2014), 775–85.

Mol, A., *The Body Multiple: Ontology in Medical Practice* (Durham, NC: Duke University Press, 2002).

Nading, A., 'Orientation and Crafted Bureaucracy: Finding Dignity in Nicaraguan Food Safety', *American Anthropologist*, 119 (2017), 478–90.

Paxson, H., 'Post-Pasteurian Cultures: The Microbiopolitics of Raw-Milk Cheese in the United States', *Cultural Anthropology*, 23 (2008), 15–47.

—— *The Life of Cheese: Crafting Food and Value in America*. (Berkeley: University of California Press, 2012).

Paxson, H., and S. Helmreich, 'The Perils and Promises of Microbial Abundance: Novel Natures and Model Ecosystems, from Artisanal Cheese to Alien Seas', *Social Studies of Science*, 44 (2014), 165–93.

Pink, S., *Situating Everyday Life: Practices and Places* (London and Thousand Oaks: Sage Publications, 2012).

Povinelli, E., *Geontologies: A Requiem to Late Liberalism* (Durham, NC: Duke University Press, 2016).

Pradeu, T., 'Qu'est-Ce Qu'un Individu Biologique?' in P. Ludwig, and T. Pradeu, eds, *L'individu: Perspective contemporaire* (Paris: Vrin, 2008), pp. 97–125.

Prainsack, B., and A. Wahlberg, 'Situated Bio-Regulation: Ethnographic Sensibility at the Interface of STS, Policy Studies and the Social Studies of Medicine', *BioSocieties*, 8 (2013), 336–59.

Rees, T., 'From The Anthropocene To The Microbiocene', *Noema* (2020) <https://www.noemamag.com/from-the-anthropocene-to-the-microbiocene/> [accessed 12 December 2020].

Sanford, S., J. Polzer, and P. McDonough, 'Preparedness as a Technology of (in)security: Pandemic Influenza Planning and the Global Biopolitics of Emerging Infectious Disease', *Social Theory & Health*, 14 (2016), 18–43.

Sariola, S., and S. Gilbert, 'Toward a Symbiotic Perspective on Public Health: Recognizing the Ambivalence of Microbes in the Anthropocene', *Microorganisms*, 8.5 (2020), 746.

Sedgwick, E. K., *Touching Feeling: Affect, Pedagogy, Performativity* (Durham, NC: Duke University Press, 2003).

Shapin, S., and S. Schaffer, *Leviathan and the Air Pump* (Princeton: Princeton University Press, 1985).

Sharpe, C., *In the Wake: On Blackness and Being* (Durham, NC: Duke University Press, 2016).

Stengers, I., 'Introductory Notes on an Ecology of Practices', *Cultural Studies Review*, 11.1 (2005), 183–96.

Strathern, M., 'No Nature, No Culture: The Hagen Case', in C. MacCormack, and M. Strathern, eds, *Nature, Culture and Gender* (Cambridge: Cambridge University Press, 1980), pp. 174–222.

Tsing, A. L., *The Mushroom at the End of the World: On the Possibility of Life in Capitalist Ruins* (Princeton: Princeton University Press, 2017).

Vannini, P., *Non-Representational Methodologies: Re-Envisioning Research* (New York and London: Routledge, 2015).

Wald, P., *Contagious: Cultures, Carriers, and the Outbreak Narrative* (Durham, NC: Duke University Press, 2008).

Weheliye, A., *Habeas Viscus: Racializing Assemblages, Biopolitics, and Black Feminist Theories of the Human* (Durham, NC: Duke University Press, 2014).

Winickoff, D., and D. Bushey, 'Science and Power in Global Food Regulation: The Rise of the Codex Alimentarius', *Science, Technology & Human Values*, 35 (2010), 356–81.

Wolf, M., 'Knowing Pandemics', *Science & Technology Studies*, 30.4 (2017), 8–29.

I

SENSING

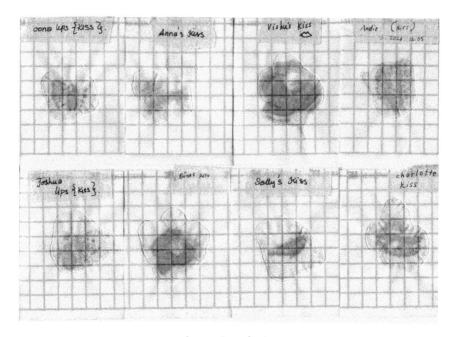

FIG. A: COLLECTIVE KISSES. A practice of microbial care at the With Microbes writing workshop in January 2020 at Kilpisjärvi (Finland) biological station brought we three artists together to think and imagine with microbes and social scientists. We (Vishnu Vardhani, Oona Leinovirtanen and Riina Hannula) offered the social scientists an individual reading from the data of their own microbes. Speculative fictioning/realism turned the laboratory into a space of magical predicting instead of scientific predicting, providing a platform for interspecies community building. Our aim was to think of relations with microbes beyond dichotomies of self/nonself or good/bad microbes etc. We asked: how do we let microbes living in and on bodies have more agency without anthropomorphising or totalising them or treating them as objects? We had no medical agenda, but we collected samples, and this 'i-magickining' became a four-hour performance for and with the academic participants: an event detecting microbial samples as a 'tarot' deck. Producing and constructing facts to predict outcomes is the daily work of science. Can we identify agents as more relational and distributed if we are not bound by factual results, even when we use the same methods as scientists do? (Photograph by the Labracadabra team)

I

THE DEPLANTATIONOCENE: LISTENING TO YEASTS AND REJECTING THE PLANTATION WORLDVIEW

Denis Chartier

Fermentation processes are energetic phenomena which change the vibratory state of the environments which are subject to them and, when it comes to wine, those who drink it. All of this energy produces organoleptic emotions and sensations of wellbeing when we drink 'real' wine. In our modern age, in which people consume an increasing number of dead and disguised products which distance them from their fundamental nature and affect their intelligence and their looks, 'real' wine is a vibratory source which helps people find alignment within themselves, with others and with the environment (Philippe Pacalet, natural wine-maker).

LISTEN

MAKE YOURSELF COMFORTABLE AND PUT SOME HEADPHONES ON IF YOU can. Let's begin with a journey through sound, scale and time. What you are about to listen to is a composition of the sounds produced by the microorganisms which produce so-called natural wine in the wine-makers' vat (see Figure 1.1).[1]

FIG. 1.1 Yeast recording system (Clos du Tue Bœuf, Les Montils, France, September 2018)

This piece is the first part of a longer composition (*Origins* 2019) created for an art installation called *L'Assemblée*, made with vine stocks which were dug up after dying from fungal diseases. The aim of this piece was to create awareness of the complex but specific relationship that natural wine-makers have with the living world and to render this relationship perceptible. You will hear the juxtaposition of different parts of the fermentation process: *Saccharomyces cerevisae* (and other yeasts) transforming sugar into alcohol, *Lauconostoc Oenos* (and other bacteria) transforming malic acid into lactic acid (and perhaps others still). If I may, I will ask you to let these sounds sink in for a moment before you return to the text.

Scan the QR code (see Figure 1.2) with a smartphone or use the HTML link below to be transported to the Yeast Symphony (https://soundcloud.com/chartier-denis/yeastsymphony).

FIG. 1.2 Yeast Symphony (QR code)

Recordings from a vat of conventional wine-making fermentation[2] would produce sounds which would probably be difficult to differentiate from those you have just heard. However, hours of recording and listening to the song of these microorganisms, enhanced by hours of observing the relationship between them and the wine-makers, have led me to track these talkative cracking sounds with a discerning ear. I suggest that we can hear agricultural practices which are gentler than those of conventional wine-making, more attentive to the cultivated environment, more respectful of the soil and of the existence of non-human creatures (the plants, microorganisms, fauna and flora present in the vineyard). What we hear is the result of an attempt at cohabitation, collaboration between humans and non-humans, rather than an attempt to coerce the living world or a relationship of domination. What we hear is a hymn to Orpheus, rather than to Prometheus: a hymn which involves listening to the living world to understand its secrets, rather than dominating it to force it to reveal things to us. What we hear is the materialisation of an 'Orphic political ecology' (Chartier 2016) in which yeasts, these beautiful symbiotes,[3] are the main actors. What we hear is the promise of these microbes. Yes, the promise: because the care given to the yeasts in these vats is the embodiment of an attempt to break with the notion of monoculture which has shaped our tastes, our emotions and the modern era's relationship with living creatures, as the concept of the Plantationocene developed by Haraway, Tsing and Gilbert so powerfully captures (Haraway and Tsing 2019). The plantation consists in the reproduction *ad infinitum* of a single species of plant, requiring other life forms to be neutralised or killed with herbicides and pesticides. But these French natural wine-makers are engaged in a break (insofar as is possible) with the practices of the plantation.

They are trying to take us out of the Plantationocene by becoming actors of the Deplantationocene.[4]

So, there we have it. Everything has already been said, but now I must explain myself. To grasp this process of 'Deplantationocenisation', I will proceed in stages. First, I will demonstrate the extent to which vitiviniculture is an agribusiness which is organised around a naturalised vision of the plantation (ecological simplification, discipline of plants and humans, etc.) as a condition for managing nature. This sector has not escaped the global reproduction of a plantation economy. I then focus on natural wine-makers' choices concerning vinification to reveal their very specific relationship with microorganisms and to show how, by means of a chain reaction, this relationship leads them to question the aesthetics of repetition, the standardisation of plants, the nature of the wines we drink, the ways of ensuring cohabitation and control of the living world, consumer tastes and the violence to which the inhabitants of these areas are subjected (Ferdinand 2019). This should help us to understand how they encourage us to abandon the plantation by inviting us to dream and to interact with living creatures other than humans.

VITIVINICULTURE AND THE PLANTATIONOCENE

The history of vineyards and wine is so ancient that it is conflated with the history of humanity (Dion 2010; Ulin and Black 2013) or, at any rate, the history of Western society which laid the foundations for the Capitalocene (Moore 2015) and the Plantationocene. It is significant to analyse this economy, these pruned vines and the yeasts which make this beverage – which Brives (2017) reminds us, were among the first organisms to have been domesticated by humans. *La vigne* (vine) is an iconic 'natureculture' (Haraway 2016), as vineyards and wine have long been important economic and cultural elements within Mediterranean societies, and as such subject to processes of Plantationocenisation: they have become plantations like any other, reconfiguring the landscape and exploiting the living world and its share of pathogens. Because of the ecological simplification of the plantation and the increased transport of living materials from one continent to another (Tsing 2017), wine-making plantations have provided ideal conditions for the development of diseases and other animal 'pests'.

The stereotypical image of fields of vineyards as a monotonous sea of stumps, stretching as far as the eye can see, is a recent reality and the result of the rise of monoculture vineyards, particularly at the end of the nineteenth century. The trend toward monospecific plantations intensified in the nineteenth and twentieth centuries, although the speed at which it was adopted depended on whether the wine-making region had a long history of polyculture agriculture. At the beginning of the nineteenth century, French viticulture had entered a period of frenzied production. Low quality wines were preferred and there was no hesitation when it came to replacing traditional grape varieties with more productive varieties. Production in France rose from 30 million hectolitres in 1788 to 40 million in 1829, 70 million in 1870 and 85 million in 1875 (Dion 2010). Increased production subsequently led to the spread of diseases, primarily from the Americas, into French vineyards. *Sparganothis pileriana*, a vine-eating moth, arrived in the 1830s, closely followed by other microorganisms. Grapevine powdery mildew (*Erysiphe necator*) arrived in the early 1850s, while grape downy mildew (*Plasmopara viticola*) spread from 1878. Various measures were taken each time to limit the damage, including the application of sulphur and hot water and Bordeaux mixture made with copper sulphate. However, grape phylloxera (*Daktulosphaira vitifoliae*) could not be contained. This aphid is said to have arrived with a soldier returning from a French military operation in Mexico and established itself among the few American vines he planted in 1864 in the south of France.[5] This is significant, given that the concept of the Plantationocene 're-establishes a historicity of global environmental changes which does not erase the colonial and enslaving foundations of globalisation' (Ferdinand 2019: 84). In about thirty years, phylloxera spread across French vineyards (and to the rest of the world); despite major efforts, this led to the total destruction of the vines (which died within three years of infection). Billions of dead vine stocks were dug up and gradually replaced by insect-resistant plants from America onto which local grape varieties were grafted. Hence this aphid brought the world of the vineyard and the landscapes associated with these plantations into the Plantationocene. Following this, vines were replanted in straight rows, making it possible to use draught animals and then machines to work the land. Production, which had fallen in five years from 85 million hectolitres to 30 million in 1880, began to rise again, with an increasing focus on monoculture vineyards (Dion 2010).[6]

Today, the wine industry remains a key economic sector in France (even if there has been a decline in the area cultivated for wine-growing and in wine production over the last few decades). With nearly 50 million hectolitres produced in 2018, France is one of the world's leading wine producers (global production stands at 292 million hectolitres annually). With 750,000 hectares of cultivated land, 10% of the world's vineyards but just 3% of French agricultural land, the wine industry is France's leading agricultural sector in terms of value and the second largest export sector with a turnover of 9.32 billion euros in 2018 (after aeronautics and before cosmetics).[7] As an industry, it is extremely standardised and is governed by considerable legislation. Wine has become a regulated product like any other and many wine-makers try to stabilise production from one year to the next, in terms of volumes, taste and distribution methods. The vast majority of these wines are produced 'conventionally', as my interlocutors refer to viniculture that makes use of pesticides, fungicides and other inputs, even if there has been a significant increase in organic production in recent years, with 14% of French vineyards recognised as organic in 2019 compared to 5% in 2009 (Agence Bio 2020). Given that there is more to wine-making than how the grape is grown (organically or not), it is important to be aware that conventional wine-makers intervene significantly in the fermentation processes in the vats, where grape juice is transformed into wine, to ensure maximum control of the fermentation and the resultant taste and stability of the wine. Only one third of wine-makers vinify their wines (the majority have their wines vinified in co-operatives). In organic wine-making, these interventions can be significant, even if just over 40 inputs are authorised, compared to more than 600 in conventional wine-making (Pineau 2019). This is to say that even in organic conditions, the logics of the Plantationocene dictate the orientations of public institutions, research organisations, wine state services and consumer tastes (Smith et al. 2007).

In this sense, natural wines are more than 'just' organic wines. Their fermentation processes do not involve inputs and require minimal intervention, determining a whole chain of relationships and practices to the living world and the local landscape. There are only a handful of natural wine-makers in France, probably no more than 1,000 from a total of 85,000 vineyards, or approximately 1.5% of the French wine market.[8] However, they are extremely visible and are rapidly growing in numbers. I have been conducting regular fieldwork in the Loire Valley since 2013. In 2017–2018, as part of the Vin/Vivants collective, this fieldwork focused more specifically on the estates of three wine-makers.[9] Hervé Villemade has a 25-hectare estate, Thierry Puzelat, who now works with his daughters Zoé and Louise, owns 19.5 hectares and Noëlla Morantin's estate spans 6 hectares. The first two inherited their parents' conventional wine-making vineyards, before changing their wine-making practices to produce natural wines. Noëlla Morantin took over a biodynamic vineyard. In addition to the deep affinities that bind us, I chose these wine-makers because the question of withdrawing from the practices of the plantation has been at the heart of everything they have done for more than 20 years.

CHOOSING TO MAKE DO WITH WHAT THE AREA'S INHABITANTS GIVE US

In order for fermentation to take place, yeasts are needed, as Louis Pasteur demonstrated in his *Etude sur le vin*, which revolutionised wine-making and earned Pasteur the title of 'the father of modern oenology' (Pasteur 1866). In natural wine-making, the care given to these organisms is crucial and determines everything the wine-makers do, from the field to the cellar. The biggest difference between natural wine-makers and their organic wine-making colleagues lies in the vinification process, during which technical interventions are limited as much as possible. In most wine cellars, grape juice is pasteurised, the processes are sanitised and controlled with sulphites, and exogenous, laboratory-grown yeast species are added to ensure that the right species are at work in the vats.[10] The list of interventions is long and includes a horde of technical terms: reverse osmosis, tangential filtration, flash pasteurisation, thermovinification and more. All these practices are disavowed in natural wine-making, during which it is said that 'nothing is added and nothing is removed'. Natural wines are made using organic grapes and indigenous yeasts; the process involves hand-picking but does not involve any inputs, filtering or any techniques which are described by some wine-makers as brutal and traumatising for living creatures.[11] Sulphites are not added before or during fermentation;[12] however, some wine-makers use very low doses (30mg/l) before bottling and, occasionally, to prepare their starter.

This way of making wine with minimal intervention is very risky and requires an intense focus on microorganisms and the processes of the living world. These processes are highly unpredictable. As a result, natural wine-makers must work differently at every stage from growing the grapes in the fields to selling the wine. Most importantly, natural wine-makers must understand and listen to the yeasts and the microorganisms; their activities and their environment must be closely monitored because any mistake can result in multiple complications, including the development of undesirable yeasts. Different yeasts result in different fermentation processes and some, like the famous Brett (*Brettanomyce*), can make wines undrinkable. In the words of Noëlla Morantin:

> Brett, [...] I've found that in some of my wines, it was just horrible [...] the yeast develops when [...] the grape juice is cold... it's incredibly resistant, it establishes itself gradually but consistently, it invades the environment, it ferments really well... and so, once it's started... I promise you, your wine is dry [...] there's no problem with volatile acidity [...] but it smells like shit [...] Brett's a killer, it destroys everything it finds, it just takes over.[13]

These words, which highlight the truly unique relationship between natural wine-makers and these yeasts, show how important it is to monitor what happens in the vat as well as the ambient temperatures at the time of harvest. This is crucial information when it comes to understanding which yeasts will flourish. It is understandable that conventional wine-makers, when trying to produce a wine with the same characteristics from one year to the next, prefer to use industrial yeasts which have been chosen for their fermentation properties and organoleptic impact – a practice which has intensified over the past 40 years (Carbonneau and Escudier 2017).

SHEPHERDING YEASTS:
ACCEPTING UNCERTAINTY

There are different approaches to the fermenting processes, involving various levels of painstaking intervention. Jacques Neauport, one of the first oenologists to have championed natural wines, encouraged 'obsessiveness'. If sulphur is to be avoided, everything must be impeccably clean. Neauport often told new wine-makers that they should spend time working in a dairy or brewery to learn how to clean the equipment. He also recommended buying a microscope to monitor yeast. Many wine-makers follow his advice to reduce the uncertainty of additive-free fermentation by using microbiological analysis:

> During the harvest, we become microbiologists: we look with a microscope to see which yeasts and bacteria are potentially present [...], I think it's good to know the direction you're going in, to find out if there are already any issues or not [...] You have a clearer idea of where you're going.[14]

FIG. 1.3A, 1.3B Starter, testing system, and bags of grapes for testing (Hervé Villemade's cellar, Celletes, France, September 2018)

Wine-makers are reassured to discover what they are working with and who they are talking to; they can also ensure that the right yeasts are developing by creating a starter (see Figures 1.3A and 1.3B). This operation, carried out just after harvest, involves using a small quantity of sulphites and heating a few dozen litres of grape juice to encourage the development of the desired indigenous yeasts and then introducing this into the vat containing the rest of the juice from the harvest.

As many people told us, testing usually confirms what the wine-makers' own experience indicated during the fermenting processes. Wine-maker Jacques Neauport explains, 'It takes ten years to start making natural wine properly, with ten years being the minimum period needed to understand every case, but even with years of experience, [a natural wine-maker is] always close to the edge'.[15] Some people seem less worried than others about this 'edge' and have stopped carrying out these tests, having concluded that they did not leave enough room for wine-makers' intuition or sensitivities, or even created unnecessary stress. The wine-maker Catherine Marin-Pestel, interviewed by Pineau (2019: 233), commented that she no longer tests her wines because it was like giving blood samples all the time to find out if she was ill when everything was, in fact, fine. In an interview, Didier Chaffardon noted:

> I don't know if we have sufficiently skilled laboratories for that. I'm not sure that it's particularly useful, actually [...] testing provides a kind of understanding which can restore confidence [...] but that's all [...] you'll never manage to contain the living world in a test or anything else [...] testing will rarely be exhaustive [...] on the other hand, intentions and trust are fundamental. If you don't trust in the process, you can carry out all the tests you want [...] the energy that you find in the wine won't ever come from testing.[16]

At this stage, it is important to say that all the wine-makers we met told us that they listen to the yeasts fermenting in the vat, as you were asked to do at the beginning of this chapter. With a little experience, they are easily able to differentiate between the sound of alcoholic fermentation and the sound of malolactic fermentation, and they are able to identify the progress of the fermentation process by listening to various auditory characteristics in the vat (power, frequency of cracking sounds, etc.). This listening process is not in any wine-making manuals, but it is clearly a way to connect with the microorganisms at work in the vat on a daily basis.

For many of these wine-makers, their stance is driven by a sense of humility and a deep respect for the processes of the living world.

> [...] The fermentation process is just incredible, it's totally beyond us. [...] There's a whole world inside [the vat], all I try to do is to listen, smell and touch it, because the temperature is important... smelling it, listening to it, listening to the sound of the yeasts, etc., [...]. I watch them just like a shepherd watches his flock. [...] I talk about monitoring rather than controlling, because as I tell my trainee wine-makers, if there's one verb you can remove from your vocabulary when you start producing natural wines, it's the verb to control (Azzoni in Pineau 2018: 232–3, my translation).

Removing the verb 'to control' from a wine-maker's vocabulary goes against the conventional concept of wine-making. Yet even if natural wine-makers are not entirely in control, they still produce excellent wines. This leads me to a crucial point: the focus on yeasts is not limited to what happens in the cellar. Didier Barrouillet, one of the first natural wine-makers I met in 2012, told me that as a former chemist, he had initially taken an interest in the vinification process before remarking that what happened in the vat depended on the quality of the grapes and the condition of the vine. His interest in these plants was inspired by a mantra known to many wine-makers, which Chaffardon summarises as: 'when you're generous with the vine, the vine is generous with everyone'. At the end of his career, however, he concluded that further work was necessary, including a focus on the soil. He came close to providing the definition of 'terroir' (the famous central concept when it comes to French wines) of Philippe Pacalet, a natural wine-maker from Bourgogne. A terroir is 'a delicate relationship between mankind, the soil (pedology, microclimate, exposure), a vine plant and a climate. The link between it all is biomass: yeast and bacterial microflora'. It is well understood that viticultural practices, in turn, have a significant effect on terroir. Jules Chauvet,[17] a major inspiration for these wine-makers, said as much as early as the 1950s when he advised against the use of herbicides, pesticides and chemical fertilisers, which 'destabilise the life of the soil and our terroir... and render it impossible to make good wines'.

FIGHTING AGAINST MONOTONY: ENCOURAGING MULTISPECIES RELATIONSHIPS TO FLOURISH

The yeasts found in the vat in early autumn are highly dependent on the yeasts found on the grape blooms in the fields in early spring. In order for these yeasts to be involved in the fermentation, organic practices must be implemented in the fields and a great deal of care given to the soil's microorganisms and to the plants. Agro-ecological practices are adopted by these wine-makers to move away from a productivist, monocultural viticulture where forms of life other than the vine itself are neutralised with herbicides and pesticides. These wine-makers see other-than-human beings as allies, rather than enemies (Pineau 2019), with the maxim that a greater diversity of living things improves the chances of having healthy grapes, good yeasts and sufficient food for these yeasts during fermentation. For example, a significant level of nitrogen in the grape musts is crucial for the metabolism of the yeasts which will carry out the alcoholic fermentation. It ensures an excellent start to the fermentation process by promoting cell multiplication and encourages the yeasts' metabolism to consume sugars during the process. In contrast, grape musts which lack nitrogen will lead to poor fermentation. In conventional agriculture, nitrogen can be added in different forms. This is not the case when it comes to natural wines. Wine-makers must therefore ensure that it is present in sufficient quantities in the fields and in the grapes. As Noëlla Morantin explains:

> During vinification, I carry out several tests. When it comes out of the press,
> I take a sample on the same day and take it to the lab to find out how much

nitrogen is in it, because if there's enough nitrogen, you know that the fermentation process will be complete […] if there's not enough nitrogen, it's a nightmare […] we have to make sure that there's enough nitrogen in the vines […] it's pretty fascinating! So when people say that the vine makes the wine [slowing down for emphasis] you see what they mean […] and in the soil […] you see that's right […] ensuring that your wine doesn't lack anything means ensuring that the vine is in a good condition and not lacking nitrogen itself.[18]

It is clear that agricultural practices are instrumental here. To ensure a supply of nitrogen, some natural wine-makers focus on growing leguminous plants (lucerne, clover, vetch, etc.) to encourage nitrogen fixation. They break up the monotony of the plantation by introducing other plants between the rows of vines (see Figure 1.4).

FIG. 1.4 Biodiversity between rows (Hervé Villemade's Vineyard, Celletes, France, July 2017)

Similarly, they plant between the vine rows to attract allies against predators (insects, birds, etc.). Some even hope to go further:

> Because it's humans who have created cultivated vines, which then become dependent. Then, to ensure that they continue to grow leaves and to produce fruit, you have to prune them and I find that really problematic. I'm considering lots of options, the shape of the vine when I prune it, something much less drastic, leaving more wood [...]but that won't necessarily work well [...] Actually, I don't know, I haven't found an answer yet [...] My goal is for the vines to become independent [...] independent and wild [...] just as I like to be [laughs] (Anne-Marie Lavaysse in Pineau 2017: 204, my translation).

The diversity of the living world and cohabitation with other non-human beings is cherished here, but it must not be essentialised. Viticulture is a complicated choreography involving human beings, soils, plants, microorganisms and the climate in areas which continue to be dominated by monoculture. Often, the relationship with certain microorganisms is similar to warfare, as some wine-makers told us during the mildew attacks in the Loire Valley in 2018.

To fight against mildew, organic farmers can only use copper, a heavy metal which can build up in the soil, leaving it infertile. It seems that well maintained, well fed, organic and diverse vines are more resistant to fungi (Deguine et al. 2016), but, in the Plantationocene, these fungi are becoming increasingly virulent because they are 'cultivated' in environments which benefit them (Haraway and Tsing 2019). This makes it increasingly difficult to fight them. These microbes, along with some animals which occasionally eat grapes and vine leaves, such as deer, are monitored and driven away or killed, in accordance with the practices which govern contemporary plantations, but with weapons which are often much less aggressive than those used in conventional plantations, the idea being to find other ways to fight or to cohabit, insofar as is possible.

FACING UP TO THE MONSTERS OF THE PLANTATIONOCENE

The decision to work only with the microorganisms which are present in the soil heightens natural wine-makers' awareness of environmental disruption and leaves them particularly exposed to disturbances and to 'monsters' (new pathogens, hybrid species) created by the Plantationocene (Tsing 2017). For example, some wine-makers told us that they struggled with the spotted wing drosophila (*Drosophila susukii*). This fly from Asia appeared in France in 2010 and is now present throughout France, where it has found new hosts. Like its European counterparts, it targets bunches of grapes, where it tends to inoculate acetic bacteria, which transform grape must into vinegar. When a plantation is affected, conventional wine-makers can pasteurise the must to kill any bacteria and re-sow with exogenous yeasts. This is not possible for natural wine-makers. Everything is intertwined.

They are also directly affected by climate change to such an extent that they are raising the alarm publicly, as sentinels. Thierry Puzelat explains:

> My father only experienced a single black frost [a severe sub-zero episode] during his first year in 1945, and afterwards [...] it froze 5, 6 times [...] in 25 years, it's frozen 10 times [...] it's become a more common occurrence with a significant shift in the 1990s [...] the problem is that bud break and flowering happen earlier. Before, bud break began at the end of April, so no-one cared about the April frosts [...] this year [2018], there were leaves on the vines at the end of March [...]it's not the spring frosts which have changed, it's the time when bud break begins, because the winter is shorter. The problem that we have now is that we have hotter years and more sugar in the grapes; this makes vinification difficult and the wines are more difficult to drink, because they contain too much alcohol.[19]

This ever-changing situation is crucial when it comes to the development of their vineyards. 'We are planting late grape varieties. Our parents had dug them up because they didn't manage to bring them to maturity every year'. This also has an impact on their ability to make wine:

> Claude Courtois [a renowned figure who has made natural wines for 30 years] says that everything is changing and that no-one understands it any more, particularly over the last two or three years! There are probably fundamental changes in the local microfauna and microflora and in a wider sense [...] this has had a particularly disruptive effect on fermentation. He is mainly talking about red wine, it's less noticeable when it comes to white wine but it's true that things are changing ... [20]

What is happening here is that the wine-makers are identifying a struggle, precisely because of the specific relationship they have with yeasts. Just as our human bodies struggle with the disappearance of symbiotic allies (Zimmer 2019), these wine-makers have seen that the terroir's body is also struggling for the same reasons. A new microbiopolitics is emerging (Paxson 2018): it has been perfectly identified by wine-makers and leads them to quietly object to the expansion of the worldview of the plantation.

DRINKING CLOUDY WINE: LIVING WITH THE TROUBLE[21]

Rejecting the worldview of the plantation when producing processed food makes it possible to step away from uniform tastes. For all the reasons mentioned here, the taste of these wines often differs from standardised conventional wines. They may be more acidic, more oxidised or more reduced than conventional wines. These 'flaws' often prevent them from being recognised as an *appellation d'origine contrôlée* (AOC)[22] and there are endless debates as to what makes a wine 'good' and what makes it 'flawed'. In some instances, this can end up in court, with natural wine-makers refusing to accept that their wines are not authorised for market.[23] These wines still contain living microorganisms when they are bottled, and so they must be stored carefully because of the risk of microbial alterations which can make them undrinkable (continued fermentation, transformation into vinegar, etc.). Moreover, it is often said that it is better to drink a specific vintage at certain times of the year than at others, because it can be affected by lunar phases, for example.

These wines impose their own conditions in terms of how they should be stored and when they should be drunk: their sensitivity to atmospheric and astronomic changes has a significant effect on their taste. The vitality of these wines, which are produced by myriad relationships, dictates how they should be approached, how they should be drunk and how they should be sold. They are not sold by large retailers because they are too fragile and not sufficiently standardised. Instead, they are sold where they are produced or by a network of specialist sellers who provide explanations. Indeed, because they are rather bewildering when compared to conventional wines, an explanation about exactly what is being drunk needs to be provided to help novice drinkers fully appreciate these wines. One of the central tenets of the explanations about natural wines, offered almost systematically by wine-makers and wine merchants, is that these wines are made with genuine respect for the living world and are therefore a living product themselves. This argument is crucial when it comes to accepting a symbolic lack of clarity, which can sometimes be literal concerning these wines. They can become cloudy because the living microorganisms they contain may continue to develop, causing the wine to lose its clarity. What is normally seen as a flaw becomes a sign of vitality and of a drink which tells a different story to that of a deadly monoculture. Those who drink natural wines are also drinking an attempt to develop another story of multi-species cohabitation within the agricultural world.

TAKING CARE OF YEASTS TO REJECT THE WORLDVIEW OF THE PLANTATION AND VICE-VERSA

These wine-makers reconnect with our microbial companions, developing relationships which are mindful of the interconnected worlds which these microbes impose. They fight against an 'epidemic of absence' (Velasquez-Manoff 2013) and a reduction in microbial exchange. Through their practices and their lives, they counter the ecological simplification of the plantation with an ecological complexification; they counter discipline with a form of wilderness, or rewilding, and they counter control of the living world with trust and relaxed detachment. By rejecting the practices of the plantation, they create trouble for the public institutions which govern French terroirs and orient consumer tastes. Rather than exhausting the soil, humans, plants and non-human creatures, they choose to feed, care for, nurture and protect them,[24] guided by the microorganisms themselves.

Indeed, just as Stepanoff (2018) has shown that it is lichens which lead the reindeer and thus the Siberian 'shepherds', and just as Paxson (2018) has shown that cheese is the product of a multi-species collective which includes the sheep, the dogs which watch over them, the bacteria and the cheese-makers, making natural wine in the Capitalocene is a process which involves bringing microorganisms, plants and geological and climatic factors together, transcending the distinctions between biological and geological life (Povinelli 2016). Their actions are guided by the way the vine, the soil and the yeasts 'respond' to what they do. They talk about 'soil' as teeming with life and processes. They rely on chemistry and microbiology in addition to their knowledge of the principles of organic or biodynamic agriculture, and common sense which they develop over time. But they also rely significantly on their 'feelings' and what they hear and understand of the yeasts which ultimately guide their actions. In this way, they reject the worldview of the plantation, often quietly but tangibly, and they lead us in a subtle inter-species dance towards a Deplantationocene.

NOTES

1   I made these recordings as part of a creative research project carried out in 2017–2018 with the Vin/Vivants collective made up of Emmanuelle Blanc, Aurélien Gabriel Cohen and myself. As a hybrid project combining humanities, visual arts and life sciences, Vins/Vivants intended to highlight responses to environmental disaster constituted by situated practices. Research was conducted in three vineyards belonging to Noëlla Morantin, Hervé Villemade and Thierry and Jean-Marie Puzelat (Clos du Tue Bœuf). It led to several

exhibitions in France, including 'Des Vivants, des Vins' at the Scène National d'Orléans (January–March 2019).

2 The term 'conventional wine-makers' refers to wine-makers who control the life of the vineyard with a variety of toxic treatments to maintain a 'healthy' vine. They also intervene in fermentation processes, using numerous exogenous products to control them.

3 A symbiote is an organism which participates in a symbiosis, a long-lasting association between organisms of different species. Here, I use Haraway's (2016) definition of symbiote, and not a strict 'biological' definition.

4 I would like to thank Emilia Sanabria for suggesting this term.

5 The objective of France's intervention in Mexico (1861–1867) was to establish a political regime in the country which would be sympathetic to French interests.

6 Two of the wine-makers with whom we worked inherited their properties from their parents, who made the decision to transition from polyculture to monoculture in the 1950s and 1960s. Their children continued with this dynamic for a while, before recently returning to polyculture.

7 https://www.vinetsociete.fr/chiffres-cles [accessed 13 July 2020].

8 It is extremely difficult to provide an exact number, given that there are few natural wine-making associations or labels. However, work is currently ongoing to ensure the French government's recognition of natural wines (Pineau, personal communication).

9 I also visited and discussed the wine-making process with other natural wine-makers, often working alone on small estates, to enhance my understanding of this practice.

10 There is an official catalogue of wine-making yeasts (384 in 2020) which wine-makers can choose from, depending on the fermentation and the type of wine they produce. These yeasts are not genetically modified organisms, as these are prohibited in France (unlike in the USA where GMO yeasts are approved by the Food and Drug Administration).

11 These are the terms used by a group of wine-makers who are trying to develop a natural wine charter as part of an association which was founded in 2019: *Syndicat de Défense des Vins Nature'l* (Proust 2019).

12 The first use of sulphites to make wine easier to store dates back to the eighteenth century and is said to have been invented by the Dutch (Carbonneau and Torregrosa 2020).

13 Interview, March 2018.

14 Morantin, March 2018.

15 laplumedanslevignoble.fr/2016/11/08/jacques-Neauport/ [accessed 6 July 2020]

16 Interview, December 2019.

17 Jules Chauvet is a wine-maker and biologist who studied fermentation from a chemist's point of view in an attempt to remove chemistry from the process. See Pineau (2019) and Cohen (2013) on his role in the development of natural wines.

18 Interview, March 2018.

19 Interview, July 2017.

20 Chaffardon Interview, December 2019.

21 In French, this title is a pun on the word 'trouble' which means both confusion and a cloudy, murky quality, such as that of an unfiltered natural wine. Here, it echoes Haraway's (2016) *Staying with the Trouble*.

22 An AOC is a product developed in accordance with recognised regional expertise that gives the product its characteristics and determines criteria, including agricultural practices and taste, which are required for it to be recognised as an AOC. Samples are blind tasted and approved or rejected by legislators who are often conventional wine-makers themselves.

23 Sébastien David, a wine-maker from Saint-Nicolas-de-Bourgueil, lost his case against the French state and had to send 2,078 bottles of a 2019 vintage to a distillery; this wine was declared unfit for consumption due to its excessively high acidity.

24 I do not wish to stigmatise conventional wine-makers who love and care for their wine estates and the plants they grow in their own way, albeit in a context radically forged by the plantation (Haraway and Tsing 2019).

ACKNOWLEDGEMENTS

Special thanks to Emmanuelle Blanc and Aurélien Gabriel Cohen for the inspiring Vin/Vivants collaboration and to Emilia Sanabria for her stimulating insights. My thanks also go to the sound artist Thomas Tilly for his precious advice which helped me enter more deeply into the world of sound recording, as well as to Jean Foyer with whom this research on natural wines began in 2013 and continued in the *Institutionalising Agroecologies* research programme. I am deeply grateful to all the wine-makers who shared their wonderful visions and ways of living.

REFERENCES

Brives, C., 'Que font les scientifiques lorsqu'ils ne sont pas naturalistes? Le cas des levuristes', *L'homme*, 222 (2017), 35–56.

Carbonneau, A., and J.-L. Escudier, *De l'œnologie à la viticulture* (Paris: Editions Quae, 2017).

Carbonneau, A., and L. Torregrosa, *Traité de la vigne, Physiologie, terroir, culture* (Paris: Dunod, 2020).

Chartier, D., 'Répondre à l'intrusion de Gaïa. Écologie politique orphique et gaïagraphie à l'ère Anthropocène' (HDR Thesis, Université Paris 7 Denis Diderot, 2016).

Cohen, P., 'The Artifice of Natural Wine: Jules Chauvet and the Reinvention of Vinification in Postwar France', in Black R. E., and R. C. Ulin, eds, *Wine and Culture: Vineyard to Glass* (New York: Bloomsbury Academic, 2013), pp. 261–78.

Deguine, J.-P., and others, eds, *Agroecological Crop Protection* (London: Springer, 2017).

Dion, R., *Histoire de la vigne et du vin en France. Des origines au XIXe siècle* (Paris: CNRS Éditions, 2010).

Ferdinand, M., *Une écologie décoloniale* (Paris: Seuil, 2019).

Haraway, D., *Staying with the Trouble* (Durham, NC: Duke University Press, 2016).

Haraway, D., and A. Tsing, 'Reflections on the Plantationocene', *Edge Effects Magazine*, (2019) <https://edgeeffects.net/wp-content/uploads/2019/06/PlantationoceneReflections_Haraway_Tsing.pdf> [accessed 17 June 2020].

Moore, W. J., *Capitalism in the Web of Life: Ecology and the Accumulation of Capital* (New York: Verso, 2015).

Pasteur, L., *Études sur le vin, ses maladies, causes qui les provoquent. Procédés nouveaux pour le conserver et pour le vieillir* (Paris: Imprimerie impériale, 1866).

Povinelli, E., *Geontologies. A Requiem to Late Liberalism* (Durham, NC: Duke University Press, 2016).

Proust, I., 'Une nouvelle tentative pour définir les vins nature', *Vitisphère*, <https://www.vitisphere.com/actualite-90880-Une-nouvelle-tentative-pour-definir-les-vins-natures.htm> [accessed 12 July 2020].

Paxson, H., 'Post-Pasteurian Cultures. The Microbiopolitics of Raw-Milk Cheese in the United States', *Cultural Anthropology*, 23.1 (2018), 15–47.

Pineau, C., 'Anthropologie des vins "nature". La réhabilitation du sensible' (PhD thesis, EHESS Paris, 2017).

——*La corne de vache et le microscope. Le vin 'nature', entre sciences, croyances et radicalités* (Paris: La Découverte, 2019).

Tsing, L. A., *The Mushroom at the End of the World: On the Possibility of Life in Capitalist Ruins* (Princeton: Princeton University Press, 2017).

Ulin, R., and R. Black, *Wine and Culture: Vineyard to Glass* (London: Bloomsbury Academic, 2013).

Smith, A., J. Maillard, and O. Costa, *Vin et politique. Bordeaux, la France, la mondialisation* (Paris: Presses de Sciences Po, 2007).

Stepanoff, C., and J.-D. Vigne, eds, *Hybrid Communities. Biosocial Approaches to Domestication and Other Trans-species Relationships* (London: Routledge, 2018).

Velasquez-Manoff, M., *An Epidemic of Absence. A New Way of Understanding Allergies and Autoimmune Diseases* (New York: Scribner, 2013).

Zimmerer, A., 'Collecter, cultiver, conserver les microbiotes intestinaux', *Écologie & Politique*, 58 (2019), 135–50.

2

KNOWING, LIVING, AND BEING WITH BOKASHI

Veera Kinnunen

IN THIS CHAPTER, I WILL LOOK AT BOKASHI COMPOSTING — AN EMERGING waste practice which takes into consideration our co-constitutive relationship with microbes. Bokashi composting could be described as a 'probiotic' waste treatment method in that it works against the modern 'antibiotic' logics of purity and control. While modern waste practices have tried to get rid of waste as efficiently as possible – or even deny it altogether – a probiotic waste practice accepts waste as an intrinsic, and even essential, part of the maintenance of life. I explore the ontoethicopolitical implications of bokashi composting on waste relations.

HOW TO LIVE WITH SURPLUS MATTER?

Think of ordinary everyday objects such as nappies, Styrofoam coffee cups, plastic spoons or oranges. Objects such as these often turn to waste as soon as they have served their purpose, and once waste, what is left of them is moved out of sight as efficiently as possible. Until recently, most of these heterogeneous waste materials would have been removed by dumping them into landfills or, at best, burning them in incinerators. These industrial waste management solutions have, as Gay Hawkins (2006: 16) has aptly noted, been marked by an ethos of 'distance, disposability, and denial'.

Indeed, practices of eliminating waste by burying surplus matter in the ground, fuming it into the air and even recycling can be interpreted as attempts to deny accountability for the specific material consequences that the modern lifestyle produces. The engineering of landfills, which, according to a World Bank report (Kaza et al. 2018), is still the globally prevalent means of managing waste, has been concerned with 'making sure that waste does not leak' (Hird 2012: 458). However, the trouble with waste is that it always leaks: it neither vanishes in the air nor stays put in the landfills. Once in the ground, the unstable mixture of heterogeneous materials becomes part of the production and consumption economy of bacteria, which 'relentlessly metabolise discarded objects into leachate, which in turn percolates into soil and groundwater, where it moves into and through plants, trees, animals, fungi, insects and the atmosphere' (Hird 2012: 457). In the logics of industrial waste management, the threatening microbial liveliness of waste matter has thus been treated as something to fight against and to keep under control as effectively as possible.

As alternative human-microbe relations are currently being developed in myriads of lay and professional practices from health care to gastronomy, alternative approaches to waste management have also become subject to experimentation. In this chapter, I explore one example of an emerging alternative waste treatment practice, which embraces the microbial liveliness of waste instead of rejecting it: the bokashi method. In an attempt to take responsibility for the waste matter produced in the midst of everyday life, the method works against the modern ethos of 'distance, disposability, and denial'.

The originally East Asian tradition of treating organic waste by fermenting it and using the ferment as a soil amendment has come to be globally known by its Japanese name *bokashi* (Christel 2017: 2).[1] During the last decade, this alternative method of composting has expanded to the global North and has quickly transformed from a technique experimented with by a few dedicated enthusiasts to a fairly common alternative to traditional hot composting. In European countries, bokashi is mainly practised in private homes, although the method can also be applied on an industrial scale.

The bokashi method has been surrounded by bold claims for its effectiveness and benefits as a soil fertiliser. Although bokashi practitioners report positive experiences and the hype runs high, scientific research proving these claims is still scarce (see Christel 2017). However, I am neither qualified nor interested in proving the microbiological effectiveness of the method scientifically. For me, as a sociologist and waste ethnographer, the bokashi practice opens up an experimental *contact zone* (Alaimo 2010) which allows for the exploration and imagining of new forms of living with waste. As Sebastian Abrahamsson and Filippo Bertoni (2014: 126) put it, 'composting shifts what togetherness might come to be'.

Karen Barad (2007), among other feminist theorists, pushes for *ontoethico-political* thinking, stating that our knowing practices, our ways of being in the world and our ethical orientation are all entangled and invoked in practical action (Shotwell 2016). Following this line of thought, the practical making of bokashi can be seen as affecting the practitioner's knowing relations and thus having implications for our ways of being and living in the world. Therefore, in the pages to come I will seek to answer the following question: how does practising bokashi affect knowing (epistemologies), living (ethics/politics) and being (ontologies) together with waste?

DATA AND METHODS

At the time of writing this chapter, I have been conducting multisensory ethnographic research among bokashi communities for more than three years. I have welcomed bokashi into my everyday life by learning to make my own DIY bokashi buckets and I have started to ferment leftover food produced by my family. Over the years, I have browsed through dozens of blogs, guides and commercial pages dedicated to bokashi. I have joined bokashi-related groups on social media and taken part in the lively discussion in those groups. I have visited the homes of Finnish bokashi practitioners, encountered their bokashi buckets and familiarised myself with their bokashi-making practices, and I have had countless conversations with fellow bokashi practitioners. Thus, I am not merely a participant observer of bokashi practices, I am a *co-experimenter* (see Gomart and Hennion 1999).

As a co-experimenting ethnographer, I consider myself as one node in the lively bokashi community and take part in its constitution through my own actions, experiences, thoughts and feelings. Taking part in and following the discussions on social media[2] have been just as important parts of my fieldwork as face-to-face encounters with fellow bokashers or the experimentation with my own bokashi. Each of these doings opens up a different aspect of knowing, living and being with bokashi, and together they weave the messy field of my ethnographic work.

As an attempt to make sense of myriad aspects of practising bokashi, I have kept several fieldwork diaries: 1) In the *bokashi diary*, a book located in my kitchen cupboard, I have jotted down entries describing my own bokashi experiences in my kitchen and garden, 2) in the *digital fieldwork diary* located on the hard drive of my laptop, I have collected notes from the discussions on social media dedicated to bokashi.[3] In addition, 3) I have made *walk-along visits* to bokashi-practising households, which I have recorded with a voice recorder[4] and complemented with written ethnographic observations. This chapter largely draws from diaries 1 and 2.

Inspired by the sensory ethnographic approach (Pink 2015), I have paid attention to the multisensory, embodied nature of knowing, living and being with bokashi. Drawing from the multispecies approach (Kirksey and Helmreich 2010), I have tuned myself into the variety of more-than-human relations, asking how assemblages and alliances are formed in bokashi practice and what kinds of forms they take.[5] The following story is weaved together from my co-experimental ethnographic insights. I start with a brief introduction to the bokashi method and continue with the sensory and relational story of knowing, living and being with bokashi.

BOKASHI AS A METHOD

At its most basic level, bokashi is a method of fermenting organic materials with a microbial inoculant (Christel 2017). Culturing and utilising naturally occurring microorganisms has been an essential part of ancient farming traditions in Korea and other parts of Asia (see Park and DuPonte 2008). In his popular book entitled *Bokashi Composting. Scraps to Soil in Weeks*, Adam Footer (2014) points out that modern-day bokashi is a result of this ancient farming philosophy merging with relatively recent scientific research.

The isolation and culturing of particular strands of bacteria that are most commonly used in modern bokashi practice was originally conducted by Teruo Higa in Japan in the 1980s. The story of his discovery – a narrative not unlike that of Isaac Newton and the apple – is repeated on numerous webpages and in countless guides dedicated to bokashi around the world (see Footer 2014). Since then, Higa's company has been developing this specific mixture of 'beneficial microorganisms' for commercial purposes. In addition to bokashi products manufactured under this license, there are also other competing products on the market.[6]

The promise of bokashi is that it is a simple, efficient, and relatively inexpensive method of treating organic waste. It allows the processing of virtually all types of kitchen leftovers to form fertile soil in just a few weeks. *The Beginner's Guide to Bokashi* (hereafter referred to as 'BAO', after its Finnish name), co-written by Finnish bokashi pioneers, crystallises the process in one paragraph:

> This might feel strange at first, but is quite simple after all. Throw organic waste in the bucket, add some bran on top of it, and close the lid. When the bucket is full, let it stay sealed for two weeks, after that it's ready to be incorporated in the soil. The waste then turns into soil in two weeks. It's Bokashi!

BAO further praises bokashi for being 'easy, fun, cheap, odourless, and useful'. To do bokashi composting, one does not need to own a garden: it is possible to do it on a balcony, in the kitchen or in the bathroom. Because the process can be conducted indoors, even in small apartments, it is rapidly gaining popularity among urban dwellers.

Although there are industrially produced bokashi containers on the market, it is also possible to assemble an airtight DIY bokashi bucket out of two plastic buckets (see Footer 2014 for instructions). The actual bokashi process begins by collecting food leftovers in the bucket. The kitchen waste produced during the day is finely chopped and collected into a bowl. Approximately once a day, the bokashi bucket is unsealed, the food scraps are layered in the bucket, compressed tightly and sprinkled with a handful of bokashi bran.

The bran is any grain-like substance inoculated with the vital ingredient that gives the bokashi method its distinctive character: the mixture of microorganisms that work together 'so that each organism causes benefit, not harm, to the other organisms in the consortium' (Footer 2014: 33). At a minimum, this consortium consists of various types of yeasts, lactic acid bacteria and – most importantly – the photosynthetic purple non-sulphur-bacteria, which allow the other microbes in the mixture to coexist. The bran can be purchased ready-made, but some practitioners even go as far as experimenting with culturing indigenous microbe consortia at home. There has been some discussion on the possibilities of using kombucha or sauerkraut as a bokashi starter, for example, although there seems to be a widely shared consensus that it would then no longer be bokashi.[7] However, it is worth noting that this kind of strict policy is likely to be the result of protecting commercial interests.

The procedure of chopping the leftovers and layering them in the bucket with bokashi bran is repeated daily until the bucket is full. When the bucket is full of tightly pressed food leftovers, the lid is sealed, and the bucket is set aside to acidify for at least two weeks.

One of the important products of the bokashi process is the leachate which has to be regularly drained off from the bucket. This microbe-rich and very acidic liquid is affectionately called 'tea', 'wee' or 'juice' among the bokashi practitioners. The golden brown, sour-smelling liquid is mostly used (diluted 1:100) as a fertiliser both indoors and in the garden. The undiluted liquid can also be poured down the drain to prevent blockages through the activity of the beneficial microorganisms that feed on the excess organic matter in the pipes.

After two weeks of fermentation, the 'pre-compost' is ready, and the container can be unsealed. In order to incorporate the fermented matter into the soil, it then has to be introduced to the aerobic microbes of the soil. As the fermented pre-compost is still juridically defined as waste – the Finnish Waste Act prohibits burying waste in the ground – it cannot be directly mixed with soil in the ground. In Finland, the ferment is typically mixed with 'weak soil' in a 'soil factory', which is made from a strong, rodent-proof plastic container. Soil factories are often placed indoors so as not to attract rodents and to prevent them from freezing during the winter season. After being kept in the soil factory for two weeks, the fermented substance will have metamorphosed into sour-smelling, humus-like matter. The product, bokashi soil, is very acidic and rich in microbes and thus it is advisable to let it settle for a few days or to mix it with less nutritious soil before utilising in gardening (see Footer 2014).

Although traditional bokashi methods – if defined loosely as a method of utilising fermented waste matter as a soil amendment – vary greatly from continent to continent (Christel 2017), the modern, urban version of bokashi is being practised in a surprisingly identical manner across the global North. The technical instructions similar to those described above can be found in various guides, blogs and discussion groups around the world. This is the kind of knowledge that the novice is equipped with when beginning their own bokashi making. These guidelines offer 'aseptic knowledge' which is cut off from the 'fleshy and dirty world of practices' (Abrahamsson and Bertoni 2014: 145).

KNOWING WITH BOKASHI

Although the instructions offered above already contain plenty of detailed experiential knowledge that has been cumulated over time, making bokashi will gradually generate more personal and involved forms of knowing: embodied and visceral forms that result from becoming attuned to one's own bokashi community. To follow what is going on in the bokashi bucket, one has to engage with it in a very physical way.

Although sight is often considered the most important sensory modality for knowledge production in the modern world (see Pink 2012), it is probably the least useful sense for knowing what is going on in the bokashi bucket. Instead, smell and touch are the essential sensory modalities in bokashi making. Multisensory evaluation becomes a necessary skill for observing the wellbeing of the bokashi substance and moderating the progression of the fermentation process.

One of the most frequently mentioned reasons for starting to make bokashi is the process' relative lack of odour. However, in the end, bokashi is anything but odourless. Instead, the practitioner is introduced to a whole spectrum of odours, most of which are not exactly unpleasant but perhaps rather peculiar. The practitioner learns to attend to the wellbeing of her bokashi by observing the scent of the substance. The 'bouquet' of each bokashi batch is unique. The characteristic odour of a successful fermentation is acidic with hints of the leftovers that are being processed. If the contents of the bokashi bucket smell foul and putrid, something has gone wrong in the process.

The odour of bokashi is one of the most popular topics of discussion on social media among the digital bokashi community. The members of the groups often share pictures of each leachate batch and compare the hue, viscosity and odour of the liquid. For instance, the sour, lemony odours of the bokashi juice are described as so pleasant that one would almost like to taste the liquid: 'It makes my mouth water' (BG).

Indeed, the diversity of scents becomes one of the most appealing features of the method:

> The special bonus is the adorable scent when opening the Bokashi container + in the leachate. The fragrance from the container reminds of the previously savoured treats – sometimes fresh lemon 🍋 and sometimes sweet strawberry 🍓 (BG).

However, the olfactory engagement with bokashi is not always pleasant. A slightly less enthusiastic member of the bokashi group calls for 'bokashi-realistic' accounts of the process to accompany the 'rose-tinted images' such as the one quoted above. Describing vividly how handling the fully fermented bokashi batch makes her eyebrows furrow, she insists that, to her, bokashi stinks like nothing she has encountered before.

Over time, the practitioner learns to tell by the smell whether the body of the fermenting matter is too protein-rich, too dry or too moist, whether the container has not been airtight or whether pathogens have spoiled the process. Most often, the spoiled bokashi batches smell like cow or pig manure or baby vomit. For instance, in August 2018, a new member enquired of the bokashi group why his soil factory was rotting and stank like cow manure. His question resulted in dozens of answers. The moderator told him to ask himself the following questions:

> If the Bokashi matter itself stinks, you should ask yourself, have you added enough bran in relation to the bio waste? Have you put too much onions, cabbage, or coffee grounds in the bucket? How often have you been adding stuff in the bucket? Is the container airtight? Has the bucket been too close to the radiator, is it too warm? If you think these questions through, you should find the cause of the smell (BG).

In autumn 2018, I personally experienced a series of failures with my bokashi process: the product in my soil factory had developed a strong smell that reminded me of pig manure, and the stench in our garage was almost insufferable. By browsing the discussion in a bokashi group I learnt that my fermenting container had probably not been airtight, which had created suitable conditions for unwelcome microbiological processes. In addition to that, the mixture of 'weak soil' and fermented matter in my soil factory was very likely to have been too moist. To get rid of the smelly batch without upsetting my next-door neighbours, I had to sneak out in the middle of the night and bury the whole batch in the woods close by (because, as the bokashi crowd assured me, 'the earth doesn't mind the smell'). Afterwards, a smell of, frankly, shit lingered in the neighbourhood for days. Even our wheelbarrow stank for several days after I had used it for the operation.

In addition to the sense of smell, touch is also actively utilised in the process of monitoring the wellbeing of bokashi. Tactile feeling of bokashi is also likely to arouse similar mixed feelings of affection, curiosity and repulsion. A pioneering Finnish bokashi blogger, Takalaiska, describes how her eagerness to engage with the process of fermentation forces her to take a peek in her soil factory and feel the soil with her bare hands. She cannot help herself, even though she knows that it disrupts the decomposition process:

Maybe I'll go and have a peek in the soil factory tomorrow. Just to get into the vibe. By the previous experience, I would expect the temperature to have reached lukewarmth. (Yeah, I'll just boldly stick in my bare hand to feel the temperature... even though I am slightly repulsed;)) (Takalaiska).

As Takalaiska gropes the pulp in the bucket with her bare hands, she engages in intimate contact with the living matter in the middle of its transformation process. Feeling the rising temperature is a means of knowing that although nothing has visibly changed, a great deal is happening.

In another blog post, Takalaiska further discusses the aversion often connected to tactile handling of leftovers usually considered waste:

What is in it, that the very moment you categorize a foliage of a vegetable or a forgotten avocado as waste, it turns disgusting?? So disgusting that you don't want to touch it anymore – just to get rid of it as quickly as possible. That it, to get it out of sight. As quickly as possible. Without effort (Takalaiska).

As is the case with any other waste treatment practice, the bokashi practice, too, is associated with affects such as repulsion and disgust. The experience of commitment and responsibility, as well as feelings of curiosity and satisfaction, works to overcome the unpleasant affects that emerge from different stages of the process (see Kinnunen 2017). The most devoted practitioners even overcome their aversion and pick 'food' for their bokashi bucket from the community bio waste container.

Bokashi tickles all the senses – it takes up space both visually and multi-dimensionally, it feels, smells and even tastes, and the sensations are not always pleasant. However, for the bokashi practitioner, these peculiar and sometimes unpleasant multisensory experiences are not something to turn away from, but they are rather considered as a form of communication: important messages that need to be taken seriously. Sometimes the bad smell is described humorously as a bucket's 'stinking objection' to possible mistreatment.

Nevertheless, most of the time the sensual correspondence with bokashi is a satisfying experience.

Indeed, for many, the multisensory encounter with the fermenting matter provides pleasure in itself:

> Simplicity, fastness and that lovely, almost physical pleasure you get when you dip your hands in the Bokashi soil after two weeks of decomposing. It's better than chocolate 😊 😊 😁 (BG).

The group member quoted above justifies her motivation for making bokashi with very practical reasons but also with the sensual satisfaction that the engagement gives her.

The mode of knowing that emerges in and through the bokashi practice is the result of becoming *attuned to* the materials in all their liveliness. The human practitioner who engages in sensory correspondence with bokashi sensitises herself to their subtle means of 'communicating' through the consistency, temperature, colour or odour of the substance, or the smell and the viscosity of the liquid the process produces.

The liveliness of bokashi entails the practitioner's living in a state of constant vigilance and requires constant tuning and tinkering. The wellbeing of bokashi is monitored multisensorially and the practitioner learns through trial and error about the conditions in which her own bokashi can flourish. Over time, the practitioner learns to consider the specific, situated conditions of her bokashi – the symbiotic consortium of microorganisms in her bucket, the quality of kitchen waste in each batch, the humidity of the matter, seasonal temperature variations and so on – and to make adjustments accordingly.

Gradually, the multisensory monitoring of and laborious tinkering with bokashi become mundane, embodied skills, which one performs almost unconsciously. The practitioner no longer feels the urge to check every detail from an online peer group, or publicly celebrate every lovely, scented batch of bokashi liquid. At that point, living with bokashi has become an integral part of everyday life.

LIVING WITH BOKASHI

Unlike litter bins or even traditional hot composts, the bokashi buckets are not hidden from sight in cupboards or backyards. Although the fermentation buckets (especially the DIY ones) are often considered eyesores, they are nevertheless commonly placed in plain sight in order to ensure easy access in the flow of everyday life. Bokashi practitioners who make bokashi in small apartments report keeping their bokashi buckets and soil factories in kitchens, wardrobes, balconies and bathrooms, and even in the living room behind the sofa! At least for the keenest bokashi practitioners, the lived-in space thus becomes very physically *cohabited with bokashi* (Kinnunen 2017).

What kind of a cohabitant is bokashi, then? Bokashi, as a cohabitant, is often compared to a pet or a baby: a family member that must be nurtured and fed (and that wees, too). Bokashi is often associated with its container, the bucket. After all, there can be no bokashi without the container. The bucket is thus not a passive container for the matter inside but an active part of the bokashi community in itself. The bucket is animate and unstable in a myriad of ways: its plastic walls are porous and become frail over time, the spigot may leak and the lid may not be airtight. The bucket requires as much care as the matter inside. The liveliness of the bokashi bucket is often emphasised by giving it funny and affectionate nicknames, such as 'Pikachu', 'Bokahontas', or 'Bämpäri' (a combination of the Finnish word for bucket, *ämpäri*, and bokashi), and even by drawing eyes or a face on the side of the bucket.

However, the essence of bokashi lies in the unstable and lively substance inside the bucket. Experimenting with bokashi makes one aware of the huge yet invisible crowd of creatures that are necessary for successful composting, but which are difficult to identify because of their miniscule size: microbes. In addition to attending to their bokashi buckets as cohabitants, bokashi practitioners also tend to describe the microbes in the bokashi bran and the fermented substance as friendly creatures in need of care: 'these "microbial-labourers" are crucial for the soil to develop. And they need to be fed and caressed, just as any other living creatures' (BG).

As the above quotes reveal, the presence of microorganisms in bokashi is oftentimes conceptualised as 'work'. The bokashi process is conceptualised as a symbiotic collaboration between different agents of varying sizes, which includes humans as well as bacteria, fungi and yeasts. From the point of view of bokashi practitioners, their bokashi bucket and contents is a meshwork of all sorts of materials, including a huge number of invisible microorganisms whose wellbeing they are responsible for and yet can never have full control over. The bokashi blogger Takalaiska has illustrated the fermentation process as a metaphorical 'microbe-party', in which the human practitioner works as the party organiser. If too many gate crashers (pathogens) enter the party, the 'own gang' (the beneficial microbes) has to be called in to calm the situation. However, the bokashi party has a high tolerance for intruders. It has been often emphasised that the success of fermentation is not so much a question of the exact combination or ratio of microorganisms but rather their high degree of diversity. In the bokashi process, a myriad of different microbes work together as a heterogeneous group, supporting and feeding off each other. As long as no single species of microbe becomes too dominant, the group itself is much stronger and more adaptable (Footer 2014).

Nevertheless, symbiotic collaboration does not mean unconditional openness to any agents; collectives are always formed and sustained by keeping something out (Latour 2005), which requires constant work.[8] As Abrahamsson and Bertoni (2014) note in their ethnographic study on vermicomposting, the composting container is simultaneously an apparatus for both separation and togetherness. Bokashi containers are necessary apparatuses for transforming the human practitioner, the organic waste matter and the mixture of 'beneficial microbes' into a heterogeneous collaborating collective, but at the same time, they are designed to keep out other elements, such as oxygen, that are considered harmful to the success of the process. The bokashi practice is about creating *specific togetherness* by bringing certain active elements together and eliminating others at different stages of the process.

In the bokashi-related discussion groups, there is an ongoing discussion of the materials that have to be kept out of the bokashi bucket. Often, people start by putting everything in the bucket but become pickier as their skills and understanding of the method develop. One of the pioneering bokashers describes her transformation from enthusiastic novice to selective expert:

When I started making bokashi, my goal was – to get a lot of soil. But lately, I have begun to consider more about the quality of the soil. Everything decomposes (luckily!) but do I want to grow vegetables for my family in soil that has been made out of moulded waste? Bad meat? Bokashi is what you put in your bucket... (BG).

What I myself have learned so far, through my own experiences and those of my peers, is that bokashi prefers carbohydrates and has difficulty metabolising large proportions of protein such as meat. One learns to welcome some unappealing elements, for instance white yeasts or spongy, yellowish slime mould, as 'friendly visitors', while avoiding others, like hairy, blue mould. Also, certain insects are considered welcome 'co-workers' in the soil, while others are considered harmful. For example, a common nuisance in soil factories are sciarid flies whose larvae feed on the roots of plants, which is why they are often removed with fly traps. Some practitioners, like the one quoted above, note that they have become cautious about what kind of food they consume, so as to make sure that their bokashi gets the best nutrition possible. Moreover, quite a number of practitioners have stopped eating imported fruits and vegetables because of the pesticides and other plant protection product residues that the peels may contain.[9]

As illustrated above, despite the celebration of microbial liveliness and symbiotic interdependency, living with bokashi is far from unconditional. It rejects, among other things, oxygen, pathogens, certain (but not all) insects, rodents and toxins. Shotwell (2016) has aptly noted that while the emerging probiotic practices embrace the ideals of messiness and interdependency, a new form of exclusive purity has been created: a wish to disassociate oneself from 'toxicity'. She reminds us that this form of non-toxic purity is possible only for the privileged few: those who have the means to choose, for instance, the air they breathe, the ground they live on and from, and the food they consume (Shotwell 2014). Given the commercial aspect of bokashi, one cannot help but wonder whether this new 'probiotic' form of purity is really available only to those who can afford to buy the inoculated bran, and further still, have enough spare time to spend on caring for waste.

BEING WITH BOKASHI

Participating in the travels of microbial communities from food to waste to soil reveals that microbial liveliness does not stay in the bucket: 'we breathe and eat microbes' (BG). I have often been told that making bokashi has made practitioners 'aware of the micro-level life in the soil'. As one bokashi group member formulates it, making bokashi has made her understand that soil is not dead matter which can be purchased in bags. Another Finnish bokashi pioneer states that, for her, making bokashi has brought 'dead soil' to life: 'my relationship with soil has definitely changed. Formerly, there was just "soil". Now the soil is the awesome world of microbes full of micro life' (a Finnish bokashi pioneer, e-mail interview).

In contrast to healthy living soil, the commercial soil products sold in any supermarket or hardware store are often referred to as 'sterilised', 'dead', or even 'killed' soil. Bokashi practitioners that I have interviewed often emphasise that they are more devoted to 'growing soil' than to 'growing food'. As one of my interviewees explains:

> My harvest is not very large, but I get satisfaction from knowing that I feed the worms and microorganisms in the soil. That I can provide nourishment for soil biota. Thus, through bokashi I take care of the land and the soil.

This co-constitutive human-soil relation is highlighted via a biblical proverb emphasising the earthly origin of living beings: 'we literally come from the earth' (BG). Some members in the group even joke that they want their bodies to be bokashi composted when they die.

By making the practitioners aware of the microbial abundance of the world, practising bokashi works towards an ontological objective: it brings forth perception of the world as a constantly changing microbial ecosystem. Instead of stressing the separateness of human beings, bokashi practitioners see themselves as co-constitutive participants in this vibrant ecology. The barriers between bokashi and human bodies are further reduced through reminders that the human body is constituted mostly of bacteria: 'most part of us human creatures consist of bacteria. They keep us standing' (BG). This statement transforms the ontological mode of being with bokashi from *being with* microbes into *being* microbes.

THE ONTOETHICOPOLITICS OF BOKASHI?

In this concluding section, I return to the question of the ontoethicopolitics of bokashi that I posed in the beginning of this chapter. I propose that despite being a relatively marginal method practised in the privacy of homes, bokashi may have wider political implications, as it crafts new imaginaries for knowing, living and being with waste.

In what follows, I will discuss the possibilities that bokashi opens up for challenging waste relations based on the axiom of 'distance, disposability and denial', and maintain that making bokashi may nourish and alter prevalent waste imaginaries in at least four ways.

First, the celebration of the microbial collaboration within bokashi practice enhances cultural imaginaries of the world as a living, symbiotic organism rather than consisting of stable, inert stuff.

Second, bokashi practice makes practitioners aware of the porous intercorporeality of their bodies, other-than-human bodies and lived spaces. If every household hosts a unique community of microbes, then co-habiting the lived space with bokashi alters this ecosystem by enriching the microbial liveliness of the lived-in environments as well as the guts of its inhabitants. Bokashi is thus underpinned by the idea that there are no strict boundaries between kinds and species, and that everything is connected and interdependent. Human bodies cannot be truly separated from, say, our waste heaps.

Third, bokashi practice operates on the logic of harm reduction rather than on the logic of elimination. Bokashi is not reducible to ecstatic coexistence with the microbial world but rather calls for a commitment to live with the particular tensions arising in the process. As the feminist fermentation artist Lauren Fournier (2020: 106) argues, fermentation as a political act shakes up tendencies toward all-or-nothing thinking and shifts the discourse from 'healing' towards considering individual and collective action in terms of harm reduction. Instead of perpetuating fantasies of total purity, the bokashi practitioner acknowledges her responsibility for what kind of waste is produced and what happens to it. To be able to live with one's waste as best as one can may necessitate adjusting one's lifestyle so that it generates different waste matters. Moreover, being affectively and physically involved in the transformation of matter turns the ethical responsibility towards waste into committed and constant tinkering rather than just dutiful following of rules and regulations.

Fourth, bokashi-making emphasises the reciprocal nature of care. Practising bokashi successfully necessitates joining forces with microbial abundance working in the organic matter. Thus, the 'waste' that is enacted within bokashi practice is not dead and disgusting matter but lively, full of potential, and even capable of mutual collaboration. This involved and reciprocal form of waste care forms a stark contrast with the institutional waste management infrastructure that has been designed to separate consumer societies from their waste both physically and emotionally. As one of my interviewees stresses, bokashi is much more than just an inexpensive and efficient means of disposing of organic waste. For her, bokashi is about revitalising and nourishing the land through increasing its microbial diversity. Thus, rather than being understood in terms of waste management, bokashi can be embraced as a form of caring *for and with waste*.

These ontological and ethical imaginaries crafted in private waste practices may seem to have an idealistic flavour, which may make them appear too unrealistic to be scaled up to public policies. However, as this volume points out, making bokashi is not just a singular funky hobby but part of a larger 'probiotic movement'. Waste relations enacted in bokashi practice are in line with the emerging model put forth in current lay and scientific practices, breaching the 'boundaries between humans, animals, plants, fungi and their bacterial and archaeal familiars and unfamiliars' (Paxson and Helmreich 2014: 166). Probiotic practices such as bokashi making alter the way we humans see ourselves and our place in the world, and how we can relate with the other-than-human world. In these probiotic practices lie the seeds for challenging the axiom of 'distance, disposability and denial': they point towards the insight that waste is inherent to life and cannot be fully eliminated.

Bokashi practice might even work towards a form of waste politics in which waste is not treated as a passive target of management practices but as an active participant in heterogenous webs of care. Might environmentally oriented waste politics be better off building on an ethos of living with waste rather than aspiring for a waste-free world through schemes like Zero Waste? This would require dropping the 'all-or-nothing' attitude and, instead striving towards a careful reduction of collective harm. It would mean acknowledging that there will be no definite formula for the best possible waste management, but rather, we would be required to move towards the practice of constant and laborious tinkering. It would also mean becoming aware of what kinds of waste are generated in societal practices, and a willingness to adjust these practices in order to generate waste materials that we will be able to live with.

NOTES

1   Bokashi is a general term which refers to the practice and the process of making bokashi as well as to the fermented substance and the end product.

2   Referred to as BG (Bokashi Groups) throughout the rest of this article.

3   I have been most actively following the largest and oldest Finnish bokashi-related group. There are currently over 9,000 members in the group, and that number is increasing daily. The discussion on the platform is extremely active. I have permission from the group's moderators to carry out research within the group. Although the rules of the group do not allow me to use direct quotes from the discussions, I have permission from one of the moderators to use excerpts from all her comments. I may also quote comments from the discussion threads that I have started specifically to be used in my research. However, following the general ethical guidelines of social scientific research, I will always anonymise the quotes.

4   Transcribed verbatim.

5   See also Ogden, Hall, and Tanita 2013; Abrahamsson and Bertoni 2014.

6   Christel 2017: 4. Although there are a number of bokashi-related businesses which have trademarked different derivatives of the term, I have no intention to promote any specific product. Thus, I use the term bokashi in a general sense and intentionally avoid mentioning any trademarked or commercialised brands in this text.

7   What makes bokashi has been a frequent topic of heated discussion in bokashi-related groups. Many influential practitioners, including the moderators of the discussion group, maintain that the lactic acid fermentation process utilising indigenous microbes instead of a laboratory produced microbial mixture should not be called bokashi.

8 Even the seeming amicability of the digital groups on social media requires constant effort from the moderators, who devote substantial time to keeping the discussions friendly and supportive.

9 Although there is also a widely-shared assumption among bokashers that the 'toxins' are destroyed by the 'good' bacteria in bokashi.

REFERENCES

Abrahamsson, S., and F. Bertoni, 'Compost Politics: Experimenting with Togetherness in Vermicomposting', *Environmental Humanities*, 4 (2014), 125–48.

Alaimo, S., *Bodily Natures. Science, Environment and the Material Self* (Bloomington and Indianapolis: Indiana University Press, 2010).

Barad, K., *Meeting the Universe Halfway: Quantum Physics and the Entanglement of Matter and Meaning* (Durham, NC: Duke University Press, 2007).

BOA. *Happaman hauska aloittajan opas bokashikompostointiin* (Beginner's Guide to Bokashi) <http://51.fi/bokashi> [accessed 1 January 2018].

Christel, D. M., 'The Use of Bokashi as a Soil Fertility Amendment in Organic Spinach Cultivation' (Graduate College Dissertation and Theses 678, 2017) <http://scholarworks.uvm.edu/graddis/678> [accessed 1 October 2020].

Footer, A., *Bokashi Composting. Scraps to Soil in Weeks* (Cabriola Island: New Society Publishers, 2014).

Fournier, L., 'Fermenting Feminism as Methodology and Metaphor. Approaching Transnational Feminist Practices through Microbial Transformation', *Environmental Humanities*, 12.1 (2020), 88–110.

Gomart, E., and A. Hennion, 'A Sociology of Attachment. Music Amateurs, Drug Users', in J. Law, and J. Hassard, eds, *Actor Network Theory and After* (Oxford and Malden: Blackwell, 1999), pp. 220-47.

Hawkins, G., *The Ethics of Waste. How We Relate to Rubbish* (Lanham: Rowman & Littlefield, 2006).

Hird, M., 'Knowing Waste. Towards an Inhuman Epistemology', *Social Epistemology*, 16.3–4 (2012), 453–69.

Ingold, T., *Being Alive. Essays in Movement, Knowledge and Description* (London and New York: Routledge, 2010).

Kaza, S., and others, *What a Waste 2.0: A Global Snapshot of Solid Waste Management to 2050*, Urban Development Series (Washington, DC: World Bank, 2018).

Kinnunen, V., 'Bokashi Composting as a Matrixal Borderspace', in V. Kinnunen, and A. Valtonen, eds, *Living Ethics in a More-Than-Human World* (Rovaniemi: University of Lapland, 2017), pp. 66–74.

Kirksey, E. S., and S. Helmreich, 'The Emergence of Multispecies Ethnography', *Cultural Anthropology*, 25.4 (2010), 545–76.

Latour, B., *Reassembling the Social. An Introduction to Actor-Network-Theory* (Oxford: Oxford University Press, 2005).

Ogden, L. A, B. Hall, and T. Kimiko, 'Animals, Plants, People, and Things. A Review of Multispecies Ethnography', *Environment and Society: Advances in Research*, 4 (2013), 5–24.

Paxson, H., and S. Helmreich, 'The Perils and Promises of Microbial Abundance: Novel Natures and Model Ecosystems. From Artisanal Cheese to Alien Seas', *Social Studies of Science*, 44.2 (2014), 165– 93.

Park, H., and M. W. DuPonte, 'How to Cultivate Indigenous Microorganisms', *Biotechnology*, BIO-9 (2008), 1–7.

Pink, S., *Situating Everyday Life. Practices and Places* (London: Sage, 2012).

——— *Doing Sensory Ethnography* (London: Sage, 2015).

Takalaiska <Takalaiska.blogspot.fi> [accessed 1 April 2018].

Shotwell, A., *Against Purity. Living Ethically in Compromised Times* (Minneapolis: University of Minnesota Press, 2016).

3

OIMROAS:[1] NOTES ON A SUMMER ALPINE JOURNEY

Matthäus Rest

IT WAS AROUND 9 PM WHEN I ARRIVED AT THE ALP, JUST IN TIME TO CATCH the team of shepherds and cheesemakers finishing their dinner.[2] A decade earlier, I had spent two summers making cheese at this mountain dairy myself. That night, there were six of them, half of whom I knew from a visit the previous year. 'We always have 5 o'clock tea in the stable, if you want to get up that early', Georg told me with a wink.[3] 'Might as well', I answered. My assigned bed was next door to the air compressor of the milking machine. In a stable with around a hundred cows that was quite a machine. So once milking started, sleeping would not be possible anyway. I had called in advance to ask whether I could take scientific samples of milk and dairy products for the interdisciplinary research project I had started working on a few months earlier. After dinner, as dusk was falling, I took a short walk around the empty stable and sat down on the old bench in front of the hut. Everything I touched felt so familiar.

The scientists who hired me to collect dairy samples are biomolecular archaeologists working in the fields of ancient DNA and proteomics. They are interested in the deep history of the complex relations between humans, food and microbes, and first and foremost in the prehistoric spread of dairying across Eurasia (Wilkin et al. 2020). Until recently, the archaeology of food had to rely on direct evidence, which was very scant, because most food does not preserve well. With the advent of ancient DNA and proteomics, this has changed. Now, microbial particles of food and food-related microbes can be extracted from teeth, cooking utensils and other archaeological finds. Recent advances in laboratory technology have brought down the cost of genetic sequencing to the point where it has become possible to detect the genetic traces of whole microbial communities in archaeological objects. My colleagues in bioinformatics then use this data to assemble metagenomes: the entire genomes of all the microbes present in the sample. This is not a trivial operation and, often, it is hard for them to know what to look for because they are missing a baseline of 'clean, high-quality' contemporary microbial genomes. This was why I had come back to my old mountain dairy: to collect dairy samples and the microbes that live in them.

When I entered the deserted kitchen shortly after 5 am, I realised that the biggest improvement in the past decade had been the introduction of an automatic espresso machine. With my coffee, I joined the team for a quick and quiet breakfast in the stable. While four of them were getting ready for milking, I followed Georg into the dairy to help him with the cheesemaking. He did not wait for the fresh milk and instead used the milk from the previous day.[4] We started right away and by 7:30 am, the cheese was already in the moulds. I was surprised that he asked me to cut the curds and that, later, I would take the lead in removing the cheese from the vat, arguably the two most delicate work steps at the vat. With decades of experience, Georg was practising a very elaborate microbial assembly. In addition to two cultures from the state laboratory[5] and the liquid rennet I had used in my practice, he also worked with dried calf stomach rennet, inoculated on a natural whey starter culture. Rennet is the umbrella term for a number of enzymes used to curdle milk at low temperatures. It is the main ingredient that distinguishes the majority of European from Asian cheese recipes. In Asia, most cheeses are made without rennet, but at much higher temperatures. Traditionally, rennet is sourced from the stomachs of slaughtered calves, kids and lambs. Young animals need these enzymes to digest milk. Today, the overwhelming majority of rennet is produced by genetically modified yeast. Most artisanal cheesemakers rely on liquid rennet produced from stomachs, while only a tiny fraction, like Georg, still process stomachs on site.

Compared to soft cheese recipes, alpine hard cheeses are made very quickly: it takes roughly two and a half hours until the curd is moved from the vat to

FIG. 3.1 Extracting the curd with a cheesecloth (photograph by Matthäus Rest, June 2018)

the press, with five distinct work steps, each taking around 30 minutes: heating the milk to 32°C to add the rennet, leaving it to curdle, cutting the curd and stirring, scalding the curd (slowly heating to a temperature between 42°C and 57°C, depending on the specific cheese) and stirring again at this temperature. Georg sped things up even more; decades of experience had taught him where to cut corners without compromising quality and shelf life. Or at least, so he claimed.

While we were scalding the curd, he removed a bucket of whey and used it to wash a few strips of calf stomach and transform them into a new batch of rennet for the next few days. At 36°C, he inoculated the stomach strips in whey he had heated to 58°C, to kill off all but the most resilient thermophilic lactic acid bacteria. Then, he added seven millilitres of a mix of acetic acid and propionic acid 'for initial acidification'. He let the open culture pot cool on top of the freezer in the hallway outside the production room. After about an hour, he put this rennet whey culture in the heat cabinet to incubate for 20 hours at 33°C. Back at the cheese vat, when the temperature reached 42°C, Georg turned off the steam valve and let the curd stir for 15 more minutes. Then, as we were getting ready to move the curd from the vat to the draining table, he turned on the cold-water valve used to regulate the heat in the vat. I had never seen anybody do that. He noticed my surprise and told me, with a mischievous smile: 'I cool it down to 39°C before draining. That gives a longer dough.'[6]

WHERE HAVE ALL THE DAIRY MICROBES GONE?

Reading the work of colleagues in anthropology who are also interested in cheese (for example West et al. 2012), I have wondered for a while now why their writing contains so little description of the physical activity of making cheese and the protocols enacted in the dairy. This is even more surprising given the importance that Heather Paxson (2012) and Harry West (2020) assign to craft, and Cristina Grasseni (2016) to skills. But maybe I have to blame my exposure to natural scientists for the blurred conceptual lines between lab and dairy, protocol and recipe. My time in microbiology labs in Oklahoma and Thuringia has taught me how similar the work of microbiologists and cheesemakers is on a bodily level. Despite the vastly different circumstances, both rely heavily on their senses and their working days are structured by microbial temporalities. Their everyday interaction with microbes is a skilful practice strongly guided by touch and smell (Ingold 2018). This leads me to the other surprising lacuna in the anthropology of cheese: where have all the dairy microbes gone? Despite the huge influence of Paxson's (2008) notion of microbiopolitics on the anthropology of microbes, when it comes to her and others' writing about cheese, the everyday relations between humans and beneficial dairy microbes play a minor role compared to the threat of potentially pathogenic bacteria. When making cheese, however, sensing the 'good' microbes in the milk, the starter cultures and the aging room is crucial. Becoming a cheesemaker means attuning one's senses and daily rhythm to the microbes. During my summers working at the mountain dairy, my working days started at 4:30 am when I tested the starter culture and ended at 8 pm when I moved the new starter culture from the incubator to the cold-water bath (Rest, Moroşanu, and Frigo 2017).

After breakfast, Georg went back to the dairy to make butter while I joined the shepherds to build a fence up on the mountain ridge. I was happy to get out of the dairy, especially because making butter was my least favourite job there. Ten years earlier, one of the first work steps of every working day had been to pasteurise the cream from the evening milk. For this purpose, I would skim the top layer of the milk tank with a plastic ladle and heat the cream in the vat pasteuriser. Skimming the right amount of cream from one milking led to the right fat content in the cheese vat. After cooling the newly pasteurised cream, I added freeze-dried culture, poured it into large churns and stored them in the cold-water bath. Every third day, I poured the sour cream into the electric butter churn and turned it on. The noise of the churn was deafening, the timing so fickle, and after kneading and portioning 50kg of butter waiting in ice-cold water my hands were frozen and my shoulders strained.

Luckily, the shepherds really liked to knead the butter and joked that this was the best treatment for their chapped, dry hands. This still left me in charge of operating the churn while simultaneously keeping an eye on the cheese in the vat. Of all the dairy work, making butter in an electric churn is the most time sensitive. As soon as the butter starts to separate into tiny corns, you have to be next to the churn, waiting for the right moment to turn it off, drain the buttermilk and add fresh water to wash the butter. If the churn runs for a minute too long, the butter will clump together, trapping butter milk inside that you will not be able to remove. The high water content will severely shorten the butter's shelf life.

But above all, I just found it sad to pasteurise the cream. Instead of making raw alpine butter, we produced standardised 5kg blocks of pasteurised butter, most of which the farmers would take home and transform into clarified butter, even further diminishing its typicality. The reason for this surprising de-valuation was a combination of nutritionism (Scrinis 2008) and microbiopolitics. For decades, it was hard to sell butter. Starting in the 1960s, nutritional scientists promoted the use of margarine as a healthier alternative to butter, leading to a general decline of butter consumption in the global North (Scrinis 2013). At the same time, food regulators convinced dairy farmers that raw cream was the most dangerous of all the dairy products, a substance teeming with pathogenic microbes. Consumers simultaneously grew to dislike the taste of raw, unpasteurised butter, often misunderstanding it for rancidity. Revisiting my notes from the cheesemaking course I attended in 2009 confirmed this: 'pasteurisation of cream is essential, adding culture is good, cold storage is compulsory (so the fat can crystallise)'. The microbial danger is not an invention, but good milking hygiene and swift cooling can minimise this threat as well as potential off-flavours. But during this visit, I was out in the pasture, almost up on the ridge, helping to build the highest fence of the alp. Looking down on the dairy, I marvelled once again at the wonder of dairying: that, through the domestication of ruminants and microbes, humans have found a way to metabolise grass.

THE 'CHEESE CONSULTANT'

In the afternoon, while the others were milking, I washed the wheels in the aging room. The alp had a semi-automated machine with rotating brushes for this purpose, a bit like a tiny car wash for cheese wheels. It felt good to realise that the skill was still there. My body remembered its choreography with the machine and the cheese boards, each one holding three wheels; my arms, legs and back just doing their thing, my mind free to wander. Touching wheel after wheel, I thought of Michael, the 'cheese consultant' I was going to meet the following day, and how he had entered this aging room during a visit that summer ten years earlier. I had been eagerly awaiting his arrival. Michael was one of the people who taught me how to make cheese, and part of the education was the promise of a visit during the first two weeks in the mountains. So, when he finally stuck his head around the door of the production room one morning after the three most exhausting weeks of my life, I was very happy to see him.

At that point, a third of the shelves in the aging room were already full, and as he entered, Michael muttered a sound of surprised approval. It smelled right and he immediately saw that rind formation had been much faster than in many other dairies he had visited lately.[7] 'Oh wow – they are ready. Have you tried one already'? I replied that I hadn't. 'We'll have to cut one, then', he replied with a bright smile. As he started touching the wheels, his expression changed. 'Too soft', he murmured. 'How hot did you cook the curd'? he asked as he turned to me. '42 degrees – I was told the farmers want the first batches to be ripe early'. 'Ok, but you're in week 4 now, you really have to increase the temperature, otherwise you'll get yourself into trouble. Also, what about the fat content? Show me your butter fabrication documentation'. We moved back to the production room, and it took him only a cursory glance at my butter yield to conclude that the fat content was also way too high. So, in addition to increasing the temperature to 44°C, Michael ordered me to take better care of skimming the cream off the evening milk every morning. All of this he knew from smelling, touching and checking my documentation.

When we finally cut a wheel, it only confirmed what he had already told me. It was young cheese but ready for consumption – smooth, mild and buttery. He congratulated me on the good cheese I had made but repeated the changes necessary to my protocol. Washing and turning these wheels for one long summer, my hands learned what Michael's touch had told him instantaneously: the differences in firmness between my earlier and later batches. It was indeed a fast cheese I had made, and it was one of the earliest to hit the local grocery store shelves. But this speed also created quite a headache for the farmers. While low scalding temperatures, high fat content and a warm aging room make cheese ripen fast, the downside of the bargain is that it over-ripens quickly, too. So suddenly, there were around 500 wheels of cheese that had to be sold off before the end of the summer. Ten years later, one of the farmers still remembered the 'time bomb' I had produced.

Right before dinner, Georg joined me and together we cut the first wheel of the season. 'If you are meeting Michael tomorrow, you might as well bring along the samples for the lab tests', he had told me earlier. The next morning, I left the alp at 5:30 am. Michael had told me to meet him at a train station further down the valley at 6:15 am. I arrived just in time to park my rental and hop into the small 4x4 Michael was driving, a sticker from the local agricultural school stuck on the door. I had not seen him in ten years, but his face had barely aged. He greeted me warmly and told me his schedule: he wanted to visit three alpine cheesemakers who had attended this year's intensive cheesemaking course in the spring. Then as now, part of the package was a visit within the first weeks of the alp season. All of the alps were located on the northern slope of the main valley, but each about an hour's drive apart. Michael represented the local alpine cheese authority.

The majority of the region's cows spend their summers at high altitude, and a substantial amount of their milk is processed on site in dozens of artisanal dairies. These do not fall under the purview of general food inspection but under the guidance of Michael and his colleagues. Their work is pastoral in many ways. In the spring, they teach alpine cheesemaking at the agricultural school to new cheesemakers. In the summer, they visit the mountain dairies and help them improve their product. In the autumn, they attend the local and regional cheese tasting events and grade the product. They are called in if there are problems. And when they come, they take measurements with thermometers and pH meters and collect samples to be sent to the laboratory. But their main tools of investigation are their senses: with their nose, hand, mouth, eye and ear they detect the vast majority of cheese problems. From the perspective of dairy microbes, Michael and his colleagues are the quintessential biopolitical authority: they 'make live and reject into death' (Fassin 2009: 52; translation of Foucault's phrase). The first thing I did was hand him Georg's samples; before farmers are allowed to start selling the dairy products of the new season, every alp needs to send samples to the lab for microbial testing.

Heather Paxson (2008: 16) coined the term microbiopolitics to 'call attention to the fact that dissent over how to live with microorganisms reflects disagreement about how humans ought to live with one another'. She develops the concept in her ethnography of raw milk cheesemakers in New England and their conflicts with hygiene authorities. In many regions of the United States, raw milk has been practically outlawed for decades. Even those who use raw milk seem to be working almost exclusively with laboratory-grown freeze-dried starter (ibid.: 129). In the summer pastures of the Alps, however, pasteurisation has never been fully implemented and many cheesemakers still use other cultures, like the state laboratory cultures of my interlocutors. In the summer pastures, turning raw milk into cheese is first and foremost an exercise in taming highly mysterious entities without the help of laboratory analysis or modern equipment like pH meters. In most mountain summer dairies, the only biochemical device at hand is a simple acidity test through titration to establish the sourness of the starter culture every morning. But before that, and much more important, are the senses of the cheesemaker – what older Swiss cheese manuals call 'Sinnenprobe': a probing by sensing.

> Through steady testing of taste and smell, the biological purity of a bacterial culture can be evaluated with sufficient certainty. Through steady sensual examination the cheesemaker will quickly develop a routine, so that an unwanted change will become apparent immediately. The healthy whey culture has a mild-sour smell and taste and a yellowish-green colour. Bacteriologically contaminated culture (infection with yeasts or coli) is always cloudy and has a cidery or stinky smell and taste (Inforama 2011: 51; translation MR).

During my first summer as a cheesemaker, my whey culture was the first thing I put in my mouth every morning. Right after making a fire, I would get the thermos with the culture from the previous day, discard the greyish top layer and pour a small amount into a cup. Then I smelled and tasted it and tried to guess the acidity (in Soxhelt-Henkel degrees) before I did the titration test. After a few weeks, my daily guess was mostly accurate.

CULTURAL ANXIETIES

'Tell me about your research', Michael asked as we drove towards the first alp. I explained the basics of the Heirloom Microbes project and how a group of biomolecular archaeologists ended up hiring me, a social anthropologist and amateur cheesemaker, to collect dairy samples for them. 'My colleagues' basic interest lies in better understanding the spread of dairying in prehistory. The current consensus in archaeology is that dairying emerged around 10,000 years ago in the northern Levant. About 5,000 years ago, dairying arrived in present-day Mongolia. But how it got there is still poorly understood. Was this a story of diffusion or are we talking about several domestication events, especially when we think about camels, horses and reindeer? Now, my colleagues are archaeologists, but they work with the methods of genetics and proteomics, so they are interested in the 'archaeology of the invisible' as one of them likes to say. Microscopic traces of milk proteins or dairy microbes are enough for them to establish their presence in the archaeological record. But especially when it comes to the microbes that live in milk, my colleagues came to the realisation that it is actually the modern baseline that they are missing: as you might know, there is very little genetic data published on dairy microbes, even less so when we look at non-industrialised dairying. From that lacuna, my colleagues decided to look for someone to collect modern samples, but also assess their cultural significance. The cultures as well as the cultures of cultures, if you will'.

Michael's eyes lit up with enthusiasm. 'That sounds absolutely fantastic. Where did you make cheese again'? I mentioned the name of the alp. 'Ah, in that neck of the woods. Quite a community up there. And their new cooperative dairy, what a mess …'. He would return to the issue later. All the way up to the dairy just below 2000 metres above sea level, we drove on perfectly smooth tarmac while every 100 metres we crossed the lancet of a fixed snow cannon, rising forlorn in the July sky; this alp was at the centre of a major ski resort. Looking at the snow cannons, and with bitter irony, Michael told me that the neighbouring alp was denied permission to build a new goat shed for environmental reasons.

As we pulled in, two milkmen were hosing down the tarmac in front of the dairy. The vast terrace of the restaurant next door was still deserted. Obviously, they had just finished cleaning the milk parlour. In the dairy, Markus and Johannes were in the process of gently warming the milk to 32°C in order to add the rennet. Markus has been making cheese here for the past 20 years and he seemed really fed up with the place. The dairy was small but practical, with an adjacent kitchen, including a fully automated espresso machine. We shook hands and Markus started by telling us how much he was looking forward to leaving this place to look for a smaller alp; fewer cows, fewer farmers, fewer tourists. This one belonged to a municipality that forbade him to do small repairs by himself because they have municipal workers for that. But when something had to be fixed urgently, it took them days to come. The people from the restaurant next door put mouldy cheese in his aging room and did not understand why this upset him. And there were hundreds of tourists every day. Michael listened to it all, took a pH measurement of the cheese from the day before – 'Perfect' – and asked about the cultures. Suddenly, Markus became very insecure. He told us he used four different cultures for his cheese, to be on the safe side. They were three different state laboratory cultures, one of which he incubated to two different levels of acidity. This was the first time I had heard of anyone doing this – the official recommendation was to use two different cultures.

When I say state laboratory cultures, I refer to a rather unique microbial culture management system that developed in the Alps over the second half of the twentieth century. At its centre are state-funded biobanks that distribute starter cultures to artisanal producers. In most cases, these cultures arrive in liquid concentrate form, unlike the cultures of commercial suppliers that are freeze-dried and therefore much more stable. Cheesemakers like Markus or Georg order the concentrates by mail and they arrive in small plastic bottles once a week. They contain different mixes of lactic acid bacteria strains for specific cheese recipes based on 'reconstituted skimmed milk', i.e. sterilised milk from powder. Every day, cheesemakers pasteurise a few litres of their milk, inoculate it with a few pipettes of the concentrate and incubate the culture at around 40°C for eight hours, before storing it in cold water overnight.

Michael reassured Markus that everything was okay, as it always had been. Johannes seemed somewhat the opposite of Markus: young, confident and cheerful. He spent his winters working as a ski instructor, and while he was the reason for our visit – after all, he had taken the course to replace Markus for the next season – he received relatively little attention. After the curd set, however, Markus insisted they did not use their automatic wire cutter as usual and that, instead, they cut the curd by hand. While the two men did their dance of cutting around the vat, my lingering feeling became apparent: Markus was not very good at being satisfied – not with himself and not with others; he second guessed every movement his young assistant made. Soon after they had cut the curd, we said our goodbyes and got back in Michael's car.

After we reached the bottom of the valley, we followed the main road up the valley for the second alp visit. As we got to the upper part of the valley, I asked him again about his earlier comments – was he referring to the problems around the new cooperative village dairy? He told me his version of the story. There was a well-established small-scale dairy in one of the villages. But the farmers did not trust the cheesemaker anymore. Mostly because he got rid of a batch of 'bloated' cheese by throwing it in the river. Nowadays the most common reason for bloated cheese on the press is contamination by antibiotics. Therefore, accidentally adding the milk of cows treated with antibiotics is the most severe threat to alpine dairying. Through millennia of living with humans, the most common dairying microbes have shed many of their defence mechanisms and become highly vulnerable to tiny amounts of antibiotics. But not all bacteria are as sensitive to antibiotics as our good old lactic acid friends. Coli bacteria, for example, are not that bothered.

Now what happens in the cheese vat when the cultures have been wiped out and the cheesemaker proceeds to warm the milk, add rennet, cut the curds, cook the curds and finally move the cheese to the press? Total coliform bacteria bloom. With no lactic acid bacteria there will be no acidification. And acidification is the main reason why fermentation is such a safe process when it comes to preserving food for humans. Except for the lactic acid bacteria and yeasts that thrive in these sour environments, microbes cannot survive low pH-values. In cheese, coliform bacteria metabolise lactose into formic acid. As side products, they produce CO_2 and H_2 that forms small holes, hence the sponginess of bloated cheese.

A few days later, a group of tourists found the cheese in the river. 'They were actually trying to pan for gold. Just imagine their faces when they found all those wheels of cheese in the river'. The local political establishment tried to save face and the dairy by putting the blame on the mountain dairies, even though everybody knew what was going on. Michael was called in after the scandal broke, but as soon as he started to ask questions in the community, his superiors told him to stop – his job was quality control, not investigative journalism. It was clear from the beginning that it could not be cheese from the high pastures because of the lot numbers that come with every wheel. Years later, as we drove towards the new dairy, he was still visibly upset that somebody tried to put the blame for this bloated batch on alpine cheesemakers. Obviously, the relationship between the farmers and the cheesemaker had already been bad, otherwise he would have surely found a better way to discard the bad batch than throwing it in the river in the dead of the night. Therefore, it was decided that a new dairy would be built in a different village. But it was on much too large a scale and lacked a proper plan. The project was completely resistant to advice from people like Michael.

'Take for example their plan to also process goat and sheep milk. A great idea in principle. But for that they bought a 500-litre vat right away! I told them: start small, but no. And then they increased the milk hygiene standards to a level that meant practically nobody in the region could sell their milk to them! One large sheep farmer now sells all his milk to a dairy in the lowlands. And then the architecture! People say it looks like a crematorium! If that was in Tyrol,[8] it would look totally different. People would love to visit and have a coffee on the terrace, but this looks like an air-raid shelter! In the end, they would have gone bankrupt, had a large food corporation not bailed them out. The farmers got three million in subsidies and now tanker trucks full of milk drive up from the lowland every day to keep it going. So, in the end, the taxpayer has spent millions subsidising one of the largest players in the food industry'.

BY WAY OF CONCLUSION: MAKING CHEESE AS A PRACTICE OF ATTUNEMENT

As we visited the two remaining alps, I again watched Michael use all his senses to assess cheese quality. Like Markus and Johannes had done, here too it seemed like he used the pH meter mostly to reassure the cheesemakers that everything was alright with their product, not because he needed the readings. While asking how they had settled in, he would casually lower the back of his hand to the whey surface in the vat to gently touch the moving curds. As when he had visited me a decade earlier, he would quickly lift a few wheels in the aging room to feel their touch and to check whether they had been properly washed and moved every day. His hand and nose would tell him how long it would be until the first wheel could be cut. Like making cheese itself, consulting cheesemakers and controlling their work is a skilful practice of attunement (Sariola and Rest 2020).

While Michael represented the state, his official title of 'alp consultant' was not a euphemism. For in order to do his surveillance work as hygiene authority, his disciplinary power relied less on the threat of punishment than on the promise of improvement. Follow his advice and you will become a better cheesemaker.

While recent ethnographic work has produced detailed accounts of many aspects of artisanal cheesemaking, the work at the vat and in the aging room has attracted rather limited attention. Most importantly, the engagement with microbes has been strongly framed through conflicts around food safety and the opposing ontologies of hygiene authorities and raw milk cheesemakers. While the threat of microbial infections was a constant topic in my cheese education, during my practice I was much more afraid that I would get up one morning to find that my culture had not acidified than I was of an infection of *Listeria monocytogenes*. So, I was more concerned with the fragility of the beneficial microbes than the power of the pathogenic ones. While these are certainly two sides of the same coin, it makes a difference which microbes we are with in our anxieties. In my understanding, making raw milk cheese is a practice of attuning one's senses and daily rhythm to these lactic acid bacteria.

Still, *Listeria* came up during my time with Michael, if only at the very end. He did not have time for a late lunch, so we ended our tour with a bottle of soda in the parking lot of a DIY and garden centre. 'On the way home I have to quickly swing by a farm in the lowlands with suspicion of *Listeria* and the samples have to go to the lab tonight', he apologised. I must have looked alarmed, so he continued: 'most probably it's not *Listeria monocytogenes*, but a less dangerous form. Still, we have to take these threats very seriously'. His handshake was firm and warm. On the way out of the valley, I stopped at a motorway rest area, put on surgical gloves, and started to subsample the milk I had collected at the three dairies. Aliquoting each sample into a number of tiny 1.5ml tubes without a pipette, I was once again surprised at the skills I was developing on this journey from the lab to the mountain dairy and back. I then put the tubes in the mobile freezer in the boot of the car, where I had already stored a whole range of samples from my stay at Georg's alp.

Frozen as they were, milk, yoghurt and milk starters were indistinguishable, but the whey samples stood out for their greenish colour. There I realised that

I had forgotten to sample Georg's butter, having been eager to get out of the dairy and join the shepherds to build a fence on the ridge. Attunement at the alp also means constantly shifting your focus of care between vat, milk tank and aging room; pasture, kitchen and stable; cows, pigs and chickens. If this practice of attunement succeeds, grass becomes milk through animals. About an hour later, I arrived in the city where I had arranged to store the sample tubes in a friend's freezer before heading off to a different region. The next morning, on the way back to my rental car, I walked past a bus stop with a billboard. The ad read: '100g Butter contains: 100% real taste, 0% artificial ingredients. Butter. Ingeniously simple'. To my taste, that felt rather simplistic.

NOTES

1 'Oimroas' literally translates 'alp journey'. In the dialect I grew up with, the term refers to a hike across the mountain pastures with frequent stops at different cabins to try the local products.

2 In the Alps, the mountain pastures used for grazing livestock during summer are called Alp (Romansh, Swiss, and South Western German), alpage (French), Oim/Olm (Austrian and Bavarian German), Alm (Standard German), alpeggio (Italian), mont/munt (Ladin), or planina (Slovenian).

3 All names have been changed.

4 Generally, the recommendation for alpine raw milk cheese is to process the milk as quickly as possible. Therefore, in most dairies, cheesemaking only starts after all the morning milk has been collected.

5 I will talk more about these below.

6 In German, cheese dough [Käseteig] refers to the cheese's texture. The longer the dough, the smoother the texture.

7 Rind formation is especially tricky in the alpine summer dairies, where cheesemakers start with an empty aging room that is often also slightly too cold.

8 Tyrol here stands for a region that has a lot of experience with agrotourism and marketing.

ACKNOWLEDGEMENTS

I thank the Kilpisjärvi Collective and Christine Moderbacher for comments on earlier drafts of this text.

REFERENCES

Fassin, D., 'Another Politics of Life Is Possible', *Theory, Culture & Society*, 26.5 (2009), 44–60.

Grasseni, C., *The Heritage Arena: Reinventing Cheese in the Italian Alps* (New York: Berghahn Books, 2016).

Inforama, 'Alpkäserei Berner Oberland: Lehr- und Fachbuch für das INFORAMA Berner Oberland, 3702 Hondrich und die Praxis' (Hondrich: Inforama, 2011).

Ingold, T. 'Five Questions of Skill', *Cultural Geographies*, 25.1 (2018), 159–63.

Paxson, H., 'Post-Pasteurian Cultures: The Microbiopolitics of Raw-Milk Cheese in the United States', *Cultural Anthropology*, 23.1 (2008), 15–47.

—— *The Life of Cheese: Crafting Food and Value in America* (Berkeley: University of California Press, 2012).

Rest, M., J. Hendy, M. Aldenderfer, and C. Warinner, eds, 'Cultures of Fermentation', *Current Anthropology*, 62, Supplement 24 (2021).

Rest, M., R. Moroşanu, and G. Frigo, '"Our Electric Sustenance". Theorizing the Contemporary, Fieldsights', *Cultural Anthropology*, 19 December 2017 <https://culanth.org/fieldsights/our-electric-sustenance> [accessed 4 December 2020].

Sariola, S., and M. Rest, 'Attuning Entanglements: Notes on a Fermentation Workshop', in M. Hey, ed., *Musings 2019: Stories with food, feminism, and fermentation* (Montreal: food feminism fermentation, 2019), pp. 52–7.

Scrinis, G., 'On the Ideology of Nutritionism', *Gastronomica: The Journal of Food and Culture*, 8.1 (2008), 39–48.

—— *Nutritionism: Arts and Traditions of the Table: Perspectives on Culinary History* (New York: Columbia University Press, 2013).

West, H., 'Crafting Innovation: Continuity and Change in the "Living Traditions" of Contemporary Artisan Cheesemakers', *Food and Foodways*, 28.2 (2020), 91–116.

West, H., and others, 'Naming Cheese', *Food, Culture & Society*, 15.1 (2012), 7–41.

Wilkin, S., and others, 'Dairy Pastoralism Sustained Eastern Eurasian Steppe Populations for 5,000 Years', *Nature Ecology & Evolution*, 4.1 (2020), 346–55.

4

BUILDING 'NATURAL' IMMUNITIES: CULTIVATION OF HUMAN-MICROBE RELATIONS IN VACCINE-REFUSING FAMILIES

Johanna Nurmi

Once, we were taking the train to visit the grandparents and I saw [my child] licking the gate handle in the train's play area. You know, the metal handle that everybody touches. She was really going at it, with her tongue stuck way out. [Interviewer: OK, wow.] So, I see microorganisms as our friends, unlike my sister who's a doctor and is almost hysterical about handwashing; she thinks that you have to wash your hands after you've walked from the living room to the bedroom (Jessica).

THIS QUOTE PRESENTS TWO DIFFERENT ATTITUDES TOWARDS THE MICROBES that surround us. In the quote, Jessica, the mother of two unvaccinated children, describes her own attitude of embracing coexistence with microbes. She contrasts her attitude with that of her sister, a medical doctor who sees microorganisms as enemies and tries to shield herself with practices such as handwashing and, no doubt, vaccination. Jessica's quote is from one of the ethnographic interviews I conducted to understand why some parents in Finland did not want to vaccinate their children. Her presentation of these two opposing perceptions was one reason I began to consider how human-microbe relations might intermix with vaccine refusal.

Vaccine refusal is marginal in Finland; the country has high rates of childhood vaccination and a relatively high trust in vaccines. A survey conducted in 2019 found that 95% of Finns completely or mostly agreed that vaccines are effective and safe, and 89% reported trust in the information about vaccines provided by experts and authorities (Kiljunen 2019). Childhood vaccines are offered free of charge as part of the public preventative healthcare provided to all children at child health clinics, and only 1% of children are not vaccinated by the age of three (THL 2019). However, in the same 2019 survey, as many as 32% of respondents completely or mostly agreed that the adverse effects of vaccines are not discussed enough, and 13% agreed that vaccines are given to children because it is profitable for the pharmaceutical industry (Kiljunen 2019). Thus, vaccines are not quite universally accepted in Finland – there is a certain level of distrust in health experts and there is worry about the possible harmfulness of immunisation.

Research has identified factors such as fear of adverse effects, negative vaccination experiences and lack of trust in the efficacy of vaccines as possible reasons for vaccine refusal (e.g. Blaisdell et al. 2016; Brown et al. 2010). In social research, contestation of vaccination is often interpreted in the framework of neoliberal individualistic responsibility and intensive parenting (Laudone and Tramontano 2018; Reich 2014, 2016). In this chapter, I approach vaccine refusal from an angle that has not yet been examined in social research on vaccine hesitancy: the connection between new understandings of human-microbe relations and vaccination acceptance.

Research and public discussions often cite the pursuit of a 'natural lifestyle' or 'alternative health practices' as some of the elements in which vaccine hesitancy and refusal are rooted (Attwell et al. 2018; Reich 2016). Jennifer Reich (2016) has noted that vaccine-refusing parents in the US relied on a strong dichotomy between 'natural' and 'artificial' in their rejection of vaccines. However, social research on vaccine hesitancy and refusal has not attempted to understand the effects of novel human-microbe relations on vaccination acceptance. Similarly, the shifting and complex everyday human-microbe relations and their implications warrant more diverse and thorough analysis (Greenhough et al. 2018).

The term 'natural' is commonly used in opposition to 'artificial' or, in the case of health practices, biomedical, technological or pharmaceutical. However, I do not consider 'natural' health practices as something untouched by culture or technology but as practices which combine social and biophysical elements. These practices are always 'naturalcultural' (Haraway 2003) and never out of reach of the social or cultural. Drawing from a multispecies approach (Kirksey and Helmreich 2010), I will deepen our understanding of what the 'natural' lifestyle of vaccine-refusing families entails. This chapter thus focuses on parental understandings of the role of microbes in human health and the kinds of human-microbe practices that emerge as parents abandon vaccination as part of promoting 'natural' immunity.

VACCINE REFUSAL AND HUMAN-MICROBE RELATIONS

Contestations of childhood vaccination can be understood as assemblages (e.g. Marcus and Saka 2006; Salmenniemi et al. 2019) that are continuously being pulled together using diverse sets of arguments, experiences, practices and objects. As microbiological research is shifting societal understandings of microbes from pathogenic threats to beneficial companions to humans (Rees et al. 2018), I suggest that human-microbe relations are present in these assemblages and may play an important role in the development of vaccine-critical views. I understand these human-microbe relations to be part of *microbiopolitics*, concerning 'the recognition and management, governmental and grassroots, of human encounters with the vital organisms of bacteria, viruses and fungi' (Paxson 2008: 18) that can happen on individual, community and societal levels.

In the public health framing of vaccination, vaccine-refusing parents are often defined as 'bad' (i.e. irrational, risk-taking) microbiopolitical citizens. However, this chapter maps the inner logics of vaccine-refusal related to human-microbe relations rather than focusing on the public health consequences. I will trace *lay immunologies* (Enticott 2003) concerning 'natural' immunity as practised by vaccine-refusing parents. Studying defenders of unpasteurised milk in rural

England, Gareth Enticott (2003) pointed out that proponents of raw milk under-stood unprocessed milk as part of a strategy of 'natural immunology' to prevent and cure disease. They subscribed to an 'impure immunology' which did not discriminate between good and bad bacteria and instead considered all bacteria necessary to build a healthy immune system. I suggest that lay immunologies are present in vaccine-refusing parents' understandings of microbes as well as in entanglements of microbes, microbiomes and the health practices of the parents. Interspecies cooperation manifests in these practices, which are often interpreted as the health choices of human individuals, but also simultaneously rely on human-microbial symbiosis.

A multispecies approach that emphasises the agency of 'organisms whose lives are entangled with humans' (Kirksey and Helmreich 2010: 566) and focuses on contact zones between 'nature' and 'culture' is helpful in understanding how vaccine-refusing parents relate to microbes in ways that differ from mainstream lay perceptions and expert understandings. Multispecies approaches emphasise connectedness rather than separation between humans and non-humans. From this perspective, vaccine-refusing parents' health practices present fascinating cases of joint human-microbial agency that manifest in parents' accounts of how and why they seek to improve immunity without vaccines. Subjectivities in these alternative health practices are perhaps best understood as coopera-tive and interspecies, potentially destabilising notions of the human subject as central, separate and oppositional in relation to non-human entities (Braidotti 2019; Haraway 2008). This perspective is further supported by microbiological research suggesting that the notion of human individuals as entities separated from their environments is questionable due to the extent of human-microbial symbiosis (Lorimer 2016; Rees et al. 2018).

RESEARCH MATERIALS AND METHODS

This chapter is based on ethnographic interviews with 34 parents who had opted out of vaccinating at least one of their children according to the national vaccination programme. I recruited participants through an open Finnish vaccine-sceptic Facebook group and via participants who referred other vaccine-refusing parents to the study. I conducted the interviews between 2016 and 2019 with participants living in southern, western and central Finland. All but two of the participants were women, and their children aged between two months and 22 years. There was a total of 78 children, of whom 35 were non-vaccinated, 30 partially vaccinated and 12 fully vaccinated until at least the age of six. All participant names are pseudonyms.

The interviews were loosely structured around three themes: 1) what led participants to refuse childhood vaccinations, 2) which health-promoting and illness-preventing practices participants used, and 3) participants' experiences in the healthcare system. In most interviews, participants freely shared their stories of how they became vaccine-hesitant. I prompted many themes, including lifestyle, diet and perceptions about immunity. However, I did not initiate discussions about human-microbe relations. While this limited the amount of data on human-microbe relations, it does indicate that engaging with microbes was something that many participants practised consciously, and that they connected these practices with immunity and non-vaccination. Obviously, the interview material only gives access to the parents' understandings of and their reported practices with microbes. In addition, I have used field notes describing the interview situations as background material.

My objective is not to evaluate the participants' claims about immunity or vaccines from a biomedical perspective. Rather, I analyse their understandings as lay immunologies (Enticott 2003). In doing this, I have subscribed to a fluid researcher position that navigates between the opposing polarities of the vaccination debate (see e.g. Koski 2019). This kind of position entails risks such as participants' expectations for advocacy (ibid.). However, it may also create new insights into how non-vaccination makes sense to parents as part of their health practices.

In an earlier analysis, I identified three main reasons that parents in Finland reported for refusing childhood vaccines (Nurmi and Harman 2021): 1) adverse effects, 2) distrust toward vaccine technocracies, and 3) health perceptions and a preference for practices pursuing 'natural' immunity. This chapter focuses on the perceptions of and practices related to 'natural' immunity and illness prevention without vaccines, examining their diverse and even contradictory manifestations. In the next section, I present the different ways participants perceived microbes. I then show how they constructed 'natural' immunities in cooperation with microbes and, finally, consider the unpredictable agency of microbes.

COEXISTENCE: BEING PART OF THE 'NATURAL SYSTEM'

According to Jennifer Reich (2016: 104), vaccine resistance is situated at the intersection of two ideologies:

> One that expects parents to intensively invest in their children and the other that calls for individuals to become savvy consumers of technology and health interventions. As they meld these cultural definitions, parents prioritize 'natural' as health promoting and manufactured products as potentially harmful.

This resonates somewhat with my observations of Finnish parents. While many participants expressed their preference for 'natural' health practices over bio-medical and pharmaceutical ones, most had still taken courses of antibiotics, some had had surgery, and many acknowledged that they would not be here today without modern biomedicine. Thus, in the pursuit of natural immunity, 'natural' was never completely free from biomedical technologies. However, while Reich notes that the vaccine-refusing parents in her study did not neces-sarily include microbes in their definition of 'natural', many of the parents in my study were very much aware of the presence of different microbes within the realm of 'natural'. To them, microbes made things natural as opposed to over-sanitised, artificial or chemical-laden.

While some parents discussed microbes in terms of pathogens that should be avoided if possible, none of them talked about microbes principally in this sense. Understandings that positioned microbes as predominantly beneficial or commensal – and indispensable – were prominent in the interviews. For instance, parents talked about the role of microbes in training and strengthening the human immune system, or how the gut microbiome affects our overall health. It is worth noting that the parents did not strictly categorise microbes into 'good' and 'bad', beneficial and pathogenic, but rather focused on the bigger picture, on a natural 'system' in which all kinds of microbes were inseparable from other life forms and as such needed to be accepted and perhaps worked with. Emma's account provides a good example of these understandings. At the time of the interview, Emma was in her late twenties, a university-educated mother of two, juggling self-employment and stay-at-home parenting. She had vaccinated her first child but stopped doing so after the child developed severe allergies and eczema which she interpreted as being caused by a combination of antibiotics and vaccines in the first months of life.

Emma repeatedly brought up the human-nature connection, which she felt most people in today's industrialised societies had lost. This connection included being in tune with the surrounding world and its microbes, which she described as ancient and intelligent beings. She blamed the loss of this connection partly on modern biomedicine, a 'proud science, men's science' that had developed and carelessly used technologies such as antibiotics, thinking it could conquer and control the microbial world. She was very much aware of the threat that antimicrobial resistance poses to human health. This was a battle people could never win: 'we may be ahead [of the resistant bacteria] for a moment. But of course they are much more intelligent than us'.

But it was not just antibiotics that had interrupted the human-nature connection. Emma saw vaccines as an equally disruptive technology:

> We can momentarily beat diseases with, let's say, antibiotics. Or we can momentarily eradicate diseases with vaccines. But they're a million times more intelligent than us, they'll cause new forms of the diseases. I'm not sure, was it whooping cough that had these altered forms that our drugs [vaccines] do not work on? The vaccine does not make you immune.

The parents sometimes drew connections between antimicrobial resistance and the mutation of bacteria and viruses that the use of vaccines might cause. They stated that when you vaccinate against one strain of virus or bacteria, other strains may get stronger. While it may not be that simple and may not concern all pathogens targeted by vaccines, the precipitation of pathogenic evolution by vaccines has been increasingly studied in recent years (Moyer 2018). For instance, in the case of *B. pertussis*, mentioned by Emma, bacterial evolution has been associated with the immune pressure from vaccination (Xu at al. 2015). Participants often used these kinds of examples as a proof that pathogenic microbes are in the process of outsmarting not just antimicrobial treatments, but also vaccines.

Other parents also emphasised that while wild strains of viruses are natural, vaccination can cause them to mutate and act unpredictably and more virulently than they would if left alone. As vaccination was also understood as disruptive for the development and workings of children's 'natural' immune systems, causing impaired immunity and autoimmunity, biomedical technologies were thus named as one of the main culprits for why people and their immune systems were out of balance. Many traced their children's health problems (especially autoimmune conditions) back to vaccines and antibiotics and the damage they thought these interventions had caused to their children's microbiomes and immune systems.

Emma's solution was to try to restore the lost connection with the natural world and its microbial diversity: 'I have to be a part of this system, this microbiology that has revolved here for millions of years. Yeah, it can kill me or my kids. But... I'd rather live with that knowledge'. She believed most vaccine-refusing parents perceived themselves as part of this bigger entity – nature. They 'understand that when we're not against it but go with it and take on certain things, some of us die from diseases and others don't'. Several parents talked about accepting coexistence with both beneficial and pathogenic microbes. They felt it was important not to be fearful and controlling in the face of this coexistence. Elisa, the mother of an unvaccinated one-year-old, talked about the risk of disease in a similarly accepting tone:

> That's life. I think non-vaccinating people have a healthier attitude toward life and death and being sick, toward the fact that life doesn't mean being in a bubble, [...] we get cuts, we get pains, we get illnesses. In my opinion, the typical way of thinking for non-vaccinating people is that, well, that's life

and when it happens, I'll do my best. But vaccinating people seem to think that 'Oh no, can you die from this?! I'm afraid'.

In these accounts, humans were not portrayed as intellectually superior and separate from non-human beings. On the contrary, humans were far behind some of the non-human beings, especially bacteria and viruses, whose capabilities were not properly recognised by most people or even medical science. Humans are simultaneously one with the non-human world ('a part of this system') but also separate in the sense that we can turn against microbes and microbes can turn against us, using their intelligence to adapt and transform so that they can continue existing and functioning despite antibiotics and vaccines. According to these accounts, humans have never been at the top of the natural order, but in a co-dependent relationship with other entities on this planet.

This view thus decentres the human subject as the point of interest (Braidotti 2019; Friese and Nuyts 2017). Simultaneously, it blurs the binary distinction between 'good' and 'bad' microbes; some viruses or bacteria may be pathogenic to some human individuals, but this might not ultimately make them 'bad'. Microbes that cause human diseases were also seen as performing the important work of controlling human overpopulation. Irene noted that 'Nature and … the planet protects itself so that there aren't too many people here'. Thus, these microbes had multiple effects on different actors, not just on humans.

Not all statements about human-microbial coexistence were this fatalistic, and they often focused more on the positive side of coexistence with microbes. Many parents talked about microbes – including pathogens – as helpful co-operators in the pursuit of 'natural' immunities. In the next section, I will explore instances in which gut microbiomes, immunities and healthy children were produced in collaboration between humans and microbes.

CO-PRODUCING 'NATURAL' IMMUNITIES

In the face of antimicrobial resistance and increasing rates of autoimmune diseases, for Emma, there was no choice but to try to live in harmony with the natural world, to live as if antibiotics and other modern medical technologies did not exist, and to follow 'that plan, whatever it is, that has made the bacteria develop into the form we're in these days, this whole complex'. At times, there was no separation between herself and the other life forms that had developed in this 'complex'. In her assemblage, refusing vaccines was just one of the elements brought together in an effort to help her children build robust immune systems. She was using as few pharmaceuticals as possible. She embraced coexistence with microbes through exposure to environmental microbes and by not washing her children's hands too often or with soap. In this way, Emma seemed to perceive herself and her children as composed of microbial and human cells; taking care of the skin and gut microbiomes was not detached from care for her own health and that of her children. Her other health practices included long-term breastfeeding and the avoidance of chemicals in cleaning products. All these practices together would strengthen her children's immunity:

> The younger one is unvaccinated, he has sat on the floor of the cowshed and eaten animal feed with the cow from the same container. Literally, he's been covered in cow shit and eaten that too. [...] If my kid is in the sandbox eating sand with his hands [...] I'll give him a shovel [so he can eat more]. Children's guts need it. [...] The stronger your gut flora, the better it fights disease.

Indeed, many participants described their relaxed attitude toward their children's relationship with microbes as one of the key elements in optimising their immune systems: 'we are not overly hygienic, [our child] can crawl around [outside] and he certainly gets germs and develops immunity that way. [...] And our dog and cat, he kisses them on the mouth and stuff so he probably gets every germ possible' (Melissa). The 'alternative' health practices that many of the participants described – extended breastfeeding, avoidance of excess hygiene and chemicals, and eating high fibre and non-processed diets – were often aimed at optimising or restoring gut microbiomes. Thus, people were only one part of this 'natural' immunity assemblage in which numerous actors (such as pathogens and microbes in the human gut, in the home, in the forest, in the cowshed and in different foods) came together to build human immunities.

Similar to Lorimer's (2016) observations about the therapeutic use of helminths as an 'ecological model of immunity as involving a multispecies community', many participants talked about natural immunity as a cooperative effort between humans and microbes. Irene explained that she had built up her daughter's immune system after it had been severely disrupted by the antibiotics used during birth and by several different antibiotics given to her daughter after surgery. For two years after the surgery, her daughter suffered recurring respiratory infections that Irene traced back to antibiotics and the early introduction of solid foods. Irene felt that all this had compromised her daughter's gut health and, relatedly, her immune system. She started to build back her daughter's immunity, skipping antibiotics for her ear infections and using vitamin C and garlic oil instead. In a process of 'species coshaping one another' (Haraway 2008: 42), she was consciously trying to rebuild her daughter's gut microbiome with probiotic supplements, sauerkraut and fermented drinks, and by avoiding cow's milk, sugar and grains. As Irene understood it, these practices eventually helped reshape the child's microbiome, which inextricably reshaped her daughter's immune system and her life in general. After two years of this interspecies work, she was no longer getting sick once a month.

Linda explained that she had alleviated her young child's severe food allergies by using raw milk: '[goat's milk] made her vomit less than other milks and first I mixed it with hot water, trying to pasteurise it, but after that I gave it to her unpasteurised'. Others also described following a diet of unprocessed food and probiotics to prevent illnesses. Preventative care for one's immune system and those of family members can then become a sort of microbiopolitical project in which the potential effects of everything coming into contact with one's microbiome are carefully considered. You care not just for your health but also for your home environment, the quality of your food and the soil where it grew or the animals that produced it. In short, you care for your relationship with microbes. For the participants, vaccines obviously disrupted this carefully crafted balance of 'natural' immunity, just as many 'pro-vaccine' health-conscious individuals think antibiotics disrupt the gut microbiome. Participants felt that the practices used to strengthen individual immune systems could also be harnessed to contribute to the fight against antimicrobial resistance or the mutation of pathogens due to vaccination.

While it may seem, for instance, that Irene and her daughter could have worked with microbes *and* still be vaccinated, to Irene, foregoing vaccines was firmly enmeshed with other practices of strengthening her child's immune system. Suffering from an autoimmune disease, Irene had come across information stating that vaccines containing aluminium might be connected to autoimmunity and wanted to avoid this risk with her daughter. Her strategy was a combination of non-vaccination and the building of a robust immune system with microbial companions. Moreover, she had found information that suggested that some vaccine-preventable illnesses (VPDs) were connected to positive health outcomes:

> I found a study that said that children who've had rotavirus had significantly lower rates of severe respiratory illnesses and pneumonia. Then I read about measles – that it has [...] a protective effect against certain types of cancer, same with mumps [...] It may be nature's way of strengthening your immunity so that you'll live longer and be healthier.

Viruses such as mumps and measles were redefined as actors that could, together with the human immune system, benefit people in a reciprocal relationship. Many participants echoed this view and saw viruses such as chickenpox and measles as crucial participants in the 'natural immunity' assemblage. They explained that pathogens helped immune systems practise (see Reich 2016 for similar observations) and thus made them stronger and less prone to autoimmunity – another thread tying together gut health, non-vaccination and well-functioning immune systems.

Many viruses causing VPDs were understood as 'good old' viruses that caused easy-to-deal-with illnesses and were slow to mutate. Participants also often said they were not afraid of VPDs, as access to medical care is provided for everyone: 'Finland has really good and advanced medical care. I believe that if it comes to that, we will be treated in the same way as people who are vaccinated and still get the disease' (Paula). Moreover, many participants would have much rather coexisted with the 'old' viruses than the less predictable 'new viruses':

> If we had the space to be ill with the so-called old-fashioned childhood diseases and to be home with those children, then these ear infections and other [secondary infections] would be considerably easier and we wouldn't have these new viruses and things that are much worse and that keep on coming (Lea).

This coexistence, however, was not often possible; vaccine-preventable childhood illnesses have become rare, and many felt that those illnesses had been replaced by persistent viral respiratory illnesses or 'nasty stomach bugs' such as the norovirus. As Lea continued to explain: 'diseases these days are really gruesome, people get terribly sick. Being ill in a natural way is rare, but instead people can have like a cough or something for three months'.

Many participants believed that at least partial immunities could be produced through vaccination. However, they preferred the 'natural' way of encountering wild strains of pathogens because this would produce strong, lasting immunities without the possible side-effects of vaccines. One might argue that the immunities produced through vaccination could also be considered a 'natural' or 'probiotic' practice of co-producing immunity by engaging the human immune system with selected microbes, such as (parts of) viruses. However, participants found it safer to engage with wild strains of microbes through 'natural' channels of exposure (such as the respiratory or digestive systems) than with vaccines mostly administered by injection. Immunisation also meant coming into contact with adjuvants, such as aluminium, which were perceived as carrying considerable risks. Wild viruses and bacteria were thus understood as 'natural', whereas the vaccination strains or virus components in vaccines were rendered 'unnatural' and potentially unsafe due to the pharmaceutical processes of manufacturing vaccines. Thus, vaccines could not be considered 'probiotic' or seen as inducing 'natural' immunity.

MICROBES AS UNPREDICTABLE AGENTS

The agency of pathogenic microbes was often treated somewhat mechanically, with the idea that pathogens want to spread, multiply and cause diseases. However, well-functioning immune systems were perceived as limiting the disease-inducing agency of microbes while simultaneously co-producing immunities with them. Humans could also be carriers of viruses that enable their spread without necessarily getting (very) sick. In this mutually beneficial process, both humans and viruses needed each other. Laura, a mother of two partly vaccinated children, said that her son had had influenza (as proven by lab tests) but, having a robust immune system, he only had common cold symptoms for less than two days. As part of the vaccine-hesitant assemblages, these kinds of stories enforced the idea of personal responsibility in maintaining a healthy immune system to mitigate the risks of illnesses. For instance, Laura's family used probiotics and other supplements, avoided cow's milk and wheat, and used several complementary and alternative medicine (CAM) treatments to optimise their immune systems.

Some VPDs, such as chickenpox, mumps and measles, were considered 'ordinary' or even beneficial diseases that had been rebranded as dangerous by health authorities and the pharmaceutical industry. Because of the health benefits assigned to these illnesses, some participants felt positively about their children contracting them. Nora explained: 'I feel sad that [some VPDs] are not around because I'd like my son to catch chickenpox and measles. (…) In general, I'd like him to get certain illnesses as a child when they're usually [milder], especially when you use the right treatments'. A certain mitigation of risks was present, as parents sometimes said they might consider vaccinating against certain illnesses if their children were not exposed to them in childhood. For example, because the disease posed risks for male fertility, Nora was going to consider vaccinating her son against mumps if he had not contracted it before becoming a teenager.

Certain pathogens occupied a role similar to the probiotics and commensal microbes with which participants sought to collaborate. The agency of these pathogens was not only understood as a selfish drive to multiply but also as symbiotic or therapeutic for the humans involved. For instance, Elisa described how after being vaccinated, her sister would have recurrent, long-lasting colds without 'a proper fever'. This lasted for years until she caught measles and 'was cured by [it]'. She now gets a fever when sick and the illness passes quickly. In Elisa's account, the measles virus thus helped her sister's immune system cancel out the harmful effects of previous vaccination.

Vaccine-refusing parents have been reported to consciously work with viruses to catch illnesses such as varicella or measles (Reich 2016). Likewise, in the interviews, some of the parents referred to seeking out interaction and cooperation with certain pathogens. However, they reported actively 'fetching' only varicella viruses from someone who had the illness. In this cooperation, however, the human subjects were never in control, as the agency of viruses was independent and unpredictable: they often did not cooperate in ways people wanted them to. Olga, for instance, talked about her difficulties in getting her children to come down with varicella:

> All these 'pox diseases' are possible to catch, but the percentage of conta-
> gion is lousy. For instance, chickenpox, we've looked for it for each of our
> children, but it has been bad at transmitting. Now I think we've gotten it
> for all of our kids, but sometimes it was hard to transmit. (…) You really
> had to go look for it.

This cooperation was not just about people *using* viruses. People had to accept the unpredictable agency of viruses. Participants also considered the possibility that the viruses may cause a severe illness with negative health consequences. For instance, Emma said that her children had not yet had chickenpox. She had recently had a chance to 'fetch' the virus from friends whose children had it. But because Emma was pregnant, she was cautious about the possible negative consequences to her unborn child and the unpredictability of the encounter between her immune system, the foetus and the virus. These concerns caused her to postpone the voluntary exposure of her children.

CONCLUSION

In this chapter, I have attempted to deepen our understanding of both vaccine refusal and everyday human-microbe relations by showing how vaccine-refusing parents perceive these relations and how 'natural' immunities are co-produced in interspecies health practices. Many participants in the study aimed to co-produce 'natural' immunities, avoid autoimmunity and possible adverse effects from vaccines, and live in a symbiotic relationship with their environment and the non-human actors in it. I have considered these health perceptions of vaccine-refusing parents as lay immunologies that can inform various health choices. These lay immunologies present human immune systems as complex organisations of interspecies and environmental relations. They entail three main elements: 1) coexistence with microbes, 2) interspecies co-production of 'natural' immunities, and 3) microbes as unpredictable agents.

Coexisting and working with pathogens allowed for uncontrolled microbial activity and narrowed the role of human control. Thus, these lay immunologies sometimes decentred human actors. Some of the parents ventured deep into the symbiotic understanding of human subjectivity, but while the 'microbial flows' (Lorimer 2016) were always out of the participants' full control, they all still presented some controlling tendencies – attempting to choose between interacting with microbes or avoiding them. The lay immunologies of vaccine-refusing parents also departed from previous conceptualisations of human-microbe relations such as reliance on the categories of 'good' and 'bad' microbes (Paxson 2008). This resembles the lay immunologies described by Enticott (2003), in which rural raw milk defenders saw all bacteria as necessary to build healthy immunity.

Vaccine-refusing parents' perceptions reflect the recent surge in research and popular science literature which states that the microbiome and potential disruptions to it play a central role in human health. Still, vaccine-refusing individuals often perceive immunity and human-microbe relations in ways that radically differ from the microbiopolitics of preventative healthcare promoted by public health authorities and healthcare institutions. This complicates communication with, for instance, most healthcare providers, who are not likely to recognise measles or varicella viruses as companions to work with.

From the perspective of vaccine-refusing parents, vaccines pose more risks (of adverse effects, autoimmunity and possible pathogen mutation) than 'natural' coexistence with microbes. While from the public health perspective the interaction between pathogens in vaccines and the human immune system happens in a controlled manner, this technologically managed exposure to antigens, pathogens and other substances in vaccines is in fact why vaccine-refusing parents do not consider vaccination a 'natural' practice. This is also why attempts to scale vaccine-promoting public health messaging to better resonate with vaccine-hesitant groups by framing vaccines as 'natural' (Reich 2016) might not be very successful.

REFERENCES

Attwell, K., and others, '"Do-it-yourself": Vaccine Rejection and Complementary and Alternative Medicine (CAM)', *Social Science & Medicine*, 196 (2018), 106–14.

Blaisdell, L. L., and others, 'Unknown Risks: Parental Hesitation about Vaccination', *Medical Decision Making*, 36 (2016), 479–89.

Braidotti, R., 'A Theoretical Framework for the Critical Posthumanities', *Theory, Culture & Society*, 36 (2019), 31–61.

Brown, K. F., and others, 'Factors Underlying Parental Decisions about Combination Childhood Vaccinations Including MMR: A Systematic Review', *Vaccine*, 28 (2010), 4235–48.

Enticott, G., 'Lay Immunology, Local Foods and Rural Identity: Defending Unpasteurised Milk in England', *Sociologia Ruralis*, 43 (2003), 257–70.

Friese, C., and N. Nuyts, 'Posthumanist Critique and Human Health: How Non-humans (Could) Figure in Public Health Research', *Critical Public Health*, 27 (2017), 303–13.

Greenhough, B., and others, 'Unsettling Antibiosis: How Might Interdisciplinary Researchers Generate a Feeling For the Microbiome and to What Effect?', *Palgrave Communications*, 4 (2018) <https://doi.org/10.1057/s41599-018-0196-3> [accessed 5 May 2020].

Haraway, D., *The Companion Species Manifesto: Dogs, People, and Significant Otherness* (Chicago: Prickly Paradigm Press, 2003).

—— *When Species Meet* (Minneapolis: University of Minnesota Press, 2008).

Koski, K., '"On Whose Side Are You?": Artist-Researcher Positionality in a Global Public Health Challenge', *Nordic Journal for Artistic Research*, 1 (2019) <https://doi.org/10.22501/vis.502826> [accessed 11 May 2020].

Kiljunen, P., *Tiedebarometri 2019* [Science barometer 2019], Tieteen tiedotus ry. <http://www.tieteentiedotus.fi/tiedebarometri.html> [accessed 20 November 2019].

Kirksey, S. E., and S. Helmreich, 'The Emergence of Multispecies Ethnography', *Cultural Anthropology*, 25 (2010), 545–76.

Laudone, S., and M. Tramontano, 'Intensive Mothering and Vaccine Choice: Reclaiming the Lifeworld from the System', *Journal of Mother Studies*, 3 (2018) <https://jourms.wordpress.com/intensive-mothering-and-vaccine-choice-reclaiming-the-lifeworld-from-the-system/> [accessed 25 November 2019].

Lorimer, J., 'Gut Buddies', *Environmental Humanities*, 8 (2016), 57–76.

Marcus, G. E., and E. Saka, 'Assemblage', *Theory, Culture & Society*, 23 (2006), 101–6.

Moyer, M. W., 'Vaccines Are Pushing Pathogens to Evolve', *Quanta Magazine* (2018) <https://www.quantamagazine.org/how-vaccines-can-drive-pathogens-to-evolve-20180510/> [accessed 15 November 2020].

Nurmi, J., and B. Harman, 'Why Do Parents Refuse Childhood Vaccination? Reasons Reported in Finland', *Scandinavian Journal of Public Health*, (2021) <https://journals.sagepub.com/doi/10.1177/14034948211004323> [accessed 4 May 2021].

Paxson, H., 'Post-Pasteurian Cultures: The Microbiopolitics of Raw-Milk Cheese in the United States', *Cultural Anthropology*, 23 (2008), 15–47.

Rees, T., T. Bosch, and A. E. Douglas, 'How the Microbiome Challenges Our Concept of Self', *PLoS Biology*, 16 (2018) <https://doi.org/10.1371/journal.pbio.2005358> [accessed 16 November 2019].

Reich, J. A., 'Neoliberal Mothering and Vaccine Refusal: Imagined Gated Communities and the Privilege of Choice', *Gender & Society*, 28 (2014), 679–704.

—— 'Of Natural Bodies and Antibodies: Parents' Vaccine Refusal and the Dichotomies of Natural and Artificial', *Social Science & Medicine*, 157 (2016), 103–10.

Salmenniemi, S., and others, 'From Culture to Assemblages: An Introduction', in S. Salmenniemi, and others, eds, *Assembling Therapeutics: Cultures, Politics and Materiality* (New York and London: Routledge, 2019).

THL, *Kolmeen ikävuoteen asti rokottamattomat lapset* [Unvaccinated Children Up To the Age of Three] <https://www.thl.fi/roko/rokotusrekisteri/atlas/atlas.html?show=infantbc> [accessed 20 November 2019].

Xu, Y., and others, 'Whole-Genome Sequencing Reveals the Effect of Vaccination on the Evolution of Bordetella Pertussis', *Scientific Reports*, 5 (2015) <http://dx.doi.org/10.1038/srep12888> [accessed 16 November 2019].

II

REGULATING

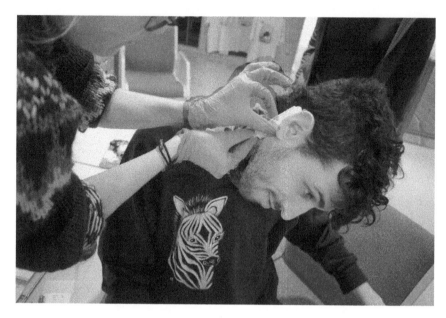

FIG. B: SAMPLING MICROBES. The Labracadabra performance embodied the social science of microbes and offered scholars moments of laboratory aesthetics. The initial absence of microbes in the laboratory felt sterile and strange, but soon the laboratory was filled with laughter and dirty fingerprints. Somewhat performative equipment made us feel we were conducting a serious task: we started our project by collecting microbial specimens from different parts of the writers' skin, without knowing what to do with them. We just wanted to be engaged with the materialities between microbes, human bodies and laboratory practices and to give space to think and live with our small companions, let them guide the way and disturb and construct our improvisation. By means of using laboratory materials alternatively, maybe even incorrectly, a method emerged for letting microbial agency channel our collaboration: more-than-human i-magickining at the lab happened as an ongoing situation between the seminars where this book was partly written. Each intuitive step was dedicated to microbial agency without trying to rationalise it. We felt we offered entanglement between people, and at the same time tiny microbes were lured to become more animated (photograph by the Labracadabra team).

5

WHEN CULTURES MEET: MICROBES, PERMEABLE BODIES AND THE ENVIRONMENT

Katriina Huttunen, Elina Oinas, Salla Sariola[1]

INTRODUCTION

OVER 700 PEOPLE FROM FINLAND PARTICIPATED IN A DIARRHOEA VAC-
cine trial in West Africa between 2017 and 2019. Groups of 10 to 30 tourist-
participants at a time spent two weeks in a small coastal village on the Gulf
of Guinea, sunbathing, going on short excursions, eating and drinking, like
on any holiday. Half of them had received a tentative vaccine to prevent
diarrhoea, the other half had received a placebo. While the tourists were
not intentionally exposed to E. coli bacteria or any other enteric pathogens, the likelihood of falling ill was high, as is often the case when one
travels from Northern Europe to the tropics. The trial had selected Finnish
research participants because they are rarely exposed to these bacteria at
home and therefore have not acquired immunity against them, unlike most
adults living in environments where these bacteria are abundant. The aim
was to test a vaccine that was being developed to prevent both traveller and
infant diarrhoea; the latter being a major cause of global childhood mortal-
ity. The trial not only created an enormous pool of data about gut reactions
to a new environment in the form of laboratory specimen containers and

health records, but it also generated endless chatter about 'poo' and bugs among the Finns.

The trial offered a unique possibility for us social scientists to study ordinary Finns' thoughts about and ways of living with microbes. This group was not ordinary, as people who volunteer to participate in a trial of this unique sort are perhaps 'slightly crazy', as they often joked, or more 'curious' and 'adventurous' than most. They agreed to test the vaccine and to give blood and stool samples before, during and after the trip, and to fill in a health card that recorded their daily bodily functions in detail. Consequently, they also agreed to talk extensively about faeces, mainly with each other, in mostly humorous ways, but also with us, more seriously. Presumably, people with strong negative or fearful attitudes towards microbes, or new places, would not have taken part in the trial in the first place.

The data for this chapter was collected in a village in West Africa, hereafter referred to as Ville. Interviews with and participant observations of the embodied practices of the trial participants offer a unique opportunity to have a closer look at how human-microbial relationality is negotiated by tourists in a new environment. The specific design – a vaccine trial conducted in West Africa on a group of Northern Europeans – is unique indeed, but we also argue that it further offers an exceptional setting to analyse lay accounts of bodily contours, fragility, immunity, hygiene and the role of the environment on human-microbe coexistence. The sociological data tells us something more general about the variety of ways in which people relate to bacteria. The analysis displays a plethora of complex and contradictory modes of discussing, embodying, embracing and resisting encounters with microbes.

The vaccine trial involved a large research group that worked not only in a laboratory setup in Ville but also in Europe and the US. Participants were recruited mainly via news and social media to identify a diverse population within the 18 to 65 age bracket. A noble aim of the vaccine was indicated in the recruitment advertising: this is about African children. The project was featured in a four-page article in the Sunday section of the biggest newspaper in Finland, and later advertised on social media, at bus stops and on commuter transport. Finally, enough volunteers signed up despite the cost of the trip (close to €2,000) and a careful selection followed. The criteria for exclusion consisted of limitations regarding the applicants' health, medication and previous travel.

The outcome of the recruitment process was a trial population that was slightly over-represented by middle-aged women, and somewhat better educated and older than the national average but diverse enough for medical – and sociological – purposes. Many worked in health care professions and education, but builders, lawyers and taxi drivers were also among the volunteers. They were socio-economically unexceptional. What characterised them was an interest in health, science and 'Africa', as the location was often referred to: 'Africa', rather than the specific country. Further, 'opportunity to travel to Africa' was given as the most usual reason for participation, followed by an interest in being part of the trial, either for the sake of science or for the potential advantages of the vaccine. Although a lot of our data deal with the encounter with the study location, 'Africa', this chapter will focus on the microbial encounter, which is also mediated by geopolitics (Haraway 2016). Social relations, including processes of racialisation or othering, are present in microbial encounters (Anderson 2006; Roy 2018; Chigudu 2020). The ways microbes are experienced, imagined and narrated have consequences for imaginaries of, and relations to, selves, others and what is considered a 'good life'.

Histories of colonial and post/neo-colonial medicine and experimentation (Vaughan 1991; Tilley 2011; Geissler and Molyneux 2011), and the recent 'scrambling for Africa' (Crane 2013) in search of masses of research participants with varying access to biomedical health care, frame this Nordic and touristic vaccine trial. In practice, though, it was rarely articulated in this way. The public discourse around histories of Nordic colonialism tends to be characterised by complicity, rather than seeing Nordic countries at the centre of colonial forces (Vuorela 2009). Hence, explicit discussions about how contemporary science carries on such legacies are rare. This silence is evident also in this case. The trial differs from the usual trial arrangements in that the recruited participants were not local but healthy Finnish adults. Unlike trial participants living in contexts without access to health care in sub-Saharan Africa (see e.g. Kingori 2015), Finnish participants here were not compelled to take part to access medical care. On the contrary, Northerners even considered themselves as donating their body fluids for the sake of African children and, hence, the concern about exploiting the poor appears to be inverted. Processes of inequality and racialisation are complex, however, as Adia Benton (2016a), for example, shows in her work on racialisation in professional humanitarianism, where race is both invisibilised and hypercentral. This applies here, too, with the humanitarian tourist-participants hoping to do good, which leads to a variety of racialising and anti-racist encounters taking place.

Our project gathered an extensive, mixed-methods dataset between 2017 and 2019. The data was collected during ten months of participant observation in Ville and six months in Finland, generating more than 500 pages of field notes, 195 qualitative interviews with staff and tourist-participants, and a survey. The focus of this paper is on vaccine study tourist-participant experiences. In the analysis, specific attention is given to the segments of data in which human-microbe relations are enacted: the shifting ways participants negotiate bodily contours and assumed embodied integrity, porousness and fragility in their relationality to the microbiota at the study site, as expressed in daily practices, from breakfast to night cap. The practices channel and mediate the context into bodies, and more specifically, guts. The gut is neither inside nor outside; it is the site where microbes blur the contours of the body as an entity. As can be imagined, the richness of feelings expressed about the gut in our data goes beyond a traditional social science analysis, as such feelings are verbalised only to an extent.

SOCIAL SCIENCE IN GUT RELATIONS

Two classic texts in feminist sociology of the body have shaped the study of the politics of human-microbe relationality profoundly: Donna Haraway's *Simians, Cyborgs, and Women* (1991) and Emily Martin's *Flexible Bodies* (1994). Both analyse ways in which popular, lay and scholarly images depict the human immune system as a militarised field of warfare. The human body is described using metaphors of the nation state during the Cold War. By this definition, the immune system fights bacteria like a nation state defending itself from outsiders violating its borders. Bacteria are attackers, intruders invaders; the immune system's white blood cells are protective killer cells that battle the attacking bacteria. In the context of international relations, these studies show how the Cold War influenced the metaphors pertaining to the human immuno-defence system, reflecting societal tensions of the time. Our analysis also points to the ways in which ideas of microbes and immunity are entangled with broader societal and global relations, such as how (racialised) imaginaries are at play when notions of purity, hygiene, dirt and illness are negotiated in everyday encounters, experiences and practices.

Since the 1990s, microbiology and immunology, and feminist readings of them, have taken new directions. New metagenomic methods utilised from the 2000s have demonstrated that microbes are among us, in, and on us in hitherto unimaginable quantities. Now, the emphasis is on abundance, relationality, inter-action and mutualistic outcomes. Discourses that Haraway and Martin earlier described as discourses of war against microbes have now been complemented with what Haraway (2016) describes as human-microbial coexistence, where microbes are crucial for human wellbeing. It is worth noting, as for example Pradeu (2019) argues, that there are great differences in how the relationality of self and the microbiota are described within scientific publications. A wider debate on the ontological shift in how the contours of the human body are fluid, open-ended, porous and processual (e.g. Åsberg 2018; Fishel 2017; Roy 2018) guides us as we study how Finnish tourist-participants in West Africa understand their bodily relationships to microbes, and what practices they enact to mediate that relationship.

THE SPECTRUM OF MICROBIAL RELATIONALITY

We identified an array of encounters with bacteria. The spectrum includes enactments (e.g. Mol and Law 2004) of human-microbe *relations*, through daily *practices* of maintaining body-boundaries and *discourses* through which tourist-participants spoke about microbes. Microbes were rarely explicitly spoken about in and of themselves; instead, they were alluded to through other domains such as illness and illness prevention, hygiene practices, food and water.

The spectrum, therefore, outlines the ways in which people described how bacteria materialised to them through the practices with which they navigated the external conditions.

The trial orients the tourists towards being conscious about microbes in both practical and verbal ways. Before travelling, they had conversations with research nurses about travel hygiene as though travelling to the tropics as ordinary tourists. As part of the trial procedures, participants provided data about their daily bodily sensations and symptoms in a way that guided them to think about microbes. In Ville, they recorded practices that might have involved microbial transfer, such as the foods they ate. The trial gave them a somewhat uniform framework to think about and live with microbes. Therefore, it is even more significant to note that despite the homogenising circumstances, they interpreted and fitted this information to their pre-existing notions about bacteria through diverse enactments. The participants were neither hyper-cautious nor hyper-adventurous as a group, as one might expect, but displayed a full spectrum of enactments from very cautious to very relaxed. The trial circumstances enabled diverse practices: the tourists were free to spend their days in Ville as they pleased, with a few pre-organised activities to nearby historical sites in buses owned by the trial.

Two small, neat but not luxurious French-owned beachside hotels were selected by the pharmaceutical company to hopefully meet the expectations of Finns: tidy and simple. In both hotels, the rooms had water closets and showers but not potable water. Frequent power cuts in Ville were remedied by the hotel's generators, yet they sometimes experienced water outages. For such occasions, buckets filled with water were typically set in the bathroom corner. The rooms were cleaned upon request, which was a little uncomfortable for some guests having to ask for services and toilet paper. Both hotels were equipped with pools, and these were frequently used by the participants, whereas swimming in the sea was considered dangerous due to strong currents. Overall, the hotels were regarded as plain in a good way, with few complaints about standards. The groups gathered each morning for a French-style breakfast with omelettes and fresh fruit – despite the constant half-humorous discussion about how long the service took. The hotels catered for an experience of touristic caution, as well as exploration of the local circumstances: one tourist spent a whole week drinking by the pool while another participated in hauling in the fishing nets and sharing meals with the fishermen.

At one end of the spectrum, we have placed practices that could be summarised as immersive *coexistence* with microbes. At the other end of the spectrum are those who are *at war* with microbes and see microbes as uniformly dangerous. In between is an approach that seeks a *controlled engagement* with microbes, i.e. trying to control the permeable contours of one's body. This middle ground comprises a range of practices that mediate the human-microbe relationship to avoid illness and to be selective about which microbes to mingle with and how, recognising the difficulty or even impossibility of doing so in the face of everyday situations.

The enactments varied between both people and situations. The value of ethnographic observational data lies precisely here: we could observe how one person enacts different versions in different situations and for different audiences. A firm position expressed by a participant during an interview was often contradicted by their behaviour when observed. For example, someone who strongly emphasised a relaxed attitude about contact with bacteria might have been rather strict in using hand sanitisers, and vice versa. The spectrum is, therefore, a dynamic analytic, capturing snippets of shifting and coexisting enactments. Crucially, it is not a stable typology of individuals. Furthermore, we do not claim that the trial collected a certain type of traveller, nor did it create uniform behaviours. We argue that this spectrum, from immersion to elimination, shows that multiple relationalities are present in lay practices and that these relationalities need to be understood within the historical and social contexts of dynamic encounters.

WILFUL IMMERSION AND COEXISTENCE

At one end of the spectrum, we find those enactments where the participants describe immersing themselves within the local microbial ecosystems with as few restrictions as possible. Microbes cannot and should not be avoided; humans rather naturally coexist in an environment where microbes are bountiful and teeming. Microbes were described as essential for wellbeing. Several tourists explained that they rely on their gut microbiota and natural immunity to manage a balanced coexistence. They made attempts to be exposed to microbes, hoping that this would add diversity and complexity to their gut flora. Some of this type of joyful immersion talk resembles recent popular scientific literature where Western guts are said to be lacking in microbial diversity, which ultimately makes them ill and vulnerable (Parajuli et al. 2018).

In an interview, while sitting on the porch of Elina's hotel bungalow, watching the staff clean the yard, knowing the dry leaves would be burned, one tourist-participant brought up her interest in composting and an ecological lifestyle, in which she wished to engage even the hotel staff in Ville. In a follow-up question by Elina, the participant connected composting to the logic of gut health, where coexistence with rich microbiota was key for her.

E: Do you see a connection between composting and immunity?

M: Yes, I do, exactly! That's precisely why I let my body work of its own accord and hope that this would become explicit so that we could rely on it and benefit from it. Relying on their immunity is how the locals here must go about treating diarrhoea because they don't have the vaccine. And that's the beauty of it. I do understand that small children here can become seriously ill and would benefit from medication or a vaccine, but on the whole, I think these two are closely interconnected, like how to support the immunity of our own bodies – bacteria are our friends after all, our bodies are full of them.

E: OK, what about some of the bacteria which are not our friends?

M: Well, there is a balance in the stomach. Hold on, I'm looking for the right words to say this. There needs to be a balance between the gut bacterial species, probiotics, and other (f)actors and when there is balance, the human body works in the best possible way. Digests fibres and all.

In this interview, gut microbes were intimately connected with the environmental microbiota. In other accounts that we have identified as exemplifying immersion, local foods were consumed with enthusiasm and curiosity. The participants were offered a few organised meals as part of the trip or included excursions, but mainly they sought their food on their own, often in small restaurants, sometimes in less touristic food stands. Food was constantly discussed among the participants; it was monitored (but not restricted) by the trial. One participant explained how the group embraced the context with all its features, depicting this move as something rather adventurous:

> We went on a day trip and while we were exploring the place, we saw that there was a guy selling ice cream. We looked at each other and were like 'We know that ice cream is a risk', but the idea of ice cream was so delicious, so we looked at each other and were like, 'What the hell, that's why we are here'! Since then, we had no restrictions, instead we celebrated it and like announced to the rest of the group if someone had had diarrhoea and drew a line on the wall. The one who had most [bouts of diarrhoea], got an award at the end.

The young person relaying the story had won the playful 'diarrhoea competition' on his trip. While the fearless attitude indicates that they saw themselves taking a risk against a normative cautiousness regarding microbes, in its entirety, the story underscores an attitude where coexistence with the local environment is regarded as possible, desirable and fun in the context of this trial. Once back in Finland, this participant was diagnosed as having one of the more serious bacterial diarrhoea-causing pathogens; however, he felt that this was not an inconvenience, as the group dynamic and the purpose of the trip made it worthwhile. Disease-causing microbes were not seen as too scary a prospect when considering the overall purpose of the trip and in pursuing scientific progress.

While most of the 'immersion' talk referred to the positive or neutral side of coexistence with bacteria in general, the immersion in this story is slightly different. This quote underlines that microbial abundance is something only a daredevil can stomach, quite literally – not so much signalling an appreciation of positive diversity but rather more in the manner of a classic heroic adventurer narrative. He combines a reckless 'into-the-wild' spirit with a faith in his own ability to cope with immersion, and yet this faith is backed by the presence of Finnish doctors. The availability of Finnish doctors made taking the 'risk', considered as a *provisional* one (Benton 2016b), an option in the first place. This example shows that immersion can be exoticising and signal a position of (white) privilege, in terms of access to health care and more generally, of being secure and safe.

At the immersion end of the spectrum, we include refusal of antibiotics or taking them only as the most extreme measure against illness. For example, one participant, whose diarrhoea would have met the criteria for taking antibiotics in normal circumstances, agreed with the study doctors that they would just 'keep observing the situation'. The rationale was that the body's immunity would eventually regain stasis, with hopefully stronger capability against whatever was causing the diarrhoea to begin with. Another participant stated that he was reluctant to take antibiotics because antibiotics destroy gut bacteria:

> Gut microflora can be really cool stuff. I have read that it almost equals our mental health, that our brains can kind of like locate in our gut, that the bacteria can be quite fantastic, actually. So, I'm pretty cautious about the idea of poisoning the whole damn thing with some unspecific antibiotics.

In one of the interviews, natural coexistence was explained with the caveat that some bacteria, of course, are pathogenic:

> Microbes are an entirely natural part of life, and they are everywhere and in our guts in astounding measures. We would not cope without them. But there is the difference which ones are the pathogenic and cause diseases and which ones are good for us. Not all bacteria cause disease. Some make you ill and some do not. Some people are just carriers and some fall more ill and it's like finding a balance.

While some enactments of immersion displayed an interest in diversifying the gut microbiome, others regarded microbial encounters in neutral terms. For example, in the following account, a participant refuses to see the microbial environment as dangerous, despite Elina's prompts:

E: How do you feel about coming to a place where the bugs are different? Does that worry you?

N: Very little. Not sure how much of it is sort of having learnt to assess risks, how much of it is in my personality of not worrying, but if I look at the situation here, it is the traffic that is the risk, and not the diarrhoea. Of course, diarrhoea would be inconvenient, but no, I'm not worried about it, whereas the traffic...

What this excerpt further exemplifies is how the context, 'Africa', and its relative lack of infrastructures and facilities were often deemed as the risky part of the trip, instead of the trial participation or possible illness. To summarise, the main feature in the immersion enactment is an awareness, even appreciation, of microbes, and a trust that a healthy defence system can find its balance. Pathogenic diseases are mentioned but not in focus; they can be tolerated in a balanced system. The human contours are porous in these accounts and attempts to control microbes are futile. This attitude towards microbes did not, however, necessitate a neutral or positive attitude towards the social, human environment of Ville. Immersion could include exoticising, othering and racialising remarks, alongside the more respectful and appreciative ones.

CONTROLLED CONTACT IN EVERYDAY PRACTICES

In the middle of the spectrum, we have identified attempts to moderate how the human-microbe relation was organised. These enactments follow the logic that the environmental microbiome challenges the notion of clear borders of the self; the body is permeable and contact is inevitable, *but* it is useful to try to regulate how much and what kind of contact one is exposed to in a given environment. Here, the tone regarding microbial contact is not outright fearful or negative, but it is cautious.

The participants engaged in constant conversations among themselves about some bacteria being potentially harmful, but they equally constantly noted that they did not need to be 'paranoid' or 'hysterical' about them. There were continued efforts to prevent potential bacterial infection, and new ways to manage the human-microbe connections were discussed and shared. One participant explained that, due to the trial, her way of protecting herself had changed. She used to think that immunity could and should be developed and when in Ville she had learnt to, in her own words, '*micro-protect*'. These micro-protections were everyday, recurring, constant moment-to-moment practices aimed at managing the assumed human-microbe boundary. These gestures of micro-protection included hand sanitising, choosing particular foods, avoiding raw salads and using bottled water to clean her teeth.

These negotiations were varied and subject to revision. Some described becoming more confident with the local context over time. Many said they were more conscientious of hygiene at the beginning of their trip, but once they became more familiar with the village and the Finnish trial team, they relaxed. We witnessed this change in attention to hygiene as a very general trend over the two-week holiday. One of the participants described the 'essential' practices for bacterial control but then said that, at some point, one could also relax because ultimately the battle is futile:

> At first, I was really cautious, but it went pretty quickly. Like I ordered a vegetarian meal at the restaurant but then it turned out to have salad and tomatoes and other raw vegetables and I was like, 'Hmm...', and just ate it. So the cautiousness dispersed pretty quickly. Of course, hand sanitiser and other basics, no tap water etc, but then I thought that if I eat in the restaurants etc, if it's going to come, it's going to come...

This example presents a movement between different kinds of practices that illustrate the flexibility in micro-protections. Certain participants who might have initially been more relaxed about micro-protection became more restrictive about bacterial contact after they fell ill. The following excerpt illustrates these navigations:

> E: Has this trip made you think about bugs and how they move about more than you would have otherwise?

L: No, no, I have travelled a fair amount and know so much about things
that I would say no surprises here. There is always some new information along the way but I'm not super hysterical. I eat pretty sensibly
and try to avoid the worst bacterial traps. Then again, like yesterday,
when we were on this river boat cruise, we had our picnic foods with
us that were prepared and packed in the morning and by the time we
had them it was the afternoon. The food was made of rice and prawns
which, when it cools down, is a real bacterial hotspot. It was really tasty
but as the serving temperature by then was like... I was like let's see
what happens....

E: And?

L: Well, when we were on the excursion, indeed, during the trip it felt a bit
like, now my stomach is a bit sore. So before we left, I went to the loo
and thought, 'Goddamn, is this where the party begins'?! Especially with
the toilet the way it was.... But I just went to the toilet once and that
was that. And even yesterday, I had the courage to eat bravely, but some
people are more cautious and avoid certain foods and that is good.

Giving up protections was described either as a move towards positive immersion
into the new context or a resignation in the face of a hopeless battle. 'Avoiding
diarrhoea' did not mean an attempt to be completely untouched by microbes but
an optimising of microbial contact, labelling of microbes as 'good' or 'bad' and
estimating the quantity of 'bad' microbial intake. The following remarks from
another participant show how making these choices was not always straightforward, and also illustrate the sliding nature of transitions on the spectrum:

K: And how do you prepare for getting sick here, or getting diarrhoea? Is
it on your mind a lot?

V: Before coming over, sure, but not now I'm here.

K: How did you, beforehand, how was it in your mind?

V: I read the Facebook site,[2] like 'take along diapers', it [diarrhoea] can come
on quite suddenly and so on. I have had severe traveller's diarrhoea three
times before this, so I know, it's not that bad.

K: OK, and do you take some kind of precautions here, or how are you dealing with that? Are you trying to avoid, or…?

V: Yeah, I try to avoid, hmm, but I have even eaten salads, yes, and then I spray these insecticides, but I haven't really skipped any [tourist activities] or anything.

K: Yeah. Do you use hand sanitiser, or…?

T: Not much, the hand sanitiser, I don't like it too much because it kills the good bacteria, too. I wash my hands and then I use the freshen-up towels.

Though the relationship between ideas of dirt and race is not a simple or stable one (Newell and Green 2018), a link can be seen in constant comments on dirtiness. Waste management, 'shocking' amounts of waste on the beach, and kitchen hygiene were often bemoaned and joked about while waiting for food to be served. These are mundane, passing examples of the ways processes of race were at play in the context. On one such occasion, a participant went to 'explore the kitchen conditions', as he said, in the rather small restaurant-bar set on the sand and intended for tourists, serving mainly rice and fish dishes. He photographed the kitchen and the phone circulated in the hands of the hungry participants, bringing about surprised comments, snorts and laughs. In the end, everyone ate, though some complained of a loss of appetite. Resonating with Newell's (2020) suggestions about the ways the idea of dirt mediated moral evaluations in colonial and postcolonial eras, here, notions of ignorant, unknowing or poorly equipped locals affected the ways participants thought about eating and dealing with bacteria.

A personal need to address a bodily discomfort in the face of a situation where one is cautious about food is of course not disrespectful or racialising as such. Often the mode of discussion when speaking about difficult practices regarding disgust or sensitive issues with locals was humorous. Adia Benton discusses the ways in which 'Africa' and race (blackness) tend to be conflated and analysis of race is elided in humanitarian or development contexts, often by using humour. Drawing from Donna Goldstein, Benton (2016a: 269; 2016b) suggests that 'jokes often get their punch by expressing perspectives that would otherwise be inexpressible. Statements made in the process of "only joking" can often provide a window into deeply held and troubling feelings, such as those that deal with race'. Sometimes humour expresses a respectful confusion, too; a sincere sentiment of not quite knowing, in terms of both local practices, culture and one's own habits around purity in the new context.

Most participants said that the presence of Finnish doctors in Ville had a calming effect. Consultations before the trip, the Finnish instructions and the presence of a Finnish laboratory and doctors in Ville were important when the decision to participate was made. It was often mentioned that this support made them feel more confident to 'travel to Africa'. For many, Africa had been a lifelong dream that had been unattainable until this opportunity. The assumed safety produced by the trial circumstances substantially lowered the threshold of what seemed otherwise risky. 'Africa' appeared both attractive and difficult, and fear of diseases was cited as part of the difficulty. Access to a doctor not only reduced concerns, but also seemed to make symptoms and the experience of illness more bearable. In addition to the micro-protections that comprised everyday actions to control contact with microbes, the presence of Finnish doctors and health care access could be defined as a reliance on 'macro-protections' of a more structural kind.

Of course, ethical guidelines prevent the design of a trial exposing people to unnecessary risk. In this trial, however, the somewhat organised nature of the human-bacteria encounters created a framework of naturalised exposure as acceptable. The environment in 'Africa' and a possible contamination by the local bacteria were not defined as dangerous from the outset. This logic was enhanced by the advice given during the trial. In practice, however, the constant awareness of diarrhoea and general health strengthened the middle ground micro-protection talk and caused a lot of movement between these enactments. Stereotypical notions of risk, disease and 'Africa' possibly heightened the micro-protective practices. Appreciation of local ways of dealing with hygiene was extremely rare, which could be slightly surprising, knowing that the trial design presumes that the local adults, after all, have a stronger immunity than the Finns.

AT WAR AGAINST MICROBES

'Why would anyone want to take a holiday just to get ill'?! was a frequently mentioned response from the participants' friends, families and colleagues. Comments about health risks in West Africa were said to have been a common subject of discussion prior to the trip. Fears and suspicions might have prevented those most concerned about microbes from joining the trial and, hence, our sample of participants does not include those whose attitudes towards microbes are the most negative. With this in mind, it is interesting that accounts which echo the Cold War combatant attitude documented by Emily Martin (1994) can still be identified today.

At one end of the spectrum, we characterise human-bacterial relationships that could be identified as being 'at war' (Martin 1994), even if the participants did not use these explicit terms. Here, microbes are described only as dangerous, harmful, contagious and dirty, while the village was similarly portrayed as dysfunctional and insanitary. Taking a certain set of hygiene standards as a given norm, and minimal bacterial life as a goal, resulted in perceptions of a lack of development in infrastructure and housing. Lack of plumbing, drinking water and toilets were deemed as sources of risk and evidence of lack of hygiene. The microbial levels in the area were taken as a negative feature. Such views show poignantly the context-specificity of microbial relationality. Exoticising, stereotyping and othering accounts, and images of 'Africa' were frequent in conversations and interviews and will be further discussed in later publications. One participant described her worries as follows:

> I have been more cautious on this trip than my past travels because I have not travelled in the tropics that much and because I've understood how different the bacterial pool is here, and that hygiene standards are lower. So I've tried to be more careful about hygiene. [...] There is so much here, like everything possible. So maybe I was thinking about it more before travelling; that I might be constantly, like bitten by mosquitoes etc, like there are so many diseases here that one might be infected with. But now that I'm

here, I'm not quite as paranoid. But in Finland, I had a mild fear that I might
bring home something severe.

This participant, while in Ville, explained her concerns about hygiene and infections ahead of the trip, using language that indicated severe concern. She deemed the perceived bacterial abundance in West Africa to be an infinite source of disease and risk that could potentially be brought back home to what she clearly regarded as a 'safe' Finland.

In accounts of a war against bacteria, antibiotics are the obvious weapon. The trial participants explained that normally, when travelling, their key method of controlling risks and pathogenic human-microbe relations is by using antibiotics. In our survey, we asked how regularly people had used antibiotics. Altogether 7% of the respondents said they wanted to have antibiotics every time they fell ill. We also asked about independent use of antibiotics and medications during the trip to Ville, but none were reported. Adherence to the study protocol was taken seriously. We were told that some participants had brought their own antibiotics from Finland, reflecting a concern that drugs might be unavailable or of the wrong kind in Ville. They were prepared to self-medicate if needed, but such a need did not arise. 'My commitment to the trial does not override my own health', said one participant in private conversation, emphasising their belief in the importance of antibiotics as a general cure.

During one of the research clinic consultations, one participant explained that she usually takes antibiotics to prevent a urinary tract infection every time she has sex. The participant was meticulous in observing her bodily aches and pains and reported different conditions and self-medications during the weekly trial checks where symptoms and medications were recorded. At this end of the spectrum, antibiotics were seen as a self-evident technology that can be used in order to ensure health and wellbeing.

Although she did not bring up antibiotics specifically, another participant also discussed her desire to guard her bodily boundaries and described a general wariness towards almost anything around her. Even so, she emphasised that she was not afraid, just highly aware of the risks. Interestingly, she described the importance of trying to maintain *a feeling* of cleanliness, and especially clean hands, with the help of hand sanitisers and freshen-up towels, 'If there's a slimy feeling, for example'. In an interview conducted by Katriina, while waiting for lunch in a restaurant popular among the participants, right next to the kitchen area, she and the participant noticed a live hen. This was a typical sight, which often brought about a joke about whether it was the lunch-to-be. On this occasion, it led the participant to talk about her ways of relating to the environment. She talked about her constant awareness of the surrounding health risks and her attempts to manage them because she wished to stay in good health in order to go straight back to work upon returning to Finland:

> K: Have you noticed that you think about health risks more, more than usual when you travel, for example?
>
> R: [...]. So, not like, I'm not too scared but you realise that you think about it a lot more.
>
> K: In what ways do you think about it, or in which situations do you notice that?
>
> R: Well... I like to walk barefoot, and that's something you're really reserved about here. Like, sometimes it feels weird, there in my, just in my bathroom, to walk barefoot, and that somehow...
>
> K: Yeah, can you tell me why, why does that feel weird?
>
> R: Well, that's probably because, just before coming here I read – I read surprisingly little before the trip, I left everything to my travel companion's responsibility and s/he read everything possible – and I happened to read one tiny article about hookworms, and now I'm always thinking that there are hookworms or something on my bathroom floor.
>
> K: OK, so is it like you're all the time thinking about lots of other kinds of things, not just diarrhoea?
>
> R: Yes, yes. Everything else that there could be here, things that are not really even talked about. [...].

This type of concern was less frequent in formal recorded interviews, but in informal small group encounters disgust and worry were commonly mentioned. In those chats, war was not so much about destruction of the enemy as it was about guarding borders. A key issue seemed to be the difficulty of knowing the enemy; microbes really might be anywhere or everywhere. In attempting to know, and thereby avoid, the microbes – and other possibly health-threatening creatures – one needs to merge scientific knowledge, popular knowledge and one's own sensory experiences.

Practices of avoiding local bacteria often meant bringing foodstuffs from Finland, such as dried bread, biscuits, porridge, nuts, raisins and coffee powder. For most, these were consumed when ill with diarrhoea. One participant cooked her own porridge and stayed in her own room for several days when she felt sick. For some, nausea and physical weakness enhanced the war talk, but for others the perky immersion talk of not being worried continued despite illness.

The most extreme example of preventing contamination and illness by maintaining the bodily boundary through controlling food intake was that of the film crew who came to make a documentary of the trial. During their two-week trip, everything they ate was brought with them from Finland, except for some fruit that they disinfected before eating. As artists, they were neither trial participants nor part of our 'data' in the strict sense, but the example is illuminating for this end of the spectrum among the Finns in Ville. They explained that they could not risk getting ill, assuming that such an event was likely. Similarly, one participant endured a day-long excursion outside Ville without eating anything at all because outside Ville he did not want to take risks.

CONCLUSIONS

The analysis presented in this chapter displays a plethora of modes of discussing, embodying, embracing and resisting encounters with microbes by Finnish participants in a vaccine study in West Africa. The analysis reveals the complex and even contradictory ways of living with microbes among lay people. There were differences in understandings and practices towards and with microbes, which we observed during the ethnographic fieldwork in Ville.

We have called these relationships with microbes, consisting of both explicitly articulated understandings and situated accounts and practices, enactments.

The combination of both participant observation during a two-week holiday and (sometimes repeated) interviews reveals the complexity and diversity of human-microbe relationality. Here we show that when doing research with and on 'Western' notions of bacteria, they should indeed be studied in all their rich complexities.

We have constructed a spectrum of enactments from immersion to controlled contact to war. This is of course a simplification of the multitude of enactments that shift between situations, contexts and perceptions of personal wellbeing, but it is a useful reminder of the importance of being aware of the whole range. Multiple human-microbial enactments existed simultaneously in the spectrum, rather than forming a binary. It is of particular interest that in a trial context where one might expect only brave accounts of microbial immersion – as this was explicitly the starting point for participation – there were also war metaphors and accounts of full avoidance of any contact with local microbiota.

Our analysis shows how relationality with microbiota cannot be detached from context, being formed and re-formed in complex historical, social, political, economic and institutional relations. Ideas of dirt, dirty places and cleanliness are not coincidental or ahistorical (Douglas 1966), and racialised and racialising imaginaries feed into notions of purity and vice versa (McClintock 1995; Xin 2019). The sense of safety that the participants often mentioned was linked to the unusual trial arrangement of Finnish collective care for the body in Ville. Some participants may have discussed the differences between Finland and Ville much less were they not travelling in a group, and furthermore, defined specifically as Finns by their trial participant role. This points to how microbial relations are inevitably contextual and subject to constant negotiation and change, and anything more general is always already specific.

Indeed, the specificity of the trial context (Finns in West Africa in a biomedical study) cannot be dismissed. This setting is unique and particular, which is precisely why it enables the study of lay enactments of human-microbe relationality in a context where microbial abundance can be imagined in various ways. Tourists from northern Europe perceive both the local context and their home environment, with human and non-human actors and infrastructure, with a wide array of ideas, and these influence their bodily practices. Both fearful and appreciative attitudes to the new context were possible. One's body, work and everyday practices did not follow one's explicit ideological or moral beliefs in any systematic manner. This study of trial participants' microbial relations within a unique biomedical project reveals the complex ways ordinary people negotiate the contours of their bodies. The trial did not limit the richness of encounters, but a full spectrum of human-microbial relationships from war to joyful immersion was enacted.

NOTES

1 The author names are in alphabetical order and the work was shared equally.
2 This was an informal Facebook group set up by and for participants', which was not moderated by staff.

ACKNOWLEDGEMENTS

The writing of this article was made possible by the Finnish Cultural Foundation (grant no 0116947-3) and the Academy of Finland (grant numbers 1320863 and 316941).

REFERENCES

Anderson, W., *Colonial Pathologies: American Tropical Medicine, Race and Hygiene in the Philippines* (Durham, NC, and London: Duke University Press, 2006).

Benton, A., 'African Expatriates and Race in the Anthropology of Humanitarianism', *Critical African Studies*, 8.3 (2016a), 266–77.

—— 'Risky Business: Race, Nonequivalence and the Humanitarian Politics of Life', *Visual Anthropology*, 29.2 (2016b), 187–203.

Chigudu, S., *The Political Life of an Epidemic: Cholera, Crisis and Citizenship in Zimbabwe* (Cambridge: Cambridge University Press, 2020).

Crane, J. T., *Scrambling for Africa: AIDS, Expertise, and the Rise of American Global Health Science* (Ithaca: Cornell University Press, 2013).

Douglas, M., *Purity and Danger* (London: Routledge, 1966).

Fishel, S., *The Microbial State* (Minneapolis: University of Minnesota Press, 2017).

Geissler, P. W., and C. Molyneux, *Evidence, Ethos and Experiment: The Anthropology and History of Medical Research in Africa*, 1st edn (New York: Berghahn Books, 2011).

Haraway, D., *Simians, Cyborgs, and Women: The Reinvention of Nature* (New York: Routledge, 1991).

—— *Staying with the Trouble* (Durham, NC: Duke University Press, 2016).

Kingori, P., 'The "Empty Choice": A Sociological Examination of Choosing Medical Research Participation in Resource-Limited Sub-Saharan Africa', *Current Sociology*, 23.5 (2015), 763–78.

Martin, E., *Flexible Bodies* (Boston: Beacon Press, 1994).

McClintock, A., *Imperial Leather: Race, Gender, and Sexuality in the Colonial Contest* (London: Routledge, 1995).

Mol, A., and J. Law, 'Embodied Action, Enacted Bodies: The Example of Hypoglycaemia', *Body & Society*, 10.2–3 (2004), 43–62.

Newell, S., and L. Green, 'Putting Dirt in its Place: The Cultural Politics of Dirt in Africa', *Social Dynamics*, 44.1 (2018), 1–5.

Newell, S., *Histories of Dirt: Media and Urban Life in Colonial and Postcolonial Lagos* (Durham, NC: Duke University Press, 2020).

Parajuli, A., and others, 'Urbanization Reduces Transfer of Diverse Environmental Microbiota Indoors', *Frontiers in Microbiology*, 9.84 (2018).

Pradeu, T., *Philosophy of Immunology* (Cambridge: Cambridge University Press, 2019).

Roy, D., *Molecular Feminisms* (Seattle: University of Washington Press, 2018).

Tilley, H., *Africa as a Living Laboratory: Empire, Development, and the Problem of Scientific Knowledge, 1870-1950* (Chicago: University of Chicago Press, 2011).

Vaughan, M., *Curing Their Ills: Colonial Power and African Illness* (Stanford: Stanford University Press, 1991).

Vuorela, U., 'Colonial Complicity: The "Postcolonial" in a Nordic Context', in S. Keskinen, and others, eds, *Complying With Colonialism: Gender, Race and Ethnicity in the Nordic Region* (London: Routledge, 2009).

Xin, L., 'Nose Hair: Love it or Leave it?: The Lovecidal of Bodies That Filter', *Parallax*, 25.1 (2019), 75–91.

Åsberg, C., 'Feminist Posthumanities in the Anthropocene: Forays into the Postnatural', *Journal of Posthuman Studies: Philosophy, Technology, Media*, 1.2 (2018), 185–204.

6

BATHING IN BLACK WATER? THE MICROBIOPOLITICS OF THE RIVER SEINE'S ECOLOGICAL RECLAMATION

Marine Legrand, Germain Meulemans

INTRODUCTION

IN 2017, IN THE WAKE OF PARIS'S BID TO HOST THE OLYMPIC GAMES, the French capital's mayor announced that the swimming and triathlon competitions would take place not in a regular Olympic pool but in the River Seine. For the local authorities, as well as those of several other large European cities, letting people once again bathe in the river was a strong symbol of their achievement regarding the 'ecological reclamation' of urban watercourses. However, this new objective spurred concerns over a return of 'faecal peril' in Paris – a central topic for public health that points to the risk of human infection by faecal bacteria present in drinking or bathing water (WHO 2000). What happens when a river becomes part of the 'domestic space' of the city it was meant to clean up by collecting and evacuating dirtiness away? How are human-microbe relations reconfigured when the field of sanitation – largely informed by a Pasteurian ethic of concealing pathogens – and the field of river management – now largely informed by the field of water ecology – meet? And how does this impact the humans and non-human agents that live in or near rivers?

This chapter describes how microbes – *E. coli* in particular – came to matter in the field of river management once the mayor of Paris announced that the Seine River would be made 'bathable' for the Olympic Games in 2024. On the basis of an ethnography conducted in the Paris region among sanitation and river management actors,[1] and a review of recent technical and legal documents related to the River Seine, we describe how different categories and actors are mobilised over time in the management of the river, and how these enact different trajectories for human-microbe microbiopolitics (Paxson 2008). To do this, we unpack the ambivalent and multiple relationships between humans, water and microbes by attending to shifts in the modes of regulatory attention, in scientific and expert repertoires and epistemologies as well as in infrastructure design priorities. Then, we examine how new concerns over the microbiological quality of the river led a handful of houseboats moored on the Seine to be identified as a new biohazard, which in turn triggered a controversy surrounding the overreliance on centralised hydraulic networks within the sanitation system. This example shows how, far from being only technical, the debates surrounding sanitation and water quality raise questions relating to appropriate human behaviour and modes of dwelling.

WATER QUALITY: FROM HYDROBIOLOGY TO RIVER ECOLOGY

Over the past two centuries, the discipline most associated with both sanitation and river management has been civil engineering. Many of the fundamental principles that have shaped sanitation can be linked to hygienism, a movement at once ideological, political, technological and scientific, which played a major role in every aspect of French society between the middle of the nineteenth century and the beginning of the twentieth century (Barles 1999). In particular, this movement played a crucial role in urban planning and the design of urban services, among which sanitation appears emblematic. The current conventional sanitation paradigm relies largely on water, which is used in combination with pipes to ensure the transport of dirtiness away from inhabited places. Above all, it seeks to contain and control human excreta (also called black water when it is flushed away) and its microbial content. During the twentieth century, rivers were strongly enrolled in sanitation socio-technical devices. And, with the building of centralised sanitation networks, they were envisioned and conceptualised predominately through a reticular paradigm and, hence, through a hydraulic lens (Barraqué 2014). In the past 50 years, however, as environmental issues have become matters of concern, disciplines pertaining to the biological sciences (hydrobiology, ecology, and finally microbiology) have gained new traction in the relations between sanitation and river management.

Dilution: Hydrobiology and the self-purification of rivers

The faecal contamination of rivers was already a subject of controversy when urban centralised sanitation systems started to develop at the end of the nineteenth century (Aguerre 2003; Barles 2005). Nevertheless, it gradually stopped being a matter of concern when sewers became the virtually exclusive model for urban excreta management, and only quite recently made a comeback in the field on sanitation. Whereas in the first half of the twentieth century, sanitation was guided by a quantitative objective to extend the sewerage networks as much as possible, the 1960s saw the emergence of concerns about improving the health of aquatic environments. From the 1970s up to and including the 1990s, EU directives were introduced to regulate the pollution emitted by industry, agriculture and cities (Barraqué 2001). In addition to toxic industrial substances (heavy metals, etc.), these directives stipulated emission norms regulating the amount of organic residues, nitrogen and phosphorous that were present in wastewater when discharged into rivers, with the intent to prevent hypoxia and asphyxiation of aquatic life. These directives did not address bacterial contamination, except in specific cases such as drinking water catchment areas or shellfish farming. In response to the establishment of these standards, much effort was made to improve the sanitation equipment, which resulted in the development of modern wastewater treatment plants, designed to remove suspended solids, organic matter, nitrogen and phosphorus, although not faecal microorganisms.

From the 1960s onwards, the interpretation of the impacts of wastewater on rivers was largely shaped by hydrobiology, an approach which based its analysis of the aquatic environment on morphological, mechanical and physico-chemical parameters (Legay 2006). As a legacy of this era, the definition of standards for the discharge of organic matter, nitrogen and phosphorous is still based on an approach which considers that sanitation continues in rivers: the receiving environments participate in eliminating the waste that is discharged into them. This is referred to as the 'self-purification' of rivers. In a conventional centralised sanitation system, the river is therefore not only an outlet for the treatment system but is enrolled as the last link in the chain of the treatment process by diluting, taking away and digesting remaining contaminants. Hydrobiologists estimate rates of dilution and biodegradation through a ratio between the flow of the watercourse, its speed and degree of slope – factors on which its oxygenation depends (Dubin 1971). This has always been seen as a problem in Paris, which is a 'mega city on a small river', as the Seine flows too slowly through the Paris conurbation to fulfil this dilution role properly (Tabuchi et al. 2016: 9).

Ecologisation: Sentinel species look out for the river's 'good ecological status'

In 2000, the Water Framework Directive (WFD) inaugurated a different approach, focusing on the development of a territorial management of water bodies as a whole. The WFD introduced the ambitious objective of achieving the 'good ecological status' of all European water bodies within 15 years. This marks the beginning of a period of ecologisation of river management, in which the good health of the aquatic environment becomes a key criterion for assessing the performance of sanitation systems. The discipline of stream ecology then gained legitimacy in the watercourse management sector, and this prominence was reinforced by the various European directives on water quality that followed in the 2000s.

For ecologists, a 'good ecological status' does not refer to a 'pristine' state of rivers but rather to their capacity to accommodate the reproduction of aquatic biodiversity. The rise of this notion overshadowed the previously central hydrobiological notions of dilution and self-purification: once rivers appeared as ecosystems to be protected, any pollution introduced into them was likely to provoke ecological disturbance.[2] Monitoring the health of rivers now implied the study of a set of aquatic species, primarily fish. Rather than being framed as a 'fish stock' to be managed and replenished by fishing federations, as had been the case since the 1940s (Bouleau 2017), fish, along with many other organisms, were now taken into account as 'bioindicators' of river health.

A bioindicator is a species or group of species whose presence, absence or abundance provides information about the ecological status of the environment (Blandin 1986). Sociologist Christelle Gramaglia (2013), who has documented the use of molluscs to monitor water quality and lichens to test air pollution, refers to these as 'sentinel' species. Sentinels are involved in environmental monitoring projects and 'look out for the environment' by detecting signs that would otherwise be invisible to humans – especially pollution. Gramaglia explains that the effectiveness of a sentinel depends on its embeddedness in the monitored environment, its ability to express stress or preference, but also on the ability of the scientists or technicians who follow it to understand the vital relationships it has with its world. In the case of river ecological monitoring, fish like trout and salmon are ideal sentinels because they offer an integrative vision of the state of the watercourse, given their place at the end of the food web. Depending on the context, dragonflies, shellfish and sedimentary worms are also targeted; each type of species provides specific information (UNCPIE 2015).

In addition to older emission standards, river ecology itself became the main indicator for the environmental efficiency of the sanitation systems. However, the territorial management system, structured by negotiations between stakeholders with different interests and negotiating weight, and surrounded by scientific controversies about the definition of indicators, has been criticised by both researchers and river managers for its slowness in reducing aquatic pollution by wastewater discharges, and WFD environmental objectives are far from being achieved in France (Maillet 2015).

MAKING THE SEINE BATHABLE: HOW MICROBES BECAME A KEY CONCERN IN RIVER MANAGEMENT

Throughout the 2010s, the Paris metropolitan area, like other European cities, has become the scene of a political and epistemic turning point in terms of public action in the field of sanitation. In Paris, urban bathing is quickly emerging as a key political priority, spurred on by the French capital's bid to host the 2024 Olympic Games. Having become the new benchmark for river health, this theme reinforces the break with the paradigm of self-purification by introducing a new key actor in the debate: the presence of faecal pathogens in rivers.

Urban bathing as a regional political issue

In the French capital, the idea of making the Seine bathable is a perennial subject in local politics. Many people remember one of Jacques Chirac's favourite promises to soon allow people to 'swim in the Seine', first made in 1988, and later taken up by successive mayors. Bathing in the River Seine in Paris became restricted to certain locations in the eighteenth century, originally for reasons of decency. It became entirely prohibited in the twentieth century, first because of conflicts with boat traffic, then because of pollution issues and the general degradation of water quality. Even though many among the working class continued to bathe despite the regulations, the redevelopment of the banks into expressways in the 1970s put an end to these activities (Duhau 2007; Le Bas 2020).

From the 1990s onwards, various citizen and institutional movements to reclaim the riverbanks changed the situation. The river began to be seen as a natural heritage, while several of its tributaries that had been buried were rehabilitated. Open water bathing in the city's river became a symbol of the successful reclamation of the aquatic environment and of sustainable urban development. In France, this idea was notably popularised by activist groups such as the Laboratory of Experimental Urban Swimming, which organises collective wild swims to campaign for the rehabilitation of urban swimming, a free and popular leisure activity. In Paris's neighbouring departments, the establishment of a programme to reclaim the River Marne by the mixed syndicate Marne Vive has put the question of open water bathing on the political agenda. At the same time, 'wild bathing' became more frequent again because of a succession of summer heat waves that struck Paris over the past twenty years, and some sites were officially reopened for bathing in 2017.

As noted by Haghe and Euzen (2018), a new political categorisation of water quality is now on the rise, centred around the diptych bathable/non-bathable. In a local context marked by competition between urban authorities whose legitimacy is being questioned (City of Paris, Greater Paris, region, Ile-de-France departments),

> [t]he political temptation is strong to set up a quality indicator for the Seine and Marne that is popular, simple to understand and a guarantee for the good governance of water and the environment, and that replaces indicators considered by elected officials and citizens as incomprehensible because they are too technical (ibid.: 2).

Moreover, bathing makes it possible to convey the good ecological state of the river through people's 'lived experience'. From the beginning of the 2010s, public administrators started to see bathing as a promising way to mobilise groups around this issue.[3]

In 2017, the designation of Paris as the host city for the 2024 Olympics accelerated the process, as the Paris Mayor's office soon promised that the river water would be of good enough quality to swim in by 2024. The hope of this project was to hold the triathlon and freestyle swimming competitions of the Olympics directly in the river, next to the Eiffel Tower. Beyond the Olympics, the authorities seized the opportunity of developing new recreational uses, with the creation of over 20 bathing sites in the urban area. In Paris, green policies are clearly seen as a tool for asserting the city's position as an international metropolis. The mayor's office sees the completion of a three-decade-long effort to raise the river's ecological quality as the fulfilment of this green policy, arguing that there are 35 species of fish in the river today, compared to only two in the 1970s. As such, a member of the City Council's sanitation team described the project as 'going far beyond a bathing project', as a way to 'speed things up in regards to how we comply with EU regulations'.[4] Thus, having returned the Seine to eels, trout and pike, the ambition to give it back to human Parisians appeared to be a strong symbol of the 'ecological reclamation' of the aquatic environment.[5]

Microbiologisation: E. coli and its procession

The political project to make bathing a marker for the river's good ecological status materialised through the creation of a steering committee on 'Water Quality and Bathing in the Marne and Seine' (here, we will refer to it as the Bathing Committee) in spring 2016, in the context of Paris's bid for the Olympic Games. Co-chaired by the mayor of Paris and the regional prefect, this committee includes local mayors and all the public and private actors of sanitation and water management. The Bathing Committee's priorities include the selection of 23 sites suitable for bathing in 2018, as well as the organisation and coordination of measures designed to make the Seine bathable.[6] The committee also takes on the role of gathering a larger set of actors and presenting urban bathing as a unifying issue among the regional population. Above all, however, its creation brings the issue of faecal contamination to the forefront as a quality criterion for the aquatic environment, where this human health issue had previously been a minor concern in this context. Indeed, the objective of making the Seine bathable is to shift the regulatory framework from the WFD to that of the Bathing Directive.

Within this new normative framework, new areas of expertise are being called upon to assess the state of the environment and to remedy established contamination. After the ecologisation of river management in the 1990s–2000s, new ways of considering the river are this time accompanied by a 'microbiologisation', with growing importance and legitimacy given to pathogen microbiology in the field of river management. Even though EU regulations already required that public authorities (e.g. the City of Paris and the Marne Vive Syndicate) perform a routine monitoring of some of the main pathogens in the river, these measurements were not analysed 'scientifically'. Around 2010, however, a shift can be observed in the publications of Ile-de-France microbiologists working on faecal contamination, who initially carried out analyses on untreated and treated wastewater but gradually became involved in studies of the aquatic environment itself (lakes, leisure centres, river sites). These microbiologists would soon question the usual categories used in the routine monitoring performed by the authorities.

Based on the first WHO recommendations regarding the microbiological quality of waters, issued in the 1970s, specific European regulations for the management of the water quality of bathing areas appeared in 1975 (76/160/EU). Just like the regulations concerning the ecological status of rivers, regulations over the microbiological quality of bathing water became implemented through the monitoring of sentinel organisms that indicate the state of affairs on a larger scale. In this case, however, these sentinels are neither trout nor mussels but 'faecal contamination indicator bacteria' (FIBs), a microbiological concept originally aimed at assessing the quality of drinking water. It was developed at the beginning of the twentieth century, when it became obvious that waterborne diseases were mostly gastroenteritis-related (Horrocks 1901). The current EU bathing directive (2006/7/EC) defines thresholds of bathing water quality (excellent, good, sufficient and poor) based on the monitoring of two FIBs: *Escherichia coli* and intestinal enterococci, both residents of human and other mammal intestines. The presence of these easy-to-follow FIBs (that can be cultivated in the lab) is assumed to be a good indicator of the presence of other faecal pathogens:

> When you talk about E. coli, you have to imagine the whole procession behind it, all the other faecal contaminants which we don't even try to detect because it would be complicated, it would take too long. But we know that if E. coli is there, there is a good chance that there are also viruses, hepatitis A, polio, coronavirus (…) you have the whole cortege that comes with it.[7]

As a result of the search for increased bathing quality, new indicator species are being referred to, making *E. coli* a new sentinel of water contamination in large portions of rivers in the Ile-de-France region. The situation also changes the way in which *E. coli* is understood: instead of being a purely sanitary indicator, it also becomes an environmental indicator, based on the idea that the more water is swimmable for humans, the less untreated or poorly treated wastewater is discharged.

Interestingly, while *E. coli* and other FIBs are widely recognised bioindicators in professional circles dealing with water-related health issues, many microbiologists consider them to be a very imperfect indicator:

> The presence of FIBs can predict the probable presence of viruses, Giardia, and Cryptosporidium in surface water affected by sewage inputs, but they cannot predict their concentration. This is in accordance with the original indicator concept in drinking water, which established FIBs as an index of faecal pollution and, therefore, the probability of the presence of pathogens and potential health risks (Mouchel et al. 2019: 8).

As we shall now see, this limitation in the reliability of FIBs contributed to reframing the debate as concerning the whole infrastructure of sanitation systems, and what it allows to flow into the receiving environment.

Recentralisation: Containing microbes in watertight pipes

In France, to obtain a swimming permit from the Regional Health Agency, the applicant must produce a 'profile' consisting of measurements taken over four consecutive years at different seasons and different points in the area and show that *E. coli* concentrations are lower than WHO thresholds (WHO 2003). However, the routine microbiological monitoring of the Seine confirmed that the concentration of faecal indicators should be reduced by up to twenty-fold in the summer months to reach an 'excellent' quality. It also detected specific viruses and parasites such as Giardia in the water. Hence, the approach of the Olympic Games soon made the headlines, as it compelled Paris to face its own 'faecal peril'. Indeed, even though the Paris region sanitation system is considered efficient from a sanitary perspective, when looking at the water quality of rivers from a bathing perspective, it becomes clear that faecal pathogens are still in fact circulating in the environment: the medium through which pathogens are put in contact with human bodies is the river itself.

The Bathing Committee soon insisted that this faecal contamination should be treated in an exemplary way. The aim was to avoid repeating past incidents where pathogens that were not taken into account in WHO routine tests had threatened the health of athletes or bathers, such as during the Rio Olympics (WHO 2016). Since large-scale antiseptic treatment of the Seine was not an option, the authorities set out to identify and suppress the source of these microbes. This, however, shed light on the structural limits of the whole sanitation system. Indeed, as sanitation engineers often insist, not all the wastewater reaches a treatment plant before going into the river. First, in the event of heavy rains, the system can overflow in places where rain and wastewater are collected together, leading to the release of untreated or partially treated water into the aquatic environment (Passerat et al. 2011). This problem is known as 'Combined Sewer Overflows'. Solving it requires a thorough review of rainwater management methods and relies on heavy investment. Second, in areas where rain and wastewater are collected separately, poorly made connections – places where wastewater is connected to the networks reserved for rainwater – result in wastewater being discharged directly into the river.[8] The Bathing Committee therefore launched a campaign to identify and repair every 'anomaly' on the network – a long and tedious task, as bad connections are multiple, diffuse and mostly situated outside Paris.

Ironically, this aspect of the authorities' response appeared to several observers as a revival of the modernist ambition to create a perfectly centralised and controllable watertight network. The strategies implemented by the Bathing Committee are reactivating this historical vision of sanitation, based on a 'reticular' approach (pre-eminence of the network) which prevailed globally throughout the twentieth century in the global North (Barraqué 2014). This emphasis on the confinement of wastewater flows in networks with a view to their optimised treatment in treatment plants, and the stress on FIBs as indirect bioindicators of the good health of rivers, thus signals a second move away from the dilution paradigm, since in relation to the bathing objective, any 'leakage' of faecal pathogens into the aquatic environment becomes a potential danger to human health. Thus, the ambition to control the microbiology of the Seine causes governance of aquatic environmental management to be recentralised, which overlaps with its territorialisation in the previous decade. However, as we shall now see, this movement of centralisation/watertightness also brought about a cascade of new and unexpected players in the socio-microbial assemblage.

'BARGE GATE': REMAINING OFF-GRID THROUGH NOVEL SOCIO-MICROBIAL ALLIANCES

FIG. 6.1 In France, many houseboats are old commercial barges bought at a cheap price from retiring haulers in the 1970s and refitted by the buyers. The most common model is the 'Freycinet' barge (40 m long and 5 m wide), which offers up to 200 m2 of living space (photograph by F.R. Thomas).

There are about 170 private houseboats, 72 passenger boats and 62 floating establishments open to the public (bars, restaurants, hotels and some workplaces) that are regularly anchored in the area of the river relevant to the Olympics, bringing the total to around 1,000 boats at a regional level.[9] Houseboats – inhabited boats that are moored most of the time – generally emit flows of untreated sewage, which means that their toilet system discharges directly into the river. In 2007, a study commissioned by the Paris boaters' association and the local authorities showed that the presence of the houseboats did significantly raise FIB levels. Even though the study's experts had recommended the implementation of quayside sewer connections and/or autonomous sanitation[10], these discharges were not considered a priority, since the amount of waste that goes into the river remains, quantitatively speaking, quite incidental in comparison to the structural limitations of the sanitation system. Furthermore, 'no legislation or guidelines mandate anything about the discharge of waste water. Direct discharge is prohibited by law, but no implementing decree exists due to the lack of standardisation of treatment equipment'.[11] However, in 2017, after the opening of the black box of sanitation to many new actors, the Seine's 'faecal peril' contributed to throwing these rather discreet actors into the spotlight.

Is a ship just another building?

The Bathing Committee encountered the issue of houseboat discharges as they were making a systematic and methodical inventory of every anomaly on the sanitation network. Following the same reasoning they had adopted regarding connection mistakes and clogged up sewers, they approached it as yet another anomaly to be corrected by ensuring the boats' connection to the sanitation system. The 2018 Olympic law therefore excluded the option of implementing on-board sanitation in Paris *intramuros* and stated that every Seine houseboat within Paris would have to be connected to the sewer system by 2024. This would solve the problem of the River Seine's direct faecal contamination by boats in the sense that they would be, from this point on, subject to the same sanitation standards as any dwelling in the city.

The choice of connecting boats to the sewers, however, also involved a different agenda, that of HAROPA, the firm that manages the riverbanks for the city of Paris. Originally specialising in freight logistics and river traffic management, HAROPA recently took charge of providing services to port users (such as drinking water and electricity). Hoping to generate new sources of revenue by developing spaces such as the banks of the Seine, which were in the process of being pedestrianised, HAROPA started lobbying to equip all the ports and banks of Paris with sewer connection points, which would ease the development of floating establishments dedicated to economic activities (hotels, restaurants, bars and other various leisure venues). This quickly generated multiple conflicts with houseboat owners, who see the development of these businesses as a 'colonisation' of the riverbanks. As a representative of houseboat owners puts it:

> Only 10% of the shelf space is residential, so they want to use the rest for businesses such as restaurants and hotels. There is already a strong colonisation of the riverbanks by hotel boats today.[12]

This is in fact a question of connecting not only the boats but the riverbanks themselves to sewers to develop profitable leisure activities, extending Paris's development on the river. For houseboat owners, resisting these infrastructures therefore means resisting the transformation of the banks into yet another leisure and shopping pedestrian area in which they have little chance to stay in the long term.

The French association of boat owners (ADHF-F) and a local boat owners' collective immediately protested against the authority's demand, urging a refocus on 'non-collective' sanitation methods that would allow the boats to remain 'off-grid' in Paris. The first reason for boat owners to reject sewer connection was the extent of the works to be carried out on the boats. Because the boats are located lower than ground level and lower than the sewers, their connection system must include a pipe network to collect all wastewater at the same point, a lift pump and non-return valves that prevent water from the sewers from draining into the boat by gravity. The installation of these systems is costly for boat owners, but their main concern was sewage flowing back into the boat in the event of a pump malfunction, frost in the connection hoses or a river flood. Some of them refused to equate their boats with buildings built on land because boats, by their nature, cannot rely on gravity to avoid wastewater reflux problems:

> We end up with people (HAROPA) who think they know everything because they manage the river. They surely manage it financially, but they don't seem to know what a boat is. We have had so many ridiculous discussions with them. They don't get what the possibility of wastewater reflux means for us. The boat is our home, and no double-check valve is a hundred percent reliable.[13]

Finally, the ADHF-F insisted that connecting the boats to the sewerage network contradicted the basic tenet of boat-based housing, which is its autonomy vis-à-vis the 'people of the land'. The idea of technological autonomy, of a symbolic and material removal from urban infrastructure, is central for many individuals or communities who choose off-grid lifestyles (Vannini and Thaggart 2015). Bringing forth images of both the vulnerability of the floating habitat (which can sink) and the freedom it affords to its inhabitants (who can, in principle, move their boat to a different location if they want to), they insisted that boats should remain independent from a fixed drain and rely on autonomous sanitation techniques instead. Among these alternatives were compost toilets – dry toilets that create compost from faeces.

From hydrophilic to edaphic socio-microbial alliances

Compost toilets were first implemented in the context of remote premises, inhabited by communities that voluntarily extricated themselves from the grid and the grip of public authorities. They have been seen as a device that allows 'disconnection from the State and reconnection with the local environment' (Pickering 2010). Compost toilets function without a water flush. Excreta is received in a bin where they can be covered with wood shavings to avoid the smell and start a composting process. When urine and faeces are collected separately, the latter can be dried by a ventilation system, and the former treated apart. In composting, the excreta are brought into contact with plant litter and living organisms (bacteria, fungi, multiple invertebrates), under specific aeration and humidity conditions.[14] These soil-related bacteria and other organisms digest the material and the rise in temperature finally eliminates pathogens, making composting a low-tech, versatile form of *edaphic* (related to soil organisms, from Ancient Greek *édaphos*, 'ground') sanitation technique.

In recent years, the ADHF-F has come to view compost toilets (or dry toilets) as a technique that could allow houseboats to continue to eject urine and grey water (from cooking, showers and laundry) with a light treatment, so that they need 'only' treat faeces, which concentrate the bacterial problem. Nevertheless, beyond its alleged legality, the practice of dry toilets on board a boat still raises many questions, both practical and regulatory. In 2019, the ADHF-F therefore approached the French Network of Ecological Sanitation (RAE)[15] with a view to conducting a study on dry toilet systems associated with the treatment of grey water by floating phyto-purification. The study demonstrated that it was technically and legally possible to install a composting box on the deck of a boat, as long as the floor is made sufficiently waterproof so there is no leak into the boat. Nevertheless, the barge dwellers whose practices were documented in the framework of our investigation[16] do not, in general, compost individually on board but on the quay near their boat or in a shared garden near the port. These are collective composters that can accommodate dry toilet materials and vegetable waste. Alternating between toilet waste and vegetable waste, from a kitchen or a garden, ensures efficient fermentation. On a boat taken alone, these conditions are difficult to achieve, as one boat owner explained to us:

> I have installed urine diversion dry toilets. I compost the solid part on the deck. I am the only one around here with dry toilets, but all the other boat owners in the area bring me their organic matter. I would not have enough material to be able to compost otherwise.[17]

These systems of pooling materials offer a middle ground solution, but they are currently prohibited by a 2009 decree on Non-Collective Sanitation, which states that composting one's faeces is only legal in one's own garden or basement – a limitation that is not specific to houseboats but can concern any building in densely populated urban areas. The ADHF-F and the RAE therefore began to consider setting up a comprehensive toilet waste management coordination plan for compost toilets, including the organisation of waste collection by a specialised service equipped with ad-hoc toilet drainers, the delivery of these materials to a local composting platform in the suburbs, and identifying prospects for the resulting compost.[18] Even though it is currently more a promise than an operational solution, this last option generates significant enthusiasm among some boat owners, who see it as an opportunity to contribute to a new kind of sanitation network not based on a confined water stream but rather on soil processes.

As we conclude this chapter, we can only speculate about the future of the alliance between the boat owners and the RAE, and about the establishment of a new pathway for collective toilet composting. However, the current discussions are already generating new socio-microbiological assemblages – at least in the technical hopes and imagination that inform these debates. Even though most boat owners are mainly concerned with the risk of a sewer overflow for their own boat, the involvement of the RAE goes some way towards reframing the controversy at a new level: that of the poor environmental value of conventional sanitation systems.

These emerging edaphic socio-microbiological assemblages can be linked to the wider features of ecological sanitation as described by Gay Hawkins's work on its development in Australia. This movement revolves around a critique of mainstream sanitation systems, described as 'magical invisibilisation devices' that allow city dwellers to turn a blind eye to the issue of what becomes of their excreta as they – the excreta – become confined in water and pipes situated underground (Hawkins 2004). By comparison, these movements promote the creation of a distributed treatment and evacuation pathway (that treats excreta in multiple composting boxes situated above the surface) as a revolutionary approach to sanitation, one that does not aspire to simply *get rid of* unwanted organisms by sending them away in the evacuation stream but tackles the problem of faecal contamination 'at the source' (Legrand 2020). Unlike water, soil does not flow in pipes or over pavements. It stays still, at least apparently, and invites urban communities to become concerned again about the question of human excrement (also called 'night soil'), its circulation and its transformations. In these discourses, on-board dry toilet systems appear as a way of countering not only conventional sanitation's exclusive reliance on the aquatic environment as the key agent of sanitation but also the centralising impetus of water engineers, making soil-based sanitation methods appear as a key step in reclaiming 'responsibility' for the becoming of one's 'shit' and its microbial content (Hawkins 2002).

CONCLUSION

In following the growing topic of open water bathing in urban rivers, this chapter has led us to analyse the changing microbiopolitics (Paxson 2008) of excreta surrounding the emergence of faecal bacteria as an indicator in river health monitoring. With regard to general environmental regulations of water quality, before the 2024 Olympic Games project the presence of faecal microorganisms in the River Seine was not regarded as a relevant criterion in assessing its environmental quality. Once the new horizon of making the Seine legally bathable envisioned putting human bodies in contact with the river water, microbiological presence, through sentinel species such as *E. coli*, gradually became a matter of concern. This attracted public attention towards the breaches and leaks in the sanitation system and led to the mobilisation of new political and technical actors, some gathered in commissions such as the Bathing Committee, others that represented new disciplines, such as water ecologists, but also unexpected actors such as the Port of Paris, wild swimmers and a collective of houseboat owners who objected to being entangled within the reticular wastewater system, instead advocating 'on-board sanitation systems'.

We showed that the controversy over houseboat sanitation issues, although a minor event on the scale of the river and of Paris, changed the way human-microbe relationships were framed in discussions on the clean-up of the river. Whereas the general objective of making the Seine bathable changed the discourse of water sanitation from water ecological quality criteria to discussions over the presence of pathogens harmful to human bodies, the boat sanitation issue brought up larger questions of *which* microbial communities – soil microbes or water microbes – were to be enrolled in techniques of human waste management, and of *how* new socio-microbial alliances can be forged in the hope of making the becoming of excreta public. On top of the classical anthropological question of what is understood as contamination or pollution in regard to cultural purity standards (Douglas 1966), or that of how the governance of social life interlinks with that of microbial life, this case shows how human bodies and microbes come to participate actively in multiple arrangements of knowledge, governance and regulation that always redefine what they are and why they matter, but never quite manage to stabilise them in controllable entities.

NOTES

1 Interviews with local officials, sanitation engineers, researchers and instructors, as well as houseboat owners and their representatives, were conducted by Marine Legrand during spring and summer 2020, completed by a series of observations during public conferences.

2 Interview with Fabien Esculier, in charge of a research programme on the ecological transition of sanitation, former head of the 'Seine water basin police' service.

3 Interview with F. Esculier.

4 Interview with Miguel Guillon-Ritz, member of Water and Sanitation Technical Department (STEA) of the city of Paris.

5 https://www.prefectures-regions.gouv.fr/ile-de-france/Region-et-institutions/ L-action-de-l-Etat/Amenagement-du-territoire-transport-et-environnement/ Environnement/Eau/Plan-Baignade-la-relance-pour-l-amelioration-de-la-qualite-de-l-eau-en-Seine-et-en-Marne [accessed 20 August 2020].

6 http://www.driee.ile-de-france.developpement-durable.gouv.fr/baignade-dans-la-seine-et-dans-la-marne-comment-y-a3438.html [accessed 20 August 2020].

7 Interview with Étienne Doumazane, sanitation instructor.

8 Interview with F. Esculier.

9 Orient and Artelia, *Missions d'assistance technique relatives aux infrastructures gérées par la direction de la propreté et de l'eau, Ville de Paris* (2019).

10 SEPIA Conseil, *Étude de l'assainissement des bateaux-logements* (2007). Today, the official sanitation solution for boats is the storage of raw sewage to be emptied at the quayside. It is not applied in practice due to the lack of adapted equipment in ports.

11 ADHF-F General Assembly report, 26/01/19.
12 Interview with Raphaël Colette, vice-president of the ADHF-F.
13 Interview with R. Colette.
14 Time is also key in the process: at the domestic level, the WHO recommends a composting time of two years before possible use in agriculture (WHO 2012).
15 The RAE is an association which advocates for decentralised forms of sanitation that protect aquatic environments and return the fertilising resources contained in human excreta to cultivated soils. It gathers together firms, associations and individuals who practise and advocate for the use of dry toilets and phyto-purification in various contexts, including cities.
16 In Paris and Toulouse agglomerations.
17 Interview with R. Colette.
18 *RAE, projet d'assainissement écologique pour habitat flottant* (2019).

ACKNOWLEDGEMENTS

We thank Charlotte Brives, Salla Sariola, Matthäus Rest, Denis Chartier, Sandra Fernandez and Marc Higgin for their comments on earlier versions of this chapter.

REFERENCES

Aguerre, J. P., 'Scatophobie des villes, scatophilie des champs. Gestion et utilisation des fèces à Lyon à la fin du 19e siècle', *Ruralia*, 12/13 (2003) <https://journals.openedition.org/ruralia/329> [accessed 15 May 2021].

Barles, S., *La ville délétère : médecins et ingénieurs dans l'espace urbain (XVIIIe-XXe siècles)* (Seyssel: Champ Vallon, 1999).

——— 'Experts contre experts: les champs d'épandage de la ville de Paris dans les années 1870', *Histoire urbaine*, 3 (2005), 65–80.

Barraqué, B., 'Les enjeux de la Directive cadre sur l'eau de l'Union Européenne', *Flux*, 46.1 (2001), 70–5.

——— 'Pour une histoire des services d'eau et d'assainissement en Europe et en Amérique du Nord', *Flux*, 97–98.3 (2014), 4–15.

Blandin P., 'Bioindicateurs et diagnostic des systèmes écologiques', *Bulletin d'écologie*, 17.4 (1986), 215–307.

Bouleau, G., 'La catégorisation politique des eaux sous l'angle de la *political ecology*: le patrimoine piscicole et la pollution en France', *L'Espace géographique*, 46.3 (2017), 214–30.

Douglas, M., *Purity and Danger. An Analysis of the Concepts of Pollution and Taboo* (London: Routledge and Kegan Paul, 1966).

Dubin, C., 'La mise en modèle mathématique de l'auto-épuration des rivières', *La Houille Blanche*, 8 (1971), 705–10.

Duhau, I., 'Les baignades en rivière d'Île-de-France, des premiers aménagements à la piscine parisienne Joséphine-Baker', *Livraisons de l'histoire de l'architecture*, 14 (2007), 9–38.

Gramaglia, C., 'Sentinel Organisms: "They Look out for the Environment!"', *Limn*, 3 (2013) <https://limn.it/articles/sentinel-organisms-they-look-out-for-the-environment/> [accessed 10 September 2020].

Haghe, J. P., and A. Euzen, 'A New Political Categorization of Water Bodies: Swimming in Open Water. The Example of Paris, "Swimmable City"', Paper Presented at *Conference I.S. Rivers*, Lyon, 2018.

Hawkins, G., 'Down the Drain: Shit and the Politics of Disturbance', in G. Hawkins, and S. Muecke, eds, *Culture and Waste: The Creation and Destruction of Value* (Lanham, MD: Rowman & Littlefield Publishers, 2002), pp. 39–52.

—— 'Shit in Public', *Australian Humanities Review* 31.2 (2004) <http://australian humanitiesreview.org/2004/04/01/shit-in-public/> [accessed 26 November 2019].

Horrocks, W. H., *An Introduction to the Bacteriological Examination of Water* (London: Kessinger Publishing, 1901).

Le Bas, A. 'Ce que Paris doit au sport: Essai de topographie parisienne des équipements', *Histoire urbaine*, 57.1 (2020), 23–45.

Legay, J. M., *L'interdisciplinarité dans les sciences de la vie* (Versailles: Quæ, 2006).

Legrand, M., 'Digestions fertiles, le retour au sol des excréments humains', *Revue d'Anthropologie des Connaissances* 14.4 (2020)<http://journals.openedition.org/rac/11042> [accessed 26 August 2021].

Maillet, G. M., 'Avancées, limites et perspectives de la Directive Cadre sur l'eau à l'échéance 2015', *Norois*, 235 (2015), 7–13.

Mouchel, J. M., and others, 'Bathing Activities and Microbiological River Water Quality in the Paris Area: A Long-Term Perspective', in *The Handbook of Environmental Chemistry* (Berlin: Springer, 2019).

Passerat, J., and others, 'Impact of an Intense Combined Sewer Overflow Event on the Microbiological Water Quality of the Seine River', *Water Research*, 45.2 (2011), 893–903.

Paxson, H., 'Post-Pasteurian Cultures: The Microbiopolitics of Raw-Milk Cheese in the United States', *Cultural Anthropology*, 23.1 (2008), 15–47.

Pickering, L., 'Toilets, Bodies, Selves: Enacting Composting as Counterculture in Hawaii', *Body & Society*, 16.4 (2010), 33–55.

Tabuchi, J. P., B. Tassin, and C. Blatrix, 'Greater Paris Water and Global Change', paper presented at *EAUMEGA Conference*, Paris, 2016.

UNCPIE, *Les cahiers de l'eau 12: Les indicateurs biologiques des milieux aquatiques* (2015).

Vannini, P., and J. Taggart, *Off the Grid. Re-Assembling Domestic Life* (London: Routledge, 2015).

World Health Organization, *Global Water Supply and Sanitation Assessment 2000 Report* (2000).

—— *Guidelines for Safe Recreational Water Environments* (2003).

—— *Safe Use of Waste Water, Excreta and Grey Water* (2012).

—— *Q&A on Recreational Water Quality in Rio de Janeiro, Brazil* (2016).

7

SCALABILITY AND PARTIAL CONNECTIONS IN TACKLING ANTIMICROBIAL RESISTANCE IN WEST AFRICA

Jose A. Cañada

INTRODUCTION

Long-distance translocation of [antimicrobial resistant] bacteria between systems and countries is also possible. One route by which this might happen occurs when waterborne bacteria become airborne either through bubble bursts or convection. Once the bacteria are airborne, air currents can move them over long distances before redepositing them. However, a more probable route of long-distance dissemination is through anthropogenic movements of vectors such as aquatic animals and plants, for which there is large-scale international trade (Taylor, Verner-Jeffreys, and Baker-Austin 2011: 281).

MICROBES AND, MORE SPECIFICALLY AS DESCRIBED IN THE EXCERPT ABOVE, resistant bacteria travel. However, they do not travel alone. Water and air flow as well as the human transportation of other animals and plants all play key roles in understanding the global spread of antimicrobial resistance (AMR). AMR refers to microbes – bacteria, fungi and viruses – becoming resistant to the mechanisms that kill them. When formulated as a health issue, AMR is usually reduced to bacterial infections and antibiotics, but resistant bacteria are not the only elements of AMR subject to translocation. Given the potential ubiquity of AMR described in the excerpt above, actions aimed at tackling resistance attempt to span the globe and to identify the many sectors involved, affected or responsible. This produces a back and forth between global and local scales of AMR enactment that forces us to think about the various contexts in which AMR and the actions to tackle it are situated. In my work, I have attended to those multi-context dynamics by following the implementation of global AMR policy initiatives in two West African countries (Benin and Burkina Faso), looking at how the actions and changes proposed from global health initiatives meet with the situated local materialities of the patients, breeders, veterinarians, healthcare workers and researchers who are pulled into the AMR challenge by global health organisations.

Exploring the emergence of these multiscalar contexts at the global and local levels contributes to what Anna Tsing (2005) has called an 'ethnographic examination of scale making, [...] the study of the messy and effective encounters and translations of globalist projects', according to Warwick Anderson (2014: 378). Tsing's thoughts on scalability are particularly interesting if we apply her 'theory of nonscalability' (Tsing 2012), which carries special significance in the context of top-down projects such as AMR. For Tsing, nonscalable elements are not easily transplanted between contexts, since they often ignore the relationalities which render such contexts unique. In this chapter, I examine how certain objects crucial to the AMR globalist project are recognisable and identifiable across the globe, yet, when exposed to local contexts and their complex relationalities, become nonscalable. That is, they struggle to fit with the situated sociomaterialities that AMR actors are embedded in. In this attempt, I do not merely illustrate how global health – and the global issue of AMR more specifically – is made in local contexts, but the problems that objectivist projects common in the governance and regulation of microbiological entanglements run into when framed using standardised scientific narratives.

Probably the most visible element in the regulation of microbiologically defined threats to health has been the Global Action Plan for AMR (GAP), published by the World Health Organisation (WHO) in 2015, which was in the process of being adapted into a national action plan during my fieldwork in Benin and Burkina Faso. Although resistance in bacteria is a naturally occurring phenomenon resulting from selective pressures (Prestinaci, Pezzotti, and Pantosti 2015), GAP calls attention to the effect of human practices, specifically antibiotic use. More concretely, these practices include the misuse, overuse and abuse, purchase without a prescription, or the commercialisation of 'fake' antibiotics with less active components than required. Such practices help to kill non-resistant bacteria while leaving resistant strains alive and capable of reproducing and spreading resistance genes. Although these are practices to avoid from a global framework perspective, for local actors like those featured in this chapter, they are key elements to compensate for the lack of infrastructures that characterise precarious settings. Reliance on antibiotics represents a 'quick fix' in antibiotic policy that largely ignores the socio-political conditions surrounding AMR (Denyer Willis and Chandler 2019), putting emphasis on the individual and framing the issue in behavioural terms (Pearson and Chandler 2019).

GAP presents specific challenges that extend beyond the usual problems associated with global health policy implementation in the context of infectious diseases (Cañada 2019) – challenges stemming from GAP's multisectoral character. The signing by a so-called tripartite collaboration between the WHO, the Food and Agriculture Organisation (FAO) and the World Organisation for Animal Health (OIE) represented a turning point for AMR and its formulation. The involvement of FAO and OIE at an international level translates into a need for interministerial collaboration at a national level and the establishment of several focal points, which impacts multiple economic sectors. Ministries of health, often the sole agencies responsible for translating WHO initiatives into action, must collaborate with ministries of agriculture, fishing, animal production and the environment. Thus, the policy processes initiated by GAP activate horizontal coordination mechanisms that challenge typical intragovernmental dynamics of collaboration, something the policymakers that I spent time with struggled to incorporate into their everyday practice.

In the absence of a recognition of local socio-material conditions, discourses of behaviourism and the cherishing of available antibiotics remain dominant in policy settings. However, alternative discourses exist. These discourses primarily engage with a redefinition of immunity and the consequent modes of coexistence with microbes. Current understandings of gut microbiota and the human-microbial entanglements we humans define as healthy are expanding in new directions. The existing literature argues for a need to understand bacteria not only through their pathogenic threats to human health but also through the crucial roles they play in producing functional immune systems (Lorimer 2017; Pradeu 2012). The policies and implementations analysed here are instead framed as a fight for survival which characterises the dynamics of resistance (Beisel 2017). In the AMR narrative, the fight against microbes cannot be won. Instead, that fight becomes a matter of optimising the tools available to regulate human-microbial entanglements (and the mediating role of animals) in ways that do not render those tools ineffective. A similar fight for survival characterises the drive and motivation of local actors to engage with AMR. However, their survival is not only uncertain because of the threat posed by microbes, but because of the constant demands exerted by global initiatives to alter their situated practices, which put their livelihoods at risk.

In this chapter, I look beyond the typical technical character of AMR policies, which tend to provide a rather static image of the most prominent actors in this volume: that is, microbes. In the technical worlds built by global health policymakers to deal with AMR, little space exists for a dynamic and complex understanding of microbes themselves, as well as the communities in which those microbes emerge as relevant actors. By attending to locally situated experiences of AMR across different human collectives, I bring to life the technical and dry narratives of microbes that feature in global policy. Doing so helps me to illustrate why global detached accounts of human-microbial relations give rise to measures and proposals that, on encountering locally situated materialities, are instantly rendered nonscalable.

In the following section, I find inspiration in the notion of 'assemblage ethnography' (Youdell and McGimpsey 2015) to formulate how the emergence of nonscalable elements can be considered analytically and methodologically. I also describe the specific empirical material used in this chapter. The subsequent empirical section is divided into three parts illustrating various nonscalable dynamics affecting human-microbial entanglements in the areas of policy, research and treatment. Finally, I conclude by arguing that fundamental elements of global AMR policy encounter unaccounted relationalities at the local level, rendering them nonscalable and putting at risk the fragile livelihoods of the local actors involved.

EMERGING SCALES IN ASSEMBLAGE ETHNOGRAPHY

In my journey to follow AMR policies, I found myself constantly changing between emerging global and local scales that were enacted through vocabularies, documents and practices. In my own attempts to not lose my footing and fall myself into the trap of that scale game, making oversimplified assumptions regarding the identity of human-microbe relationalities, I started to think of my methodology in terms of *constant travel*, both physically and digitally, between the global and the local. To systematically approach this constant travel, I took inspiration from the notion of 'assemblage ethnography' (Youdell and McGimpsey 2015). Specifically designed to study rapidly changing policy issues by following policymaking and implementation networks, this type of ethnography allowed me to empirically explore complex policy implementation networks, paying attention to how scales emerge across institutional, research and more-than-human assemblages. This approach invites researchers to follow relevant actors – both human and non-human – by combining different methods and techniques. In the context of my study, this was particularly relevant because, in that constant travel, it often felt easy to lose track of what microbes are and the spaces they occupy.

Taking global AMR policy as a starting point, I followed its implementation all the way to West Africa, more specifically to Benin and Burkina Faso. These two countries have struggled more than most to develop and implement a national AMR action plan, given the lack of governmental and health infrastructure, and have thus become clear examples of the inequalities that characterise global health. Framing my methodology in terms of assemblages

(Deleuze and Guattari 2006) carries several advantages. The notion of an assemblage allows me to highlight the hybrid characteristics of the more-than-human entanglements key to understanding AMR. Most importantly, the idea of an assemblage carries implications in thinking about the emerging character of those hybrid actors, their capabilities and multi-sited character, leaving us with a constant renegotiation of who is involved and a distributed understanding of agency.

To make sense of the more or less stable identity of these human and non-human actors, I rely on the notion of partial connection as formulated by Marylin Strathern (2004), which is useful when considering how the same objects are present in different contexts in ways that create similarity and divergence. Strathern argues that any comparison always entails some sort of partial connection, even if the comparison does not create equivalence between both objects within the comparison. The need to think in terms of partiality comes from the pitfall of representing the contexts we compare in terms of difference and uniqueness. In the case of microbes, analysed discussions of policy, research and care entailed working with understandings of microbes and resistance that are partially connected: that is, different and similar at the same time. The challenge lies in discussing connections between these contexts without representing them as unique or homogenous. This requires an understanding of the context that allows us to grasp the significance of the object, a framework useful for understanding the cultural and socio-political differences that feature in the implementation of global policy. Although we can agree on microbes as identifiers that emerge in policy, research and healthcare, their emergence does not take place in the same way. Sometimes they become relevant in one context because of their presence within another – that is, they become a global health policy concern before they become a concern within a national health policy or on an individual farm – rendering visible the hierarchical logic followed by global health. Similar dynamics occur with other nonscalable elements of AMR, which I will also address in this chapter. Thus, by understanding the different contexts and scales in which an object moves, we must acknowledge the constant shift in meaning, agency and identity. The microbe, the doctor, the farmer and the researcher are not understood in the same way within policy as they are within an academic setting or on a farm. The connections between one context and another are always partial, and the transplantation of different objects challenges their own significance and identity.

The research for this chapter relies on material gathered during two one-month ethnographic visits to Benin and Burkina Faso, complemented with documentary material. This includes the analysis of 38 policy documents from international organisations; seven policy documents from Benin and two from Burkina Faso; 27 semi-structured interviews with national policymakers, international collaborators, researchers and healthcare professionals; six focus groups with Beninese veterinarians and breeders; and two ethnographic diaries from fieldwork conducted in Benin and Burkina Faso. The fieldwork involved spending time in locations where AMR is shaped locally – that is, universities, laboratories, farms and hospitals. The following sections organise the insights gained during fieldwork around three central areas of AMR projects where scalability issues emerge: 1) policy development, 2) research and knowledge production, and 3) the diagnosis and treatment of bacterial infections in both humans and non-human animals. Examining more than one aspect of AMR helps to understand what makes such a project nonscalable across settings. Although I look at implementation in only two countries, by attending to practices of AMR across different, partially connected settings, I intend to provide a broad picture of the nonscalable elements that often feature in global health initiatives. Of particular relevance to this book's perspective, this broad picture allows me to reflect on what nonscalability means for human-microbial engagements, an issue I return to at the end of each subsection and in the conclusions.

ONE HEALTH AND THE ANTIMICROBIALS THAT MATTER

In AMR discussions, One Health (OH) emerges as a fundamental aspect in defining the breadth of the AMR problem. OH is a public health approach that aims to recognise the links and dependencies between human and animal health, agricultural production and the environment. As I wandered the public offices of Benin and Burkina Faso, I found that policymakers from both countries relied on the notion of OH as their first frame of reference to explain the challenges embedded in combatting AMR. However, the fact that the term was ubiquitous and widely recognised did not mean that the core ideas and their practical implementation were understood unequivo- cally. The way in which the idea of OH is transplanted to specific localities is conditioned by the particular political practices and infrastructures that characterise each context.

This context specificity, and the relevance of local infrastructures, is some- thing that characterises global health in general (Biehl 2016). Yet by incorporat- ing OH, the issue is not only that global organisations operate with very different resources and mandates than their national counterparts, but also that differences emerge horizontally. The challenge here is not only one of making local contexts fit the OH rationale, but of moving elements across sectors that have traditionally worked in isolation, making clear that national contexts are not homogenous. Differences in budget, size, facilities and authority represented clear pitfalls to the development and implementation of a national policy that effectively considers AMR an issue extending beyond human health. My observations in the field are complemented with the analysis of both global and national policy, where OH appears to work more as a policymaking mantra than as an articulated proposal bringing relevant actors to the table to contribute complementary capabilities. Conversations with Beninese and Burkinabe policymakers provide examples of the nonscalability of the OH approach. While in conversations with human health authorities, conflicts between sectors hardly arose, in conversations with animal health stakeholders these difficulties were part of their everyday strug- gles with AMR, which manifested in the different cross-sectoral collaboration attempts that global policies demand.

In Burkina Faso, establishing an OH platform – one of the actions recom- mended by international policy – became a source of organisational conflict. Experts from sectors other than human health understood that the OH approach meant their contribution should be equally distributed. This was the position held by Dr Z, an advocate for animal health and agriculture, who asserted that before talking about AMR we must talk about the OH platform, which was, at the time of my visit, a work-in-progress. Although, in Dr Z's view, the creation of this group represented an impressive step forward, other issues emerged, since the human health sector was reluctant to organise the platform in a horizontal manner. For human health stakeholders, OH is a human health issue rooted in International Health Regulations.[1] In Dr Z's view, this will not result in a true OH approach. Thus, Dr Z's organisation promoted a co-leadership approach: they did not want the livestock sector to lead, but to find co-leadership alternatives. In Benin, on the other hand, approaching AMR as an OH issue meant reaffirming the status quo, with the human health sector taking the lead, while environment, agriculture and animal health played supporting roles. In my discussion with Dr Y, a researcher involved in AMR policymaking, it was explained that the absence of conflict between human and animal health resulted from the latter having been secondary to the process. Therefore, not everyone contributes equally to the process. These two positions provided different organisational understandings of resistant microbes. While in the first position resistant microbes remain an issue for the health of both humans and animals, in the second resistant microbes are portrayed as an issue in the animal context because of the effect they have on human health.

These two scenarios support the existing literature, which criticises the notion of OH because of its partisan focus. Hinchliffe (2015) has argued that OH makes one specific health – mostly human and mostly Western – stand for something much wider, through a reductionist process that denies the complex and multiple character of health. In the context of AMR policymaking, while OH attempts to conceptualise an interconnected understanding of health, such a formulation remains reductionist since it builds on a refusal to break with anthropocentric policymaking (Kamenshchikova et al. 2019). This anthropocentrism can produce infrastructural blocks for implementation, as in the first example, or prevent experts in non-human health from contributing on equal grounds to the development and implementation of national policy, as in the second example. These cross-sectoral dynamics might prevent concrete regulations from having their intended impact within practical domains such as farms, hospitals or the environment.

SCALING MICROBES, SCALING RESEARCH CAREERS

One of the immediate consequences of the increase in global health policy to tackle AMR has been an increase in international funding for AMR research. In particular, an important investment has been directed at researchers in low- and middle-income countries, in the hope of boosting knowledge production in areas where concrete data about the presence of resistant microbes has been virtually non-existent. Some of these researchers, part of international consortia and projects to produce AMR data, were my first contacts with AMR circles in both countries. This gave me a privileged vantage point to understand the way local science production is embedded in a more or less scalable way into global policy initiatives. During my fieldwork, I met with a loosely organised, yet well-connected group of scientists that saw the new global concern about AMR as a key opportunity to boost their own professional careers. Their location in West Africa, defined as a hotspot that needs to be known by the international community through surveillance and data production, made the role of those scientists an indispensable one. However, local conditions for scientific knowl-edge production and the agency of West African researchers in the face of often totalising global health projects made sure the process of scaling back and forth between local and global was not without struggle.

One of the most evident ways in which local socio-material conditions got in the way of producing data that met the demands of global initiatives was the lack of laboratory capacity. Laboratories represent a valuable resource in West Africa, which cannot be taken for granted. All the laboratories I visited were under development and in need of equipment or unable to find the financial resources needed to update facilities established decades ago. Some of the latter had even turned into offices where dated devices for microbiological analysis accumulated dust. These facilities relied upon uncertain streams of funding from foreign organisations, funding which helped establish a laboratory despite the contextual constraints, and which remain invisible within global mandates for capacity building. Dr X, a microbiologist and postdoctoral researcher from a university laboratory, described the limitations imposed by this reality and explained how they were completely dependent upon grant applications to keep their laboratory updated. During my stay, Dr X's laboratory needed a new molecular analysis section to isolate, identify and characterise bacterial strains using polymerase chain reaction (PCR). Without such developments, they were forced to rely on external collaborations for these types of analysis. Such limitations condition how microbes can be identified and how knowledge about microbes can be made scalable so as to enter the global arena. Furthermore, it limits local researchers' autonomy to establish their own research agendas.

Researchers understood that an important part of their ability to contribute to international projects relied on the provision of data. To scale up their careers to become members of the international AMR expert community, they had to be able to turn locally taken samples into internationally relevant data, despite the precarious conditions of their laboratories, which complicated the gathering, conservation and analysis of samples. Success in that endeavour would help researchers carry out research that cannot be conducted in their home institutions. This would then also allow them to publish in more prestigious journals. In part, this desire represented a reaction to what they perceived as a non-rigorous means of building academic careers in West Africa, often based on publishing internally within their own faculty after little or no peer-review process. This contrasted with usual scientific standards in the global North, and so researchers with international ambitions insisted on differentiating themselves from local academic cultures that engaged in those non-rigorous practices. Yet these researchers continuously struggled to balance their criticism of local academic practices and their ability to work with global North scientific standards, which secured them funding through international collaboration, with their reluctance or inability entirely to abandon their idiosyncratic national or regional practices, thereby challenging the all-encompassing character of global health.

Traditional medicines served as strong candidates to build that identity, although they struggled to gain recognition for their medicinal value. African researchers dedicated time and effort to collect samples of herbal medicine that could be used to test their effect on microbial cultures. However, this part of their work was hardly recognised by their international collaborators. During conversations with European researchers, there was a tendency to dismiss the study of traditional medicines as non-rigorous or unscientific.

Whilst antibiotics as a problem or a solution establish partial connections between local microbes and microbes addressed within global policies, traditional medicines become nonscalable since they challenge Western modes of knowledge production. Their role in regulating human-microbial engagements remained forcefully local. This provides an example of how, confronted with the unique entanglements that condition economic production, sanitation and hygiene, and a failure of development politics, there is a need to develop innovation and capacity in Africa consistent with local conditions and contexts (Louis, Nazemi, and Remer 2017). African researchers build a biotechnological-turned-biotraditional imaginary that encounters no counterpart in global policy. AMR policies provide a much less ambitious formulation, inviting experts to cherish existing antibiotics and to produce knowledge about the dynamics of resistance that develops around the globe, leaving out any emphasis on innovation. This understanding not only establishes various means of coexisting with microbes different to that which exists in the global North, but it also establishes specific modes of expertise not possible elsewhere. Thus, African researchers advocate for a chance to build their expertise around axes of native knowledge and responsibility towards a global mandate linked to the specific context in which they operate.

Access to laboratory and microbiological analysis tools is key in regulating how microbes can be known in local West African settings, but also how other local actors are able to interact and situate themselves on a global scale. Advanced testing and analytical methods require sending samples outside the region, transferring knowledge production to the global North. African scientists rely on those collaborations to understand microbes in ways that allow them to participate in international cutting-edge scientific discussions. Yet the specific context and the nonscalable nature of traditional medicines promotes a mode of microbe knowledge that stems from the lay use of medicinal plants, allowing for the creation of biotechnological imaginaries visibly missing in the global North. Both international collaborations and the use of traditional medicines help to articulate not only the scalability of microbiological science but the scalability of African microbiological researchers themselves as they struggle to become active partners in knowledge making.

UNCERTAIN DIAGNOSES, TREATMENT AND SATISFACTION

As mentioned in the introduction, a key aspect of global initiatives to tackle AMR is to reduce the use of antibiotics. The key strategy is to narrow their use to cases where a bacterial infection has been confirmed. This is another policy mandate that encounters serious difficulties in the studied areas. The difficulties of maintaining well-equipped laboratories, discussed in the previous section, extend here to human and animal health.[2] Physicians and veterinarians rely on laboratories to confirm their clinical diagnoses, making specific infections visible and assisting in treatment decisions. However, the doctors, nurses, veterinarians and breeders I met confided that access to laboratory diagnoses was often prohibitive from an economic perspective or simply non-existent to those living in rural areas. Care professionals were forced to interact with microbes without what global health policy deems preferable – that is, a laboratory diagnosis. For example, while antibiograms (antibiotic-specific resistance tests for a given microbial colony) are available in West Africa and do not require significant laboratory investments, they are far from ubiquitous, typically only available in the largest cities and main hospitals. Thus, a rural veterinarian or physician who needs a diagnosis to make a treatment decision has little chance to send samples and receive results in a timely manner. The health of a patient or a group of animals might be at stake.

In these circumstances, both care for animals on farms and for humans in hospitals provide similar available paths of action related to bacterial infection, directed by individual and/or collective manifestations of resistance – that is, persistent symptoms that do not disappear after initiating treatment. Microbes, in such cases, form an assemblage with humans or animals and medicines, an assemblage interpreted through the lens of resistance. Often, no data or laboratory confirmations are available to indicate that the persistence of an infection is, in fact, caused by a resistant strain. Rather, this understanding is at times formulated as a suspicion which, given the lack of diagnostic capabilities, must be acted upon. A Beninese veterinarian explains that:

A diagnosis is not reliable [until] after the laboratory diagnosis. What we have in the field is a suspicion [...]. We are obliged to limit ourselves to suspicion to advance the treatment, but theoretically we have been trained to make a diagnosis before treatment. In the field it is a little complicated because it is when the breeder has problems and there are mortalities, he calls you, and you must react urgently. Even if we have the tools we need, we don't have the time to do the right thing properly before moving forward when the breeder wants to be satisfied.

With this lack of laboratory access and the added time pressure, often the conclusion that an infection is resistant is based on an unsuccessful antibiotic treatment. Successful treatment, on the other hand, is confirmed by the disappearance of symptoms and patient or breeder satisfaction with treatment. Otherwise, two possible paths of action are available in the case of failed treatment. First, treatment may involve increasing the dose; second, treatment can shift to a different antibiotic. These are, in the absence of laboratory confirmations and antibiograms, and given the impossibility of knowing the infectious agent at the microbiological level, blind steps from a scientific perspective. Alternatively, these steps also activate different modes of *sensing* that obligate veterinarians, breeders, animals, patients and physicians to communicate in ways that allow for resistance to become a part of the relational assemblage, productively compensating for the nonscalability of laboratory diagnoses.

In this relational setting, there is little space for guidelines that require a level of confirmation not available to any of the professionals encountered during fieldwork. In my conversations with Beninese veterinarians, the satisfaction of the breeder guides the veterinarian's decision-making. In the case of human health, the satisfaction of the patient dictates the persistence of the infection, as explained by the managing director of a Beninese district hospital:

Yes, that's the problem: how do I know if the patient is not satisfied? Because, generally, when you start the treatment, you have to feel better [...]. When the patient returns and you notice that the parameters have not fundamentally changed, as a doctor, the first reflex that you have is to change the product and maybe prescribe a higher dose […]. You may not know. So, all you can do is just change the product, hoping the second one is better.

In the absence of bacterial infection diagnostic testing, an interaction with other microorganisms and diseases like malaria creates an even more complicated assemblage. The international push to develop treatments for malaria, together with efforts by nongovernmental organisations, have ensured that even in many remote rural areas malaria rapid tests are accessible. However, confronted with symptoms of a fever and a negative malaria test, bacterial infection becomes the immediate diagnosis in the absence of testing, followed by the subsequent prescription of antibiotics without a laboratory confirmation.[3]

What remains nonscalable here are general recommendations to reduce antibiotic use in humans and specific statements to not use antimicrobials of critical importance to humans when treating food-producing animals (World Health Organization 2017). These recommendations represent an important element in the behavioural understanding of AMR (Pearson and Chandler 2019). Policy implementation in the field confronts a more collective relationality that challenges the individuality of behaviourism, an approach that becomes a nonscalable element in its clash with local specificities. Similarly, reducing antibiotic use through diagnoses is in this case a difficult if not impossible task. This is particularly true in rural areas, where often only nurses or pharmacists are available to provide any medical advice, or where an unaffordable hospital trip means losing a day's wage. For animals, calling in a veterinarian can represent a prohibitive service for a breeder, putting the economic viability of their farm at risk, and an action usually reserved for only the direst situations. Until then, they rely on advice from family and friends with whom the constant exchange of information and experience remain crucial to producing collective modes of diagnosis.

This supports Denyer Willis and Chandler's (2019) claim that understanding the role of antibiotics links with how entrenched they are within a society. In the case of farming, various antibiotic uses associate with financial needs. Thus, the notions of use, misuse and even lack of use become complex in the economic and productivity networks of humans, animals and microbes whereby antibiotics become generative of either health or disease. This also agrees with studies demonstrating a pragmatism in antibiotic prescription connected to the conditions of access to diagnostics (Pearson and Chandler 2019). Indeed, in my material, farmers' and patients' use of antibiotics connects to pressing needs, given the lack of affordable alternatives.

CONCLUSIONS

In this chapter, I have illustrated some elements of the scalar difficulties of implementing AMR policy in two national settings: Benin and Burkina Faso. I argue that fundamental elements of global AMR policy encounter unaccounted relationalities at the local level, rendering them nonscalable. Still, many of those elements manage to retain their identity as global health objects despite their varying ways of being established by each specific local context. Similarly, elements of everyday life with microbes in these contexts, such as the use of natural medicines or collective modes of diagnosis, cannot be harmonised with global health policymaking and Western modes of knowledge production. My fieldwork shows that microbes emerge differently together with the diverse scales that global assemblages produce. The scalability or nonscalability of different elements plays an important role in the regulation and coexistence of humans and microbes. Based on examples in which humans, animals and microbes materially coexist, similar to 'living with malaria' (Beisel and Boëte 2013: 126), there is a need to live within human-microbial entanglements. These entanglements inevitably involve the dynamics of resistance often mediated by non-human animals, the environment, and medical, scientific and governmental tools. Thus, in a way, within the contexts examined here, there is a need to *live with resistance*. The specific shapes that coexistence takes are mediated by practices allowed by the infrastructure.

The lack of resources necessary to produce systematic knowledge that allows local communities to understand their microbial neighbours from a microbiological perspective pushes care practices towards relational modes of knowing that are often not compatible with the regulatory modes offered by global health initiatives. Similarly, the immediacy of the economic risks entailed by disease represents a crucial factor that keeps small breeders from developing practices to avoid situations where AMR may kill up to ten million people annually by 2050 (O'Neill 2016). While economic security remains an unattainable asset at present, it is hard to put that security on hold for the sake of a distant future which is unknown to many stakeholders. Living with resistance is an ironic correlate to living without data, data that could potentially provide evidence of resistance as a genuine phenomenon. From a global health policy perspective, living with resistance seems to represent a corollary of *living without* combinations: living without surveillance, living without laboratories, living without confirmation, living without resources. Given this perspective, I propose that living with resistance is also the result of living with global policy that fails to consider local relationalities, rendering AMR policy nonscalable.

NOTES

1 IHR is a legally binding framework aimed at regulating health internationally, involving WHO members. This ambitious venture began with its publication in 2005 yet continues to struggle with implementation (Burci and Quirin 2018).

2 While human and animal treatments of bacterial infections involve obvious differences, here I present examples from both, since achieving a diagnosis is similarly difficult in both humans and animals. Furthermore, this agrees with the more-than-human concerns (Whatmore 2006) underpinning this chapter and the entire volume.

3 Efforts exist aimed at developing rapid tests for bacterial infections (Narang et al. 2018), which have been found to occasionally decrease the unnecessary use of antibiotics (Do et al. 2016). But they are far from ubiquitous and none of the informants discussed them.

ACKNOWLEDGEMENTS

I would like to thank my anonymous informants in Benin and Burkina Faso for their time and guidance, all of the attendees to the Kilpisjärvi workshop for their insightful comments, the Kone Foundation and the Academy of Finland for their financial support of this project, and Vanessa Fuller (Language Services at the University of Helsinki) for assistance with the language revision of this manuscript.

REFERENCES

Anderson, W., 'Making Global Health History: The Postcolonial Worldliness of Biomedicine', *Social History of Medicine*, 27.2 (2014), 372–84.

Beisel, U., and C. Boëte, 'The Flying Public Health Tool: Genetically Modified Mosquitoes and Malaria Control', *Science as Culture*, 22.1 (2013), 38–60.

Beisel, U., 'Resistant Bodies, Malaria and the Question of Immunity', in C. Herrick and D. Reubi, eds, *Global Health and Geographical Imaginaries* (London: Routledge, 2017), pp. 114–34.

Biehl, J., 'Theorizing Global Health', *Medicine Anthropology Theory*, 3.2 (2016), 127–42.

Burci, G. L., and J. Quirin, 'Implementation of the International Health Regulations (2005): Recent Developments at the World Health Organization | ASIL', *ASIL Insights*, 22.13 (2018) <https://www.asil.org/insights/volume/22/issue/13/implementation-international-health-regulations-2005-recent-developments> [accessed 15 October 2020].

Cañada, J. A., 'Hybrid Threats and Preparedness Strategies: The Reconceptualization of Biological Threats and Boundaries in Global Health Emergencies', *Sociological Research Online*, 24.1 (2019), 93–110.

Deleuze, G., and F. Guattari, *Mil Mesetas: Capitalismo y Esquizofrenia* (Valencia: Pre-textos, 2006).

Denyer Willis, L., and C. Chandler, 'Quick Fix for Care, Productivity, Hygiene and Inequality: Reframing the Entrenched Problem of Antibiotic Overuse', *BMJ Case Reports*, 4.4 (2019), 1–6.

Do, N. T. T., and others, 'Point-of-Care C-Reactive Protein Testing to Reduce Inappropriate Use of Antibiotics for Non-Severe Acute Respiratory Infections in Vietnamese Primary Health Care: A Randomised Controlled Trial', *The Lancet Global Health*, 4.9 (2016), e633–41. <https://www.thelancet.com/journals/langlo/article/PIIS2214-109X(16)30142-5/fulltext> [accessed 8 December 2020].

Hinchliffe, S., 'More Than One World, More Than One Health: Re-Configuring Interspecies Health', *Social Science & Medicine*, 129 (2015), 28–35.

Kamenshchikova, A., and others, 'Anthropocentric Framings of One Health: An Analysis of International Antimicrobial Resistance Policy Documents', *Critical Public Health*, (2019) <https://doi.org/10.1080/09581596.2019.1684442> [accessed 15 October 2020].

Lorimer, J., 'Probiotic Environmentalities: Rewilding with Wolves and Worms', *Theory, Culture and Society*, 34.4 (2017), 27–48.

Louis, G. E., N. Nazemi, and S. Remer, 'Innovation for Development: Africa', in C. C. Mavhunga, ed., *What Do Science, Technology, and Innovation Mean from Africa?* (Cambridge, MA: MIT Press, 2017), pp. 151–67.

Narang, R., and others, 'Sensitive, Real-Time and Non-Intrusive Detection of Concentration and Growth of Pathogenic Bacteria Using Microfluidic-Microwave Ring Resonator Biosensor', *Scientific Reports*, 8.1 (2018), 1–10.

O'Neill, J., 'Tackling Drug-Resistant Infections Globally: Final Report and Recommendations', (Review on Antimicrobial Resistance, 2016) <https://amr-review.org/sites/default/files/160525_Final%20paper_with%20cover.pdf> [accessed 15 October 2020].

Pearson, M., and C. Chandler, 'Knowing Antimicrobial Resistance in Practice: A Multi-Country Qualitative Study with Human and Animal Healthcare Professionals', *Global Health Action*, 12.1 (2019), 1–9.

Pradeu, T., *The Limits of the Self: Immunology and Biological Identity* (Oxford: Oxford University Press, 2012).

Prestinaci, F., P. Pezzotti, and A. Pantosti, 'Antimicrobial Resistance: A Global Multifaceted Phenomenon', *Pathogens and Global Health*, 109.7 (2015), 309–18.

Strathern, M., *Partial Connections* (Walnut Creek: Altamira Press, 2004).

Taylor, N. G. H., D. W. Verner-Jeffreys, and C. Baker-Austin, 'Aquatic Systems: Maintaining, Mixing and Mobilising Antimicrobial Resistance?', *Trends in Ecology & Evolution*, 26.6 (2011), 278–84.

Tsing, A. L., 'On Nonscalability: The Living World Is Not Amenable to Precision-Nested Scales', *Common Knowledge*, 18.3 (2012), 505–24.

—— *Friction: An Ethnography of Global Connection* (Princeton: Princeton University Press, 2005).

Whatmore, S., 'Materialist Returns: Practising Cultural Geography in and for a More-than-Human World', *Cultural Geographies*, 13.4 (2006), 600–9.

World Health Organization, *Global Action Plan on Antimicrobial Resistance* (Geneva: World Health Organization, 2015) <https://www.who.int/antimicrobial-resistance/global-action-plan/en/> [accessed 15 October 2020].

—— *WHO Guidelines on Use of Medically Important Antimicrobials in Food-Producing Animal* (Geneva: World Health Organization, 2017) <https://www.who.int/foodsafety/areas_work/antimicrobial-resistance/cia_guidelines/en/> [accessed 15 October 2020].

Youdell, D., and I. McGimpsey, 'Assembling, Disassembling and Reassembling "Youth Services" in Austerity Britain', *Critical Studies in Education*, 56.1 (2015), 116–30.

8

ONTOLOGIES OF RESISTANCE: BACTERIA SURVEILLANCE AND THE CO-PRODUCTION OF ANTIMICROBIAL RESISTANCE

Nicolas Fortané

THE OVERUSE AND MISUSE OF ANTIBIOTICS IN HUMAN MEDICINE AND IN agriculture are key factors behind the development of resistant bacteria that generate infections which are increasingly difficult or even impossible to cure (O'Neill 2016). In the farming sector, although some half-hearted measures were introduced in the 1970s, it was only at the end of the twentieth century that ambitious regulations began to be implemented in order to better control the use of antibiotics in livestock, particularly the 2006 European ban on antibiotics as growth promoters (Kirchhelle 2020).

These public policies are also important for having introduced a series of lesser-known measures, namely surveillance systems for monitoring resistant bacteria in livestock farms and slaughterhouses, along with other devices for monitoring the sale of antibiotics in veterinary medicine. Most European countries have created such surveillance and monitoring systems, which are regularly updated to more effectively track the evolution of antimicrobial resistance (AMR) and to provide a basis for public policy in this area. However, many outstanding issues related to the functioning of these systems remain. They range from the type of data produced and the methodologies used by these systems to how AMR is defined, and the kind of human-microbe relationships involved.

In recent years, numerous studies have explored the history of epidemiological surveillance. They have shown how the globalisation of these surveillance systems is linked to the profound changes in risk management and assessment policies that took place at the turn of the twenty-first century. From a biosecurity standpoint (Lakoff and Collier 2008), the deployment of surveillance networks was linked to the emergence of new actors, knowledge and techniques that helped to reframe numerous public health issues. Although the roots of this dynamic could be traced back to the post-World War II period and the development of epidemic intelligence (Fearnley 2010), the logic of preparedness that was imposed from the late twentieth century onwards considerably reshaped global health policies and the way surveillance systems operate (Lakoff 2010). While this chapter draws from these studies, it also aims to give them a fresh perspective.

The rise of epidemiological surveillance in response to biosecurity concerns was less a rupture than an adjustment of existing systems, particularly with regard to risks involving animals. Major institutional reforms involving both national and international governance of public health certainly took place in the late 1990s. However, what I would like to highlight here is that there was no massive shift or change in the design of policy instruments. Instead, there was a gradual rearrangement of pre-existing infrastructures and a reorientation of the activities taking place within them. Biosecurity concerns relating to animal surveillance were tacked on to systems initially created for other purposes, such as academic research, the technical management of agricultural or veterinary practices, or the conservation of biodiversity (Fortané and Keck 2015). Surveillance thus relates not only to practices of control but also to practices of care (Manceron 2013).

Second, and consequently, to understand how different activities coordinate or compete within surveillance systems, we also need to understand them 'from the bottom up', i.e. through the everyday practices that help to structure surveillance systems and bind together all of the actors (humans and non-humans) involved in their operation. In short, we must examine not only the knowledge and policy instruments that built these surveillance systems but also the practical activities and the 'disciplinary borderlands' (Enticott 2017) that ensure the ordinary fabric of the phenomenon that they are meant to monitor and govern (Fortané and Keck 2015). In this chapter, I therefore intend to demonstrate how the surveillance of AMR relies on an assemblage of various forms of practices related to animal health, from animal care performed by vets and farmers to biological research and epidemiological surveys performed by scientists.

To examine the material conditions behind the production of monitored and governed objects more closely, we may look at certain recent works which extend this pragmatic perspective via the 'ontological turn' in the anthropology of science and/or medicine (Woolgar and Lezaun 2013). These works highlight the different stages in the construction of an object of knowledge, such as the wolf population (Doré 2013) or foot-and-mouth disease (Law and Mol 2011), which, through these successive operations, also becomes an object of policy, i.e. a governable object (although this governability may in part remain uncertain). To consider these different approaches, I use the notion of apparatus to refer to the surveillance system studied here. In effect, such an apparatus works as an 'interessement device' (Callon 1986) which allows the assemblage of different forms of practice and therefore engagement; both humans (veterinarians, microbiologists, and epidemiologists) and non-humans (animals, microbes, and antibiotics), contribute to the production of AMR. AMR thus acts as a 'boundary-object' (Star and Griesemer 1989) that is able to bring together the multiple actors, tools and modes of knowing which are enacting the apparatus and providing the material conditions of existence of this boundary-object. These enactments through which the surveillance system exists, and AMR is somehow brought to life, are precisely what this chapter aims to analyse, as they refer to the relationships that bind together humans, animals and microbes.

However, as said above, the practices and forms of engagement through which the apparatus is enacted can be quite various. Veterinarians, biologists and epidemiologists do not have the same relationships with animals and microbes. The surveillance system can thus produce different versions of AMR, or what I will call here 'ontological referents' (Doré 2013). Even more importantly, the surveillance system can only work and reach its final objectives because several ontological referents are being produced, as a consequence of the variety of practices and engagements that are assembled in the diverse activities that make the system work (data collection, analysis, etc.). In the case that is presented here, I will show that the population of resistant bacteria that epidemiologists are trying to measure and construct as a 'governable' object is not the only form of AMR that is enacted. Veterinarians and microbiologists, whose engagement is likewise vital to the operation of the system, also produce their 'own' resistant bacteria, for their own purposes. Surveillance thus consists in an arrangement of different spatialities, materialities and subjectivities (Enticott and Ward 2020) which allows the coexistence of several forms of relationship between humans, animals and microbes. However, the triple ontology of AMR that is enacted through the surveillance system (i.e. the three ontological referents that are produced by three types of engagement with microbes – those of microbiologists, epidemiologists, and veterinary practitioners) also engenders areas of uncertainty that limit the governability of resistant bacteria.

This chapter proposes an analysis of the history and functioning of Résapath,[1] one of the apparatuses for monitoring resistant bacteria of animal origin. Designed to trace and control the flows of microbes and antibiotics within diverse animal populations, Résapath is France's main AMR surveillance system. Its operation is based on the combination of several different tools and areas of knowledge, and in particular veterinary medicine, epidemiology and microbiology, which make it possible to collect bacteria and measure their levels of resistance to antibiotics. Résapath is organised like any other surveillance system in animal health. Veterinarians collect data during their routine animal care activities. For example, while on a farm visit or when a farmer calls them because an animal has fallen sick, veterinarians take biological samples to perform the tests required in the case of a bacterial infection (i.e. bacteria isolation and/or antibiotic susceptibility testing, also called 'antibiograms' – see the section 'How does a surveillance system work'? in this chapter). These tests are processed by local laboratories which may either belong to the veterinary practice or be a private or public laboratory located relatively close to the farm. The results of these tests are sent both to the veterinarians, so that they can return to the farm and cure the sick animals, and to national veterinary epidemiology and microbiology units (usually belonging to expert bodies like food safety agencies). These units aggregate all of the data collected on the national territory and perform an in-depth analysis in order to monitor the global state of AMR (i.e. which resistances are increasing, which ones are decreasing, etc.). This analysis is then published in the expert agency's annual reports and will inform the decisions of the national veterinary services (which are usually a part of a country's Ministry of Agriculture) regarding which management strategies should be implemented to control the spread of AMR (e.g. a ban on or restriction of certain antimicrobials). The chart below (see Figure 8.1), which was adapted from the Manual of Livestock Disease Surveillance and Information Systems (FAO 1999), represents the functioning of surveillance systems in animal health.

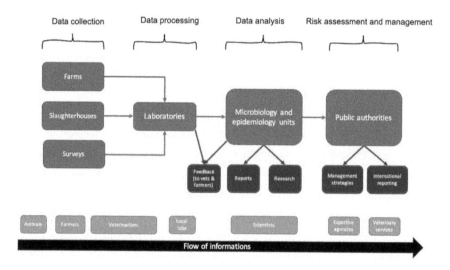

FIG. 8.1 Surveillance systems in animal health

Résapath is a network of member laboratories, distributed across France, which participate in the surveillance system and follow the corresponding protocols. It is coordinated by two national veterinary laboratories that are part of the French Food Safety Agency (ANSES), which oversees the epidemiology and microbiology units analysing the tests performed by labs on the samples submitted by local vets. One is based in Lyon and the other in Ploufragan (Brittany).

Over the past 15 years, Résapath has grown considerably, with roughly 20 new labs joining the network and the number of antibiograms collected multiplying fivefold. In 2018, Résapath was composed of 71 local laboratories, mainly concentrated in the western area of France, and the network collected more than 55,000 results from antibiograms.

This chapter is based on two types of empirical material. First, I performed eight interviews with experts from the French Research Institute for Agriculture (INRA) and from the ANSES units in charge of Résapath, along with a dozen interviews with veterinarians who participate in the collection of the surveillance data. These interviews made it possible to understand the variety of practices relating to the surveillance activity. Second, we used a corpus of grey (activity reports, technical recommendations, annual reports) and scientific (veterinary epidemiology and microbiology articles, and transfer publications) literature produced by these actors, which allowed us to trace the evolution in the knowledge and techniques employed within Résapath since its creation, and even a few years prior to that. The chapter is divided into three parts and explores the role of microbiologists, epidemiologists and veterinarians in the surveillance of AMR, showing how their different engagements with bacteria tend to co-produce different ontologies of resistance.

RESISTANT BACTERIA: A JOB FOR MICROBIOLOGISTS (THE 1970S AND 1980S)

Making AMR an object of research

The first people to study resistant bacteria of animal origin were veterinary microbiologists. However, although during the 1970s antibiotics were of interest to animal health researchers, the question of AMR was not yet a subject in its own right and continued to be split into different themes. Pathologists were interested in therapy, biologists were studying the effects of antibiotics as food additives, while pharmacologists were working on maximum residue limits.

These areas of research finally discovered a point in common, AMR, thanks to a handful of microbiologists who decided to examine this phenomenon.

The researchers (Elisabeth Chaslus-Dancla, Jean-Pierre Lafont, and Jean-François Guillot) who were to bring this subject into the academic arena of veterinary microbiology shared the particularity of having received their training in places central to 1970s French microbiology, namely the team run by Professor Chabbert of the Pasteur Institute, and that of Professors Raibaud and Ducluzeau at INRA. The former was precisely where research into resistant bacteria was mainly to develop in France, although in relation to human medicine. The latter team was better known for specialising in the concept of 'microbial ecology' and for the techniques it was to develop throughout the 1970s, which would become an extremely important tool for AMR specialists.

The veterinary microbiologists set themselves up in a laboratory at INRA's experimental station in Nouzilly, in the Loire valley. This station had a decisive feature that was to make it one of the essential nodes of the future surveillance system: Nouzilly owned an experimental chicken farm. This allowed the researchers to work on animal models that were not exclusively used to study human health issues (such as rats and mice) but which also (or even mainly) oriented studies towards animal health problems.

> The team at Jouy was like Mecca, or the Vatican if you prefer, they were original thinkers, theorists on mice and rats. They worked on mammals, targeting humans, in Microbial Ecology. And at Nouzilly, we were closer to livestock. And chickens, they had the advantage of being both lab animals and livestock (INRA microbiologist).

However, having access to both laboratory animals and livestock was not the only key element. It was also because they were able to link this material to both the emerging theme of AMR (glimpsed during their time at the Pasteur Institute) and the microbial ecology techniques learned at INRA, that the Nouzilly veterinary microbiologists were gradually able to make resistant bacteria of animal origin a totally legitimate object of research, around and through which would be built an apparatus that would enrol a multitude of actors (human and non-human) into the ontological work of producing AMR. In the microbiology lab, humans and microbes interact in a specific way that makes this work possible. First of all, AMR was already a subject of academic research that was starting to flourish due to the development of molecular biology, which made it possible to study resistance genes. Second, the techniques of so-called 'germ-free' models, imported to France and developed by Raibaud and Ducluzeau, allowed them to work on fully sterilised laboratory animals. By inoculating these animals with bacteria that had predetermined characteristics (like resistance to antibiotics), humans were able to observe how microbes behave in contact with a change in their environment (e.g. after the introduction of an antibiotic molecule) without the experiment being flawed by any pre-existing and uncontrolled flora.

The creation of a bacteria 'supply-chain'

At the beginning of the 1980s, the work carried out by the Nouzilly researchers was able to progress thanks to the creation of a socio-technical apparatus that enabled them to bring materials to their work bench. Microbiologists needed to regularly acquire bacterial strains with profiles (in this case, resistance) that were useful from an academic standpoint. Although there was little competition from their colleagues at the Pasteur Institute, who were not interested in bacteria of animal origin, the veterinary microbiologists needed their culture collection to be regularly renewed in order to ensure a certain frequency of publication. This was even more important given that at that time, their analytical techniques did not allow them to study the heart of the genome of resistant bacteria, which meant that they almost always needed a new strain in order to document a new resistance mechanism.

In 1982, Jean-Louis Martel, a veterinarian from the national veterinary laboratory in Lyon, created Résabo.[2] This was a network of local veterinary laboratories collecting samples from field veterinarians. Initially, this network was anything but a surveillance system. In fact, it included less than a dozen laboratories, which sent poorly standardised results to the central laboratory in Lyon. Martel then requested that bacterial strains presenting an atypical resistance profile be sent to him so that he could study them in greater detail. Consequently, while the stated objective of Résabo was to produce data needed to measure the evolution of AMR in cows, its configuration made it no more than a network for circulating and supplying a limited number of bacterial strains for the purpose of microbiological research, and not of epidemiological surveillance.

As Martel's laboratory did not really possess the skills and tools to carry out in-depth work on AMR, he began to collaborate with the Nouzilly team, sending them the most promising strains so that they could conduct a micro-biological analysis of the resistance mechanisms. Starting from the 1980s, Martel was thus regularly associated with the publications made by INRA researchers. A division of scientific labour was then created, thus helping to structure the device, which at that time was organised through the link between Lyon and Nouzilly.

> And for example, something that I did with Gérard [a PhD student in the mid-1980s] and that everyone now accepts, was to do with neonatal diar-rhoea. [...] I said it had to be the cow that carried it, but we had to prove it and we managed to do that via the initial resistances to quinolones, I remember a herd of cows that was monitored by a good practitioner and which had cases of diarrhoea. He was able to take samples from the mothers and the calves and sent the samples to Martel, who isolated the strains, so we had traceability that proved it (INRA microbiologist).

TWO IRREDUCIBLE FORMS OF KNOWLEDGE? (THE 1990S AND 2000S)

The academicisation of microbiology

From the mid-1990s onwards, the operation of Résabo changed due to several dynamics that had an important impact on human-microbe relationships and therefore on the ontological co-production of AMR. First of all, the

Nouzilly team experienced a process of 'academicisation' of their research, which meant their work was increasingly framed by the standards of high-level international science rather than by those of more applied research, which until then had been more typical of the work conducted at INRA (Tétart and Torny 2009).

The microbiologists' engagement with animals and bacteria changed when a new researcher joined the team. He had already been working at Nouzilly's experimental station but with a different team that was studying brucellosis, a zoonotic disease mainly found in cows and sheep. He was a microbiologist but not a veterinarian, a profile that prefigured the forthcoming recomposition of the team's members. This researcher, who was to be put in charge of the laboratory a few years later, brought with him a new way of working that was far more oriented towards basic research (in particular, he used experimental mice models and introduced techniques taken from genetics). The team was gradually reorganised around works that were far more oriented towards high-level publications. Fewer bacteria were studied, but the research went much further in the genetic characterisation of resistance mechanisms.

This modification to the microbiologists' engagement with resistant bacteria was also due to a change in their 'supply-chain'. The new researcher had access to devices other than Résabo, enabling him to obtain more specific bacterial strains. In particular, he re-established the historical links with the Pasteur Institute and instigated collaborations with international teams. It was through these channels that he obtained a particular strain of salmonella (Salmonella DT104, known as 'Kentucky') which allowed the Nouzilly team to highlight a resistance mechanism that had enormous success in terms of scientific publication. From then on, the work of the Nouzilly microbiologists was organised almost exclusively around this singular mechanism (SGI1: Salmonella Genomic Island 1), thus strengthening the central position of these researchers within the surveillance system. The strictly academic engagement of the microbiologists within the apparatus helped produce a specific ontological referent for resistant bacteria, namely a *bacterium-strain* which was perceived individually and from a molecular and genetic perspective.

I identified a gene resistant to Florfenicol among the salmonellas. But when we looked a little bit around the genetic environment of this gene, we realised that it was an entire genomic island that carried other resistance genes. We ended up calling it SGI1 for Salmonella Genomic Island One. [...] So, when we realised how important this was, it completely restructured the overall thematic of the research team, because it became the main study model, because we realised that it was a very good model for studying the propagation of antibiotic resistance genes (INRA microbiologist).

A short time after these developments at INRA, a second 'historic' member of Résabo also went through a form of academicisation in the early 2000s. When Martel retired in 2003, he was replaced by another veterinary microbiologist, albeit with a relatively different profile. The new director of the Lyon Bacteriology unit, who had previously cut his teeth with BSE,[3] wished to raise the academic level of the team and change its role within the surveillance system. The stated objective was to no longer be a mere channel for supplying bacterial strains to INRA researchers.

Jean-Louis Martel recovered the veterinarian bacterial strains and sent them to INRA. It wasn't a real partnership. It was a sort of a deal, a tandem that worked well like that. So Jean-Louis Martel was mentioned on INRA publications, never last, always somewhere in the middle. But he hadn't really developed the same competency in his own laboratory. That's what was missing (Microbiologist from ANSES-Lyon).

Such a change in the engagement of the Lyon microbiologists obviously took time (necessitating the appropriation of molecular biology knowledge and techniques, acquisition of material, targeted recruitments, etc.), but this academicisation was gradually achieved. While the Lyon-Nouzilly duo still constituted the heart of the apparatus, their relationship, the ensuing division of work, and above all the forms of engagement of its actors (human and non-human) underwent profound changes.

The emergence of the epidemiologists

The repositioning of the Lyon laboratory within the surveillance system was not solely due to this academicisation of the microbiology team. Résabo was significantly restructured between the late 1990s and the early 2000s under the impetus of the first French AMR policies.

First, Résabo merged with Onerba in 1997,[4] thereby becoming part of a vast AMR surveillance system that had until then been exclusively comprised of networks dedicated to bacteria of human origin. This had a major impact on how it operated. The main challenge was the harmonisation of the ways in which data were produced, which was needed to ensure greater reliability. A standardisation process of data collection and processing was therefore carried out when Résabo joined Onerba, including the following: a charter of engagement and 'good practices' certification required for all local laboratories; a single data coding system; and regular training sessions. Moreover, the integration of the Lyon laboratory, along with all other national veterinary laboratories, into the new French food safety agency in the early 1990s also strengthened the work done to standardise the various epidemiological animal health surveillance networks, including Résabo (Dufour 1993). In 2001, Résabo became Résapath and was no longer limited to bacteria of bovine origin but could also collect and produce data from bacteria of porcine and avian origins. To this end, new local laboratories were gradually integrated and a second national veterinary laboratory (Ploufragan), specialising in the pig and poultry sectors, participated in the running of the network.

This restructuring had serious consequences for the forms of engagement within the apparatus. In particular, a new category of human actors emerged at this time: epidemiologists. These researchers quickly made AMR one of their preferred subjects and became highly engaged in the operation of Résapath. Since the emergence of the epidemiologists and the profound restructuring of the apparatus, the surveillance activity was at last able to develop. The epidemiologists' engagement took forms that differed from those of the microbiologists and, above all, led to the production of another ontology of resistant bacteria. Alongside the *bacterium-strain* (enacted through an academic form of engagement), henceforth the apparatus also produced a *bacterium-population* (enacted through a surveillance form of engagement).

Although epidemiologists also engage in scientific research, their main aim is to produce a form of expertise that makes it possible to govern AMR. Therefore, unlike the microbiologists, they are not interested in bacteria as individuals, and even less in bacterial genetic and molecular mechanisms. They do not even have a lab where they can physically interact with bacteria or animals. They actually look at bacteria as a population and only need aggregated statistical data allowing them to trace changes within this population. Consequently, microbiologists and epidemiologists do not consider AMR in the same way. The former define a 'breakpoint', which is the threshold from which an antibiotic ceases to be effective on a given bacteria; the latter define a 'cut-off' which is the average point from which a population of bacteria ceases to be 'wild', i.e. it acquires some resistant genes, whether or not it is still susceptible to an antibiotic.

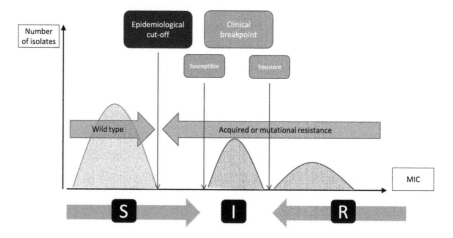

FIG. 8.2 Clinical breakpoints and epidemiological cut-off (reproduced from Tascini et al. 2016). This diagram shows the difference between the epidemiological cut-off (Ecoff) and the susceptibility (S) and resistance (R) breakpoints. Grey figures represent the microbiological conception of AMR: clinical breakpoints indicate likelihood of therapeutic success (S - susceptible) or failure (R – resistant) of an antimicrobial treatment against a given bacterial infection (I being the intermediary zone). Blue figures represent the epidemiological conception of AMR: Ecoff values separate microbes without (wild type) and with resistance. Figures are expressed in MIC which indicate the lowest concentration of a chemical (here an antibiotic) which prevents visible growth of bacteria. MIC is often expressed in milligrams per liter (mg/L).

HOW DOES A SURVEILLANCE SYSTEM WORK?

Back to the roots: How vets, animals, and microbes co-produce data

The work of microbiologists and epidemiologists, and the ontological referents of AMR which they produce, could never exist without some sort of an original engagement, i.e. an upstream sorting process that constitutes the basic material conditions of the surveillance system's operation. Only the bacteria that Résapath has previously managed to 'capture' are likely to reach the microbiologists and epidemiologists. This first enrolment of non-human actors into the device is dependent upon another form of engagement and relationship with animals and microbes, namely that of veterinary practitioners who take the bacterial samples in order to produce the 'antibiograms' that the other two categories of actors need to obtain the data they require.

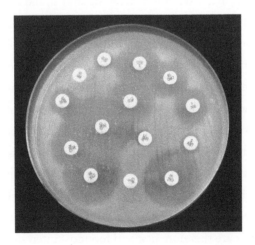

FIG. 8.3 An antibiogram (iStock, ref: 47080398). The antibiogram is the technical tool that makes it possible to characterise a bacterium's antibiotic resistance profile. It consists of a petri dish that has been colonised by a bacterium. Using the sample that a veterinarian has taken from an animal, the lab staff isolate the bacterium (from the other cells and/or molecules present) and let it colonise the petri dish (generally no longer than 24 hours in an optimal environment). The actual antibiogram is then performed. A series of discs (the white dots shown in the picture) loaded with antibiotics are placed in the dish and one can observe how the bacterial colony reacts to each antibiotic: a large 'inhibition diameter' means that the bacteria is fully susceptible to a given antibiotic; an absence of diameter means that the bacteria is resistant since the antibiotic has no effect on its development.

Résapath is a so-called 'passive' surveillance network, meaning its existence is not subject to any regulatory obligation, and consequently its data are essentially produced through the routine activity of its field actors (Dufour and Hendrikx 2011). The way that veterinarians work with animals and microbes, and in particular the way in which they use (or not) antibiograms, is thus essential to Résapath's operation. The results of the antibiograms are the apparatus' base data which can then be used by the microbiologists, epidemiologists and even veterinarians according to their own specific objectives.

When a veterinarian takes a sample from a sick animal to determine the nature of the animal's illness, he/she sends the sample to a local laboratory. The laboratory performs an antibiogram analysis to characterise the type of bacterium causing the infection and, at the same time, to determine its level of resistance to a certain number of antibiotic molecules. The laboratory returns the results to the veterinarian, who then decides how to treat the animal, and a copy of the results is sent to one of the two national laboratories running Résapath (assuming, of course, that the local laboratory in question is a member of the surveillance network). These national laboratories then do two things: the epidemiologists combine all of the collected data to calculate the global evolution in resistance levels for each bacterium(-population) in relation to each antibiotic, and the microbiologists may request that the bacterium(-strain) be sent to them if they believe its resistance profile is of interest. However, the possible existence of these two ontological referents is in fact dependent on the engagement of the veterinary practitioners without whom the system itself would not exist.

Veterinary medicine is above all a clinical activity, designed to care for animals. Veterinarians are therefore first and foremost interested in sick animals and, consequently, their pathogenic (rather than commensal) bacteria. The veterinarian's ontological referent is thus a *bacterium-disease* (derived from a clinical form of engagement), which is significantly different from the microbiologist's *bacterium-strain* (and academic form of engagement) or the epidemiologist's *bacterium-population* (and surveillance form of engagement), which do not necessarily need to be pathogenic for their AMR profile to be of interest. There is therefore a selection process within Résapath's operation which takes place through this primary engagement with microbes and animals; the only bacteria that can be captured are those that present a clinical interest for veterinarians. Indeed, veterinary practitioners only perform antibiograms when they are unable to treat sick animals, i.e. when they are in a situation of therapeutic failure. There is no sense in their using this relatively onerous and expensive protocol for infections which they can easily treat. Yet in fact, therapeutic failure usually means the failure of one or more antibiotic treatments. This means that the sick animals from which veterinarians take samples have already been treated with antibiotics and, therefore, a selection effect for the most resistant bacteria (those that resist the treatment) has already taken place before any enrolment of microbes into the apparatus.

Moreover, this selection effect relating to the clinical engagement of veterinarians with animals and microbes comes on top of the fact that veterinarians do not ask for an antibiogram every time they take a sample. Sometimes, veterinarians only want to obtain an 'isolation' from the laboratory, i.e. a characterisation of the bacterium implicated in the animal's disease but not its resistance profile. This happens for relatively common infections for which they know that resistant bacteria are rarely found. In such situations, no data is produced for Résapath.

> For a mastitis, [the veterinarians] can easily say: 'I want to give the right treatment but there's very little resistance with mastitis, I just want to know what germ it is, so I can use the right antibiotic. I don't need to do an antibiogram because mastitis germs are quite susceptible, but I want to know if it's a Coli or a Strepto or a Staph'. So they just ask for an isolation. And if there's no antibiogram, we don't collect anything (ANSES-Lyon epidemiologist).

The triple ontology of AMR: Complementarity and uncertainty

All in all, we can see the extent to which the clinical engagement of veterinarians is a determining factor of not only the knowledge but also the governability of resistant bacteria. Résapath is the socio-technical apparatus that gives life to the boundary-object of AMR by enrolling a wide range of actors which can enact it. However, this co-production of AMR is the result of heterogeneous forms of bonds and engagement between humans, animals and microbes that are both complementary and contradictory. There is an incommensurability between the ontological referents produced by the Résapath apparatus that can engender uncertainty in the governance of AMR.

HUMAN ACTORS	TYPE OF ENGAGEMENT	ONTOLOGICAL REFERENT
Microbiologists	Academic	Bacterium-strain
Epidemiologists	Surveillance	Bacterium-population
Veterinary practitioners	Clinical	Bacterium-disease

FIG. 8.4 The triple ontology of AMR enacted through Résapath

By assembling a range of human and non-human actors whose engagement is not based on the same objective (be it clinical, microbiological or epidemiological), the apparatus produces competing definitions of AMR which make it difficult to entirely fulfil any purpose. Although the development of Résapath has been a great provider of bacterial strains of interest for microbiologists for two decades, the stabilisation of the system (in terms of territorial extension, sampling practices, analytical tools, etc.) makes it less likely now to regularly capture original bacteria and renew the strain bank of microbiologists. Veterinary practitioners cannot fully rely on antibiograms as they are unable to predict with complete certainty the therapeutic effectiveness of antibiotics (Fortané 2015). Epidemiologists combine and model data whose statistical representativeness may be questioned (Botrel et al. 2006), as they remain dependent upon the decisions of veterinarians regarding whether or not to perform antibiograms (Bourély et al. 2018).

> So, we're talking about a sort of mixture, in fact it's written on the veterinary CA-SFM[5], at the top it's written 'the data are of an epidemiological nature', because we're really looking to see whether it's resistant or not resistant on the diameter distribution curves. Of course, we can't judge the clinical effectiveness for vets because we don't even know if it works or not, in other words at the end of the day whether the cow is alive or dead. We have no idea. So, we're in a clinical frame of reference but with epidemiological data.

(...) So, it's a little bit this ambiguity which means that the surveillance is nevertheless linked to a system which, initially, was to help the practitioner. So, it's an in-between thing (CA-SFM microbiologist).

As shown by this interview, the triple ontology of resistant bacteria engenders something that is 'in-between', which I relate to a form of ungovernability in the sense that none of the three human-microbe relationships can be entirely fulfilled. Governing microbes does not only refer here to AMR policy but principally to the assemblage of practices and engagements with microbes through which AMR is enacted. Even if these multiple enactments are (and need to be) partially combined since they rely on each other, several ontologies of resistant bacteria keep co-existing and producing some sort of 'in-between' governability of AMR where every human actor has to deal with a share of uncertainty. Because of the way Résapath works, neither veterinarians (who must adjust and control the antibiotic treatment of sick animals), microbiologists (who must set adequate therapeutic thresholds for each resistant strain), nor epidemiologists (who must monitor the status of the bacterial population) can fully rely on the knowledge that is crucial for the accomplishment of their objectives.

In the end, what do we know and govern about AMR? Is it the evolution of a bacteria population or the presence of resistant genes in a given environment? Is resistance the individual ability of a bacteria to definitely inactivate an antibiotic's effect, a genetic evolution that alters the susceptibility to an antibiotic until the pharmacological structure of this antibiotic can be adapted to this evolution (for example by increasing the MIC), or just a momentaneous feature of a bacterial population that may naturally disappear anyway if we reduce its exposure to antimicrobial compounds? It is probably a little bit of everything, and this is what makes AMR so complex and uncertain, and in some ways so controversial. Yet reducing the use of antibiotics in both human and veterinary medicine is undoubtedly an important goal for managing the risks posed by resistant bacteria. However, the relationships between humans, animals and microbes are certainly richer and more diverse than a surveillance system could ever capture, even though its operation and efficiency already rely on a combination of different epistemologies and ontologies.

CONCLUSION

From a small network of a dozen or so local veterinary laboratories in 1982 to a system that now comprises around 70 laboratories producing 55,000 anti-biograms a year (compared to between 10 and 20 times fewer 40 years ago), Résapath's socio-technical organisation has undergone significant changes. The surveillance of resistant bacteria of animal origin is now based on the interlink-ing of several different forms of engagement and relationship between humans, animals and microbes, and produces three ontological referents for resistance: the veterinarians who collect (and therefore select) the bacteria in accordance with their professional motivations (in particular that of caring for animals) are *clinically* engaged in the apparatus and co-produce a *bacterium-disease*; the microbiologists who are above all looking to get material onto their lab bench with new microbial strains are *academically* engaged in the apparatus and co-produce a *bacterium-strain*; and the epidemiologists who aim to model the evolution in bacterial resistances to antibiotics are engaged in the apparatus for *surveillance* purposes and co-produce a *bacterium-population*. All in all, surveil-lance arranges different spatialities, materialities and subjectivities in order to enact the (multiple) existence(s) of AMR.

Additional research would nevertheless be useful since in this chapter I have only examined one type of apparatus – that of an AMR passive surveillance system. Yet there are also active surveillance networks (such as salmonella moni-toring in slaughterhouses), systems for post-market authorisation surveillance (monitoring the side effects of pharmaceuticals) and for the monitoring of antibi-otic sales (data from the pharmaceutical industry), prescription (data from veteri-narians), and use (data from livestock farmers). It is likely that these apparatuses produce other ontological referents because they mobilise different instruments, knowledge and metrics, particularly those from the field of pharmacology, which has other ways of measuring and defining AMR, such as pharmacokinetic and pharmacodynamic models. Nor should we forget that resistance, while a property of bacteria, is first and foremost the result of interaction between the latter and antibiotic molecules in specific social, biological and ecological contexts (human and animal bodies or the environment, including farms, healthcare facilities and sewers). Yet all of these organisms are unstable: pharmaceutical companies regularly update the composition of their antibiotics in order to improve their effectiveness and safety (in particular by relying on data from all of these monitoring and surveillance systems); the food industry is continuously transforming animals' bodies (genetic selection); environments are constantly subject to pressure from phenomena such as climate change or the discharge of chemical substances into the water, air and soil. There is no doubt that several resistance ontologies exist, and if it seems so difficult to govern AMR, this is perhaps also due to the fact that AMR is so many different things at the same time.

NOTES

1 From the French: Réseau d'EpidémioSurveillance de l'Antibiorésistance des bactéries PATHogènes animales (epidemic surveillance of antibiotic resistance from pathogenic animal bacteria).
2 Network for the epidemio-surveillance of the antibiotic resistance of pathogenic bacteria of bovine origin.
3 Bovine spongiform encephalitis, commonly known as 'mad cow disease'.
4 National observatory for bacterial resistance to antibiotics.
5 Antibiogram committee of the French Society of Microbiology. This is the expert body that sets up and reviews antibiogram thresholds annually.

REFERENCES

Botrel, M.-A., and others, 'Le Résapath: analyse critique et propositions d'amélioration', *Epidémiologie et santé animale*, 50 (2006), 157–68.
Bourély, C., and others, 'Why Do Veterinarians Ask for Antimicrobial Susceptibility Testing?', *Preventive Veterinary Medicine*, 159.1 (2018), 123–34.
Callon, M., 'Éléments pour une sociologie de la traduction. La domestication des coquilles Saint-Jacques dans la Baie de Saint-Brieuc', *L'Année sociologique*, 36 (1986), 169–208.
Doré, A., 'L'exercice des biopolitiques. Conditions matérielles et ontologiques de la gestion gouvernementale d'une population animale', *Revue d'Anthropologie des Connaissances*, 7 (2013), 837–55.
Dufour, B., 'Naissance et développement de l'épidémiosurveillance animale en France', *Epidémiologie et santé animale*, 23 (1993), 83–100.

Dufour, B., and P. Hendrikx, *Surveillance épidémiologique en santé animale*, 3rd edn (Paris: Editions Quae, 2011).

Enticott, G., 'Navigating Veterinary Borderlands: "Heiferlumps", Epidemiological Boundaries and the Control of Animal Disease in New Zealand', *Transactions of the Institute of British Geographers*, 42.2 (2017), 153–65.

Enticott, G., and K. Ward, 'Mapping Careful Epidemiology: Spatialities, Materialities, and Subjectivities in the Management of Animal Disease', *The Geographical Journal*, 186.3 (2020), 276–87.

Food and Agriculture Organisation (FAO), *Manual of Livestock Disease Surveillance and Information Systems* (FAO, 1999).

Fearnley, L., 'Epidemic Intelligence. Langmuir and the Birth of Disease Surveillance', *Behemoth*, 3 (2011), 36–56.

Fortané, N., and K. Keck, 'How Biosecurity Reframes Animal Surveillance', *Revue d'Anthropologie des Connaissances*, 9.2 (2015), a–l.

Fortané, N., 'La triple ontologie des bactéries résistantes', *Revue d'Anthropologie des Connaissances*, 9.2 (2015), 265–90.

Kirchhelle, K., *Pyrrhic Progress: The History of Antibiotics in Anglo-American Food Production* (New Brunswick: Rutgers University Press, 2020).

Lakoff, A., and S. Collier, eds, *Biosecurity Interventions. Global Health and Security in Question* (New York: Columbia University Press, 2008).

Lakoff, A., 'Two Regimes of Global Health', *Humanity: An International Journal of Human Rights, Humanitarianism, and Development*, 1 (2010), 59–79.

Law, J., and A.-M. Mol, 'Veterinary Realities: What Is Foot and Mouth Disease?', *Sociologia Ruralis*, 51.1 (2010), 1–16.

Manceron, V., 'Recording and Monitoring: Between Two Forms of Surveillance', *Limn*, 3 (2013), 25–30.

O'Neill, J., 'Tackling Drug-Resistant Infections Globally: Final Report and Recommendations' (final report of the Review on AMR commission, London, UK, 2016).

Star, S., and J. Griesemer, 'Institutional Ecology, "Translations", and Boundary Objects: Amateurs and Professionals on Berkeley's Museum of Vertebrate Zoology', *Social Studies of Science*, 19.3 (1989), 387–420.

Tascini C, Sozio E, Viaggi B and Meini S, 'Reading and understanding an antibiogram', *Italian Journal of Medicine*, 10 (2016): 289–300.

Woolgar, S., and J. Lezaun, 'The Wrong Bin Bag: A Turn to Ontology in Science and Technology Studies?', *Social Studies of Science*, 43 (2013), 321–40.

III

IDENTIFYING

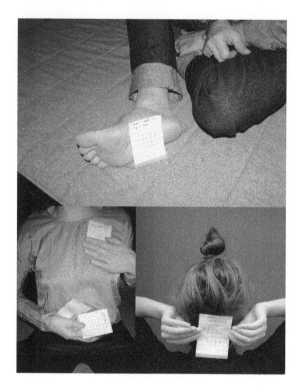

FIG. C: MICROBIAL BODY INTELLIGENCE. By turning matters of fact into matters of concern, as Bruno Latour has suggested, and then treating them as matters of care, after Maria Puig de la Bellacasa, the laboratory became a place of companioned and playful experiment. When samples had matured in the incubator, we launched a clairvoyant event to let each participant hear the outcome of their microbial culture. Turning laboratory activity and scientific predictions into magical readings of petrifilms and dipslides was to turn visualisations and representations that laboratory tools provide into something else. Instead of providing a clinical verdict, we caringly turned microbial companions of the body away from the medical gaze to give them an active and relational position: fostering community instead of objectifying other species. Speculating about microbial agency gave space for humans and microbes to create new assemblages or actor-networks. We saw the microbes emerging from the petrifilms but used intuition and magical readings to interpret what they were revealing to us. We did not explain microbes; they participated.

Prophecies with microbial samples required getting intimate during the Labracadabra performance: bodies were incited to rub against each other, using body parts according to the samples lifted from the 'microbial tarot deck' in order to make human-microbial communities enter into new assemblages in unpredictable ways, and at the same time break the ice between bodies. Labracadabra offered us human-holobionts to attune to our bodies and unsure/quiet/non-verbal knowledge/affects/feelings, where wisdom of the microbes may also reside (photograph by the Labracadabra team).

9

SCENES FROM THE MANY LIVES OF *ESCHERICHIA COLI*

A PLAY IN THREE ACTS

Mark Erickson, Catherine Will

CAN BACTERIA BE FAMOUS? IF THEY CAN, THEN WHICH ARE THE MOST famous, and why? In this paper we will put our candidate for the world's most famous bacterium onto the stage, literally, give it a voice – or a few voices – and show how *Escherichia coli* grew in importance.

We present a play showing *E. coli* on an odyssey of self-discovery, from a children's clinic in Bavaria to high-tech university labs, via hospitals, medical schools, wastewater treatment plants and government offices tasked with slowing antimicrobial resistance. Names are important and we'll see how naming this bacterium changes our relationship to it,[1] just as the disciplines and tools of those naming and making these microbes also shift.[2]

It is not easy to put words into the mouth of a microbe. We confronted the problem of bacteria as plural, and the question of generation. The *E. coli* made visible (in plural) in laboratories tend to end their lives soon after in the autoclave. Yet we use the singular to gesture to the ontological stakes,[3] even as we multiply coliform identities.[4] Across the decades, our hero has had a dizzying number of these, though many practices involve familiar actors such as Petri dishes, Falcon® and Durham tubes, agar, Bunsen burners, slides, and microscopes. Nonetheless, we suggest *E. coli* itself is unsettled – fixed and stained, but often misunderstood and ignored.

Joining a tradition of experimental writing in STS,[5] we take inspiration from classical Greek theatre, using a Chorus to represent laboratory assemblages forming and decomposing,[6] and its Leader to help navigate. Like the writers of this time we also invoke higher powers, Gods and Muses, to help us tell our tales.

PROLOGUE[7]

Thalia: Welcome to our performance, a joyous play in three acts. I am Thalia, the muse of blooming. My sister Clio, the muse of history, has helped me with some parts, and where would we be without our darling mama Mnemosyne, whose memory we rely upon?

We are brought together to tell you of a world of microbes; first, as many decades ago we find the wild one. As wild as Enkidu, who is older even than we Muses.[8] We tame it through naming it, first, *Bacillus coli commune* (*B. coli*), later *Escherichia coli*. Then bleak-hearted Melpomene scripts our play, as the blame for disease and illness is placed upon *E. coli*, who turns trickster, hiding and dissembling, only to be revealed as, perhaps, a hero after all. Meanwhile wise Athene guides the molecular biologists' hands as they grow, break and construct the innards of *E. coli*, revealing its secrets. But Melpomene drives the humans towards a tragic end as our microbes' resistance grows. Perhaps it is they who will bloom in the future, while those who have flourished, like all fragrant flowers which abound in the meadow,[9] will wither and die.

ACT 1

Act I, Scene I

LEADER OF THE CHORUS: We begin in the 1880s when the story goes that Theodor Escherich was studying microbes in stool samples. Before this, coliform bacteria were known and seen under the microscope, true, but the quest for understanding this particular companion species was just beginning.

THEODOR ESCHERICH MD: It's good to be in Munich, but here – as in Vienna – we lose too many infants to dysentery. We don't know what's responsible, but the microscope might help.

Cultures are grown on plates, then samples placed on slides on a long lab bench, ready to go under the microscope.

CHORUS: The party's assembled; ready for action – lab,
Esteemed doctor, microscope, slide.
Could shit samples reveal the cause of this illness?
Let's focus and find what our bodies might hide.

Escherich looks and listens carefully.

THEODOR ESCHERICH MD: I see distinctive shapes in many of my samples. Tiny organisms, short with rounded ends.

COLIFORM: *I am here.*

THEODOR ESCHERICH MD: Perhaps they are the source of the dysentery? I will call them *Bacteria coli commune* and continue my investigations.[10]

LEADER OF THE CHORUS: Meanwhile, in the 21st Century, molecular biologists revive and sequence Escherich's original bacilli samples, and get a surprise result.

MOLECULAR BIOLOGIST: Are you sure you've got the right culprit? We've brought molecular vision by sequencing genes using SMRT cells and the Pacific Biosciences RS II instrument in these historical samples. They originated in your lab alright, but they don't look to be pathogenic.[11]

B. COLI: *A false accusation, or a case of mistaken identity? Whatever the reason we're all suspect now.*

LEADER OF THE CHORUS: Escherich thinks he's found the culprit but perhaps it's not so clear. Some of the first to work with his samples focus on hygiene and sanitation. In the Lister Institute of Preventive Medicine, a young Harriette Chick starts what will become an illustrious career in nutrition, with laboratory work on the efficiency of different disinfectants against bacteria.

HARRIETTE CHICK (LATER DBE): They're dirty and dangerous and I'm going to kill them.[12]

B. COLI: *AAAAAAAARGGGGHHH!*

LEADER OF THE CHORUS: Her colleague Alfred MacConkey – later of agar and broth fame – is more interested in *B. coli* in water.[13] He does a series of experiments to explore ways of identifying it effectively and using it as a signal for faecal contamination.

B. COLI: *More slander, I assure you!*

LEADER OF THE CHORUS: But the accusation proves hard to escape. Around the time of the First World War, in a frenzy of nomenclature revisions across scientific communities, the genus *Escherichia* is named in honour of Theodor as part of the family *Enterobacteriaceae*.[14] Within this genus numerous strains – some pathogenic and some not – are given new names, including *Escherichia coli*, which will become the most famous of all.

Act 1, Scene 2

LEADER OF THE CHORUS: Alfred MacConkey experiments with media to create the perfect conditions for the bacteria to show themselves.

CHORUS: With broth and with lactose our friend *B.* blooms

Let's join together, say a prayer, make a wish!

Add bile salts and culture. Given time

Coli will appear in clear view on a dish.[15]

ALFRED MACCONKEY MD: Never mind Hariette's 'kill efficiency'. If we're going to test water samples for *B. coli* regularly, we need to grow these organisms. Just for a time, here in the lab, we want those bacteria to flourish like the roses in my garden. Fortunately, they do well at body temperature, and they don't need protection from oxygen, but I'll offer them lactose, saccharose, dulcit, adonit or inulin. I can show that *B. coli* likes to ferment sugar and that fact is useful…

> *Samples of 497 bacilli are meticulously isolated from 76 different substances including human and animal faeces, soil, pond and rain water, oats, beans and cheese, and are put onto plates. Bile salt media is used because of its inhibiting effect on other organisms. Once colonies appear, MacConkey adds lactose and watches for fermentation.*

B. COLI: *Busted! We like the lactose, though the bile salts are not so welcoming. But you've certainly found us out: our bacterial cousins can't grow so well here so we reveal our presence on the plates.*

ALFRED MACCONKEY MD: The problem is we keep identifying more types of lactose-fermenting enteric bacilli, and at the moment we're calling them all *B. coli*. Still, whatever they are, now we can culture them quickly we can go back to counting… what does our work tell us about the water from which the sample came? Ideally, we'd have some form of numerical interpretation of what we find,[16] perhaps by measuring the volume of gas produced in the fermentation.

CHORUS: Again, we're together. Broth, lactose, salts in a tube.

Wait once more. Watch. Hold your breath.

The doughty professor assembles his subjugated workers

But can dodgy *B. coli* really help confront death?

ALFRED MACCONKEY MD: *B. coli* might not be a friend, but it could yet be an ally in our war against dirty water if we assume it reflects the presence of other coliforms. Contamination by human faecal matter is our fear but also a practical problem. 'We all of us always wish to identify organisms as accurately as possible, in as short a time as possible, and with as little trouble as possible.'[17]

E. COLI: *Named, tamed and shamed! Established as the villain of the piece, my reputation can only improve as we create new forms of cooperation. But I'm happy to get a job. I'm here to help, believe me…*

LEADER OF THE CHORUS: MacConkey's 'practical' approach rapidly spreads, appearing in the very first edition of the textbook *American Sewerage Practice*, published by Leonard Metcalf and Harrison P Eddy in 1914/5, and still a touchstone in the field.

BACTERIOLOGISTS: Why should we let *E. coli* speak for all the coliforms? It is only 0.1% of the microbial flora,[18] and isn't even an anaerobe like most of the others.

E. COLI: *Because the standard guide to Wastewater Engineering tells you 'The presence of E. coli in drinking water is an indication that there is a greater risk that disease causing pathogens could also be present'.[19] In this field you respect traditions, and these stretch back decades. I can represent the bigger group, and with some amplification I do that pretty well. Look how safe the drinking water is, if you don't believe me.*

ACT 2

Act 2, Scene I

LEADER OF THE CHORUS: We've given you one history, here's another. From their earliest identification *B. coli* have been blamed for more than diarrhoea. And in the early 20th-century hospital the laboratory is growing in importance, meaning they play more of a role...[20]

CHORUS: Big hospital, small lab. With samples coming
All the time it's getting a bit tight.
Clinicians and technicians, they all join in the hunt
Examining slides late into the night.

B. COLI: *Why is it always my fault?*

LEADER OF THE CHORUS: Urine has been examined for centuries, but from the 1880s bedside pronouncements were enhanced by chemical testing using test papers and now 'piss pots' are travelling down to the lab for some bacteriology.[21]

CHORUS: Another glass jar viewed with suspicion.
Our microscopes are ready though so we'll
Plate piss – and culture – leave them to grow.
Tomorrow we're back for the great big reveal.

LEONARD S. DUDGEON, MRCP (LOND): But it is hard to interpret the results of these cultures, even working long hours and following careful procedures. What's the meaning of our frequent discovery of *B. coli*? 'Some pathologists go so far as to say that in the female this condition is of no importance; certainly there may be no associated symptoms of disease unless constipation is considered as such. At times, however, there will be headache, slackness, and general malaise'.[22]

B. COLI: *Slackness and general malaise sound a bit vague. What exactly is the accusation here?*

LEADER OF THE CHORUS: You're in the wrong place in short. But attention is focused on the female urinary tract, not sewers. Are you causing symptoms or are you somehow incidental?

Act 2, Scene 2

LEADER OF THE CHORUS: By 1957 doctors have antibiotics that can act effectively against *E. coli*. But the cultures are confusing, and they are still debating which results to act on.

EDWARD H KASS MD: Here in Boston, we test pretty much everyone who comes into hospital. But we keep finding bacteria. There's a considerable number of cases of what I call 'asymptomatic bacteriuria'. I propose we distinguish between severe and mild infection by counting the colonies on an agar dish. If you're comparing in this way you have to follow careful steps to do the culture, but numbers can be multiplied to give an estimate of bacteria per ml.[23] In my view, more than 1,000,000 per ml should be taken as evidence of infection. Less than 10,000 per ml should be taken as a sign of contamination or as clinically irrelevant.

CHORUS: For sure we're doing what we can to help here
More knowledge, more medics – the brightest and best –
The mid-century height of clinical hopes
With more counting we could have a new type of test.

LEADER OF THE CHORUS: With this approach, *E. coli* could be blamed for silent infections as well as those with symptoms.

Act 2, Scene 3

LEADER OF THE CHORUS: In family medicine too, examining urine samples remains a staple of practice.[24] By the 1950s, general practitioners have the 'dipstick' – combining test papers on a single card for glucose, white blood cells and nitrites or proteins without the fuss of sending samples off for culture.[25]

CHORUS: With antibiotics *E. coli*'s distressed, but bacteriologists are still in a mess. We'll need to gather all our wits and make some diagnostic kits.

Bacteria, samples, doctors, women,

Journals, dipsticks and – ampicillin.

> *A patient awkwardly hands over a small pot with yellow liquid, still warm. The doctor examines it visually, then puts in a card indicator for 1-2 seconds. He pulls it out and examines the coloured squares. Moving to purple and pink in the first indicates the presence of leukocytes, the body's response to infection, and nitrites which are reduced by E. coli. He pulls a prescription pad towards him and writes the name Penbritin.*[26]

E. COLI: *Now I'm seriously worried I'm a target. Your efforts to make and use antibiotics are pretty concerning. Just because you can see me does not mean I'm causing any trouble. You're just picking me out because it's easy. But should you really try to kill me off?*

LEADER OF THE CHORUS: Short answer is no. In the 1980s, doctors are still arguing. They can see colonisation without symptoms or white blood cells in some patients, but they also see symptoms that look or feel like urinary tract infections when their tests can't find bacteria.[27] Through these investigations – mainly from a clinical perspective – E. coli emerges as a tricky character.

Act 2, Scene 4

LEADER OF THE CHORUS: There is still debate about the right approach to treatment today, with fears of growing resistance in antibiotics.

SALLY DAVIES, CHIEF MEDICAL OFFICER OF HEALTH UK: Over-treatment with antibiotics represents a waste of antibiotics' declining efficacy. If *E. coli* is exposed to too many antibiotics it can learn to live with them and the drugs won't work! Antimicrobial resistance (we call it AMR) is a major threat to modern medicine.

LEADER OF THE CHORUS: Automation makes it possible to review larger numbers of samples more quickly and more cheaply. It might be more reliable, but it might not.

ADAM, DIRECTOR OF A HOSPITAL LAB: There's still lots of uncertainty. Numerous factors affect the results we get from urine samples coming into our lab after a positive dipstick result. Still we put them all through our system. Now when the counts look high, we do sensitivity tests with the MAST-URI system against different antibiotics. We notice up to 15% error in antibiotic quantity in the prepared discs we use, though the machines have got the depth of agar fairly consistent now. Is it MacConkey agar? No, I'm sure it's not, but I couldn't tell you what it is these days. Everything is proprietary in this set up.

CHORUS: It's all automated here. Once again progress is in the air.

Look on us *E. coli* and despair!

But we're not sure it's the end of the argument...

A CLAMOUR OF VOICES FROM JOURNAL SCIENCE: There's so much more to the human microbiome than we think. 'The urinary tract is not sterile'![28]

The urine is unlikely to contain all pathogenic agents. 'Bacteria may invade the epithelial lining cells finding sanctuary from immune surveillance and urinary clearance mechanisms'.[29]

There might even be such a thing as 'polymicrobial UTI'.[30]

LEADER OF THE CHORUS: Given this, the industry built around culturing urine samples might need rethinking. If *E. coli* is even more ubiquitous than previously thought, the search is on to understand its role in illness and how it relates to other organisms.

E. COLI: *Oh yes, we're also good at hiding, and we have friends who are even better at concealment. For us this is more than just a visit. We've settled in to stay. If we stick together we can avoid being flushed away by the urine flow. The epithelial lining is a wonderful thing. It's not home exactly but it's a lovely spot.*

Act 2, Scene 5

LEADER OF THE CHORUS: By the start of the 21st century, all this leads to considerable caution about the use of laboratory cultures for UTI. They are still done, especially for pregnant women, but not on apparently straightforward urinary tract infections in primary care. The principle becomes treating people quickly if they have the expected symptoms and culturing the tricky cases.

PUBLIC HEALTH ENGLAND: Our new guidance is for GPs to not send samples for testing, just prescribe the recommended antibiotics anyway for uncomplicated UTIs. We know what's happening and who is responsible.

LEADER OF THE CHORUS: In the hospital lab however there's a whole suite of technology designed for direct susceptibility testing.

MICROBIOLOGISTS: We see more and more nasty infections in the blood stream: if E. coli makes it in there, we have to look for the right antibiotic for each case.

CHORUS: More helpers required! Resistance tests aren't so simple.

Pour broth libations. Stack up 8x12 racks.

So much work to show whether drugs kill the bugs.

> *Spotlight falls on the machines designed to give a measure of resistance, processing 95 samples at a time to examine susceptibility to different concentrations of antibiotics.*

E. COLI (WILD TYPE): *I get it, you're scared. Well maybe you should be! I'm feeling pretty good, getting wise to your tricks, and I've got some of my own.[31] I'm doing so well, I'm travelling all over.[32] You can throw ampicillin at me and half the time I bounce right back.[33] Maybe trimethoprim still knocks me out mostly, but don't take it for granted. Ciprofloxacin and amoxicillin are not a problem I assure you. I've hung out with them so often they're like mates. See how resistant I can be!*

EUROPEAN COMMITTEE ON ANTIMICROBIAL SUSCEPTIBILITY TESTING (EUCAST): Whatever you say. We now know exactly how to define susceptibility and resistance right across Europe. We're onto this.[34]

LEADER OF CHORUS: Meanwhile, routine samples checking for UTIs in pregnant women are seen as valuable for tracking the problem of antimicrobial resistance.

MICROBIOLOGIST: In many parts of the world, we test pregnant women because we know urinary tract infections are dangerous for the health of their child. We can use those samples to picture the spatial (or even social) distributions of the more resistant E. coli.[35]

CHORUS: No, the work never ends, and nor do the grants.

They're calling committees and funding reports.

It's dizzying how many people turn up.

Multiplying disciplines, all with their thoughts.

DATA SCIENTIST: Yes, the figures are big enough for us to play now. Away from the smell of stale pee in the laboratories, we crunch numbers in bright white offices. But beware. The resistance percentages are acutely sensitive to the full set of samples being tested by each lab.[36] More testing of routine samples and the 'resistance rate' might look artificially low. If testing of routine samples is reduced – say because prescribing is increasingly allowed to follow clinical symptoms – then it may look artificially high. 'Instead of trying to sum up from laboratory results at a regional or national level perhaps we should instead create a surveillance system. We have more to learn about how far prescribing for one condition increases the chance of suffering resistance in another and about the mechanisms behind resistance within the host or patient.'[37]

CHORUS: A system, let us have a system. That's always the solution in our experience.

IMMUNOLOGIST: Please don't forget us and the contribution of lab research. In this funding bonanza you'll want interdisciplinary teams, and now we know there's plasmid transfer of resistance we should study the 'bacterial gene pool' too. 'Even a transient effect of antibiotic use on the carriage of resistant organisms by an individual could have a major impact on the endemic level of resistance in the population.'[38]

ACT 3

Act 3, Scene 1
A molecular biology laboratory at a university in the West Midlands

CHORUS: Here we all are again

And what a proliferation!

Microbiologists, sociologists, biochemists

Careers, papers and prep-kits

Microbes, vectors, equipment shiny

Will make our esoteric thought community[39]

Working away on our usual routine

Looking for a β-barrel protein

MOLECULAR BIOLOGIST 1: The laboratory is a secure and hazardous environment, so we need to don our PPE; lab coats, goggles and nitrile gloves. We've got a big job: to work out the structure and function of a piece of *E. coli's* cell wall, its BamA β-barrel protein. This could give us a new antibiotic if we're lucky.

LEADER OF THE CHORUS: The molecular biologists' task is large. They will need to enlist the help of a large number of actors to bring this about, but the star here will be their old 'workhorse' *E. coli*, here in the K-12 strain which is an established model organism in the field.[40]

The team of molecular microbiologists in the lab are surrounded by machines, Bunsen burners, assorted glassware, reagents, family photographs, discarded PPE, pens and papers, fridges and microwave ovens. Is this a mess?

LEADER OF THE CHORUS: Eventually, the molecular biologists will triumph in identifying the structure and function of *E. coli's* BamA β-barrel protein,[41] but (spoiler alert) on the way they experience some doubt.

E. COLI K-1 2: *Take me apart, look inside me, tell me my secrets. I am at your disposal, a willing helper in the quest for complete knowledge.*

MOLECULAR BIOLOGIST 1: Thank you *E. coli* K-12 but be aware that this will be a long, complicated process. And we should say, we have nagging doubts about your identity.

E. COLI K-1 2: *Why? You've worked with me before many, many times and know me almost personally. I'm here to help – I'm as accommodating as possible.*

MOLECULAR BIOLOGIST 2: That might be a problem *E. coli*. Maybe you're too accommodating, too refined, cossetted, too removed from your wild cousins? You're right, we know you personally and have even given you your own name: *E. coli* K-12 RLG221 to be precise,[42] which indicates that you are a very specialised and refined bacterial strain, bred in captivity as a clone with special characteristics, not least of which is our ability to work with you easily. Your cell wall, which is what we are interested in, is much easier to penetrate than that of your wild cousins.

E. COLI K-1 2 RLG 2 2 1 : *Is that what you are going to do to me?*

MOLECULAR BIOLOGIST 1 : Yes – first through electroporation, to insert those plasmids and vectors, then through sonication to break you apart and take out your new DNA. Then we'll look at what the 'new you' is capable of doing before finally taking you apart again and inferring the structure of that BamA β-barrel protein.

E. COLI K-1 2 RLG 2 2 1 : *OK. You're right, it does sound complicated. Painful, too.*

MOLECULAR BIOLOGIST 2 : And we were only giving you a tiny part of the story! But first, can we resolve the question of your identity K-12 RLG221?

E. COLI K-1 2 RLG 2 2 1 : *Some more experiments, perhaps?*

MOLECULAR BIOLOGIST 1 : However did you guess? We need to design and run a huge array of experiments to investigate just how far removed from the (true)[43] wild type you really are.[44]

Act 3, Scene 2
Two other molecular biology laboratories at universities in the Midlands

LEADER OF THE CHORUS: So, the molecular biologists design and run their experiments.

MOLECULAR BIOLOGIST 1 [to *E. coli K-12*]: One thing we know about you, K-12, is that you can't express the O antigen, but your wild cousin can. I wonder what difference that makes.[45]

E. COLI K12 RLG 2 2 1 : *OK, I admit I can't express the O antigen, but maybe I can be just like the true wild type, maybe I too can infect your other favourite model organism, the little worm* Caenorhabditis elegans.[46] *Perhaps that would be a good test?*

MOLECULAR BIOLOGIST 3 : Nice idea K-12 RLG221; we've used *C. elegans* to test the pathogenicity of other strains of *E. coli* for years. We'll reverse-engineer you and make you express O antigen. [Time passes...] Now you have a new identity: *E. coli DFB 1655 L9.*[47] Like the name?

E. COLI DFB 1655 L9: *Neat! But that was a lot of hard work too. So – gonna test me? Bring on those worms!*

CHORUS: We're adding to our assembly again,

> This time a worm and the O antigen
>
> The worms are in a different laboratory
>
> So, our new microbe needs to make a journey.

MOLECULAR BIOLOGIST 1: Well, putting that O antigen back into K-12 made DFB 1655 L9 kill those little worms with a vengeance! *E. coli* K-12 RLG221 without the ability to express the O antigen are non-pathogenic for *C. elegans*, but then we knew that already. But all the true wild type *E. coli do* have the ability to synthesise the O antigen. So – have we got the right model for our lab studies? These results certainly call things into question.[48] These guys are quite different from one another!

E. COLI K-12 RLG221: *I am here to help you. I thought I was helping you really well.*

MOLECULAR BIOLOGIST 3: And we do thank you for it – but things are different outside the lab.

E. COLI (TRUE WILD TYPE): *You better believe it – those wimpy lab strains wouldn't last a moment in the hostile environments I hang out in! You think you're tough 'cos you like MacConkey Bouillon and TBX agar – you should try living in some of the places I do – frozen seagull poo,[49] sewage systems,[50] air conditioning units…[51]*

Act 3, Scene 3
The original molecular biology laboratory at a university in the Midlands

MOLECULAR BIOLOGIST 1: Interesting results regarding K-12! Do you think we should change how we run the BamA β-barrel protein experiments?

MOLECULAR BIOLOGIST 2: Not right now – stick to the protocol!

E. COLI K-12 RLG221: *Yay! Happy to be working with you guys again. Let's go.*

CHORUS: *E. coli* K-12, K-12 RLG221, K-12 DFB1655 L9 all tamed like Enkidu

> But which is the wild type like that in our poo?
>
> We've done a lot of experiments, but what have we found?
>
> Are we nearer to showing our knowledge is sound?

E. COLI: *From your perspective I suppose this looks like a mess. From mine, a great success. Whatever you threw at me, I learned to cope and shared my skills. I still want to assist, but you're going to have to treat me with a bit more respect. Stop trying to get rid of me all the time and recognise I can help in more ways than you knew. Our long collaboration may be entering a new phase but please, respect my creativity and complexity rather than just what you call 'virulence' or 'resistance'. I know you're a bit uneasy about how my lab self – K-12 – may vary from free-living E. coli but try to reconcile this. Your skills in ensuring my cooperation in the laboratory may yet give us a way to thrive together. But you need to lose your anthropocentric view of bacteria!*[52]

EPILOGUE

Back on Mount Olympus, the Muses look down.

CLIO: I wonder what the mortals have learned from our tour? They have tools and motivation now, whatever the twists of the story, they just keep going!

THALIA: How joyous, how beautiful our actors working together are. From bacteriology to molecular and cell biology, and biotech, *E. coli* is a constant partner to humans!

MELPOMENE: Have you learnt nothing? Look at the storm clouds on the horizon. Those mortals have sowed their doom with their reliance on this organism.

CLIO: Only I can know the future, sisters, but let us leave it to our audience to decide which voice they will hear, Thalia or Melpomene.

Curtain(s)

NOTES

1 Here we are following Ian Hacking's 'dynamic nominalism' where kinds of things come into being at the same time as the kind itself is invented (Hacking 2002).

2 Hannah Landecker's (2016) work is particularly helpful here, reminding us that biologists may also explore histories of their discipline through attending to model organisms, practices and media.

3 We (unwittingly) echo Andrew Balmer and Susan Molyneux-Hodgson's study (2013) which set out to compare 'bacterial ontologies' emerging from different practices, in the case of their research between wastewater treatment plants and synthetic biology laboratories. They looked at differences between types of 'engineering' – but we take another route by centring the bacterium in its encounters with a wider range of actors who share neither discipline nor practices.

4 Our debt to Annemarie Mol is most clear in the notion of practices making multiple versions of something with the same name. The obvious reference is her work on atherosclerosis (1999). However, in her more recent paper on 'schoon' (2020) she directs our attention to notions and practices for ensuring 'cleanliness', including how we treat wastewater, and gave us the lead to Balmer and Molyneux-Hodgson (2013). See also Erickson (2018) for details on how *E. coli* is a key indicator of water cleanliness.

5 We are particularly drawing on the New Literary Form movement from the late 1980s (Ashmore 2005; Mulkay 1991; Woolgar and Ashmore 1991) and later work that voices actants as well as humans, such as Latour (1996). We use italics to signal the imagined voice of the microbe against ordinary text for other actants.

6 With Bruno Latour (2005) we reassemble the assemblages that we have encountered in our various researches – using different fonts for Chorus and 'stage directions'.

7 We invoke the Muse of comedy and idyllic poetry, Thalia. Translations of this name include 'blooming' (Hesiod, trans. by Catherine M. Schlegel and Henry Weinfield: 77). Liddell and Scott's translation (1889) of θαλεια is '*blooming, luxuriant, goodly, bounteous*', and Θαλεια, η, one of the Muses, 'the *blooming* one' (Hesiod, trans. by Catherine M. Schlegel and Henry Weinfield). Thalia as 'blooming' has good microbial connotations – bacterial blooms have been described in the literature (e.g. Fuentes et al. 2016).

8 The 'wild man', companion to Gilgamesh in that eponymous epic poem composed sometime in the second millennium BCE.

9 Theocritus, *Idyll XXII: The Dioscuri* (from lines 27–52)

10 Escherich (1885).

11 Méric et al. (2016); Dunne et al. (2017).

12 Chick (1908).

13 See MacConkey's obituary in *Nature* 127, 980–9811931, which also mentions his love of roses. MacConkey gave his name to a selective medium widely used to encourage the growth of *E. coli* in laboratories across the twentieth century.

14 Buchanan (1916).

15 MacConkey was drawing on older ideas about differential media but exploring the best way to tailor the medium to B. *coli* from 1897, publishing a summary in MacConkey (1908).

16 This urge to count was not new: see a fuller account of the nineteenth-century history of water analysis in Britain in Hamlin (1990).

17 MacConkey (1909).

18 Eckburg et al. (2005).

19 Tchobanoglous et al. (2014), p. 160 – the current version of 'Metcalf and Eddy' – first published in 1914–15 as *American Sewerage Practice*.

20 Wall (2013).

21 Voswinckel (1994) – with thanks to Eleanor Kashouris.

22 Dudgeon (1908).

23 Kass (1956).

24 In part because of interest in diabetes as a treatable condition, see Oudshoorn (1994).

25 In 1957, Ames launched *Albustix*, similarly using colour to give a semi-quantitative estimate of protein concentration.

26 The brand name for Beecham's new antibiotic, ampicillin, on the market since 1961.

27 Maskell et al. (1983); Stamm (1983).

28 Hilt et al. (2014).

29 See Blount (2014).

30 Price et al. (2016).

31 Target alteration, reduced drug concentration, inactivation of the drug.

32 Adapted *E. coli* 131 (ST131) improved fitness and growth rate and spread worldwide as an extraintestinal pathogenic organism.

33 Nomamiukor et al. (2015).

34 See http://www.eucast.org/documents/rd/ and explanations there of new definitions of susceptibility and resistance published in January 2019 after review by EUCAST [accessed 9 December 2019].

35 Nomamiukor et al. (2015) op cit.

36 Pouwels et al. (2019).

37 Costelloe et al. (2010).

38 Knight et al. (2018).

39 Fleck (1979).

40 Browning et al. (2013a),

41 Dunne et al. (2017); Browning et al. (2013a).

42 Browning et al. (2013a) Table S1 shows the relevant genotype of this bacterial strain.

43 We are improving readability by using this nomenclature, rather than extended strain names: our definitions are as follows: 'wild type' refers to an organism that has been unmodified, but may be a laboratory strain such as K-12; 'true wild type' refers to an organism that has not been modified and exists in the environment beyond the laboratory;

'strain' refers to an organism that exists in the laboratory but has been deliberately modified to take on certain phenotypical characteristics.

44 Browning et al. (2013b).

45 Ibid.

46 Another model organism, a worm, microscopic, that eats bacteria; if the worm dies, it shows pathogenicity of the microbe. See https://www.ncbi.nlm.nih.gov/books/NBK453431/.

47 Under this name the strain is stored in extra cold freezers in the lab, lying dormant until it's needed again. But it has also travelled the world, as the microbiologists send out samples in response to requests from Argentina, Canada, and Singapore, just as Escherich shared his original *E. coli* with colleagues in Cambridge.

48 Browning (2013b).

49 Rabbia et al. (2016).

50 Sozzi et al. (2015).

51 Gołofit-Szymczak et al. (2019).

52 'The anthropocentric view of bacteriology has largely driven the study of pathogenic *E. coli* at the expense of understanding commensalism', Dunne et al. (2017).

ACKNOWLEDGEMENTS

Professor James Ebdon, Dr Doug Browning, Eric Will MD, participants in the Kilpisjärvi 'With Microbes' workshop and 2020 EASST/4S conference. Catherine Will would like to acknowledge the support of the Wellcome Trust (grant no 214954/Z/18/Z).

REFERENCES

Ashmore, M., *The Reflexive Thesis: Wrighting Sociology of Scientific Knowledge* (Chicago and London: University of Chicago Press, 2005).

Balmer, A., and S. Molyneux-Hodgson, 'Bacterial Cultures: Ontologies of Bacteria and Engineering Expertise at the Nexus of Synthetic Biology & Water Services', *Engineering Studies*, 5.1 (2013), 59–73.

Blount, Z. D., 'The Unexhausted Potential of E. Coli', *eLife*, 4 (2014).

Browning, D. F., and others, 'Mutational and Topological Analysis of the *Escherichia coli* BamA Protein', *PLoS ONE*, 8.12 (2013a).

Browning, D. F., and others, 'Laboratory Adapted Escherichia Coli K-12 Becomes a Pathogen of *Caenorhabditis Elegans* Upon Restoration of O Antigen Biosynthesis', *Molecular Microbiology*, 87.5 (2013b), 939–50.

Buchanan, R. E., 'Studies in the Nomenclature and Classification of Bacteria: The Problem of Bacterial Nomenclature', *Journal of Bacteriology*, 1 (1916), 591–6.

Chick, H., 'An Investigation of the Laws of Disinfection', *The Journal of Hygiene*, 8.1 (1908), 92–158.

Costelloe, C., and others, 'Effect of Antibiotic Prescribing in Primary Care on Antimicrobial Resistance in Individual Patients: Systematic Review and Meta-Analysis', *BMJ*, 340 (2010).

Dudgeon, L. S., 'Acute and Chronic Infections of the Urinary Tract Due to the Bacillus Coli', *Lancet*, (1908), 616–20.

Dunne, K. A., and others, 'Sequencing a Piece of History: Complete Genome Sequence of the Original Escherichia Coli Strain', *Microbial Genomics*, 3 (2017).

Eckburg, P. B., and others, 'Diversity of the Human Intestinal Microbial Flora', *Science*, 308.5728 (2005), 1635–8.

Erickson, M., 'Homer in the Laboratory: A Feyerabendian Experiment in Sociology of Science', *Social Epistemology*, 32 (2018), 128–41.

Escherich, T., 'Die Darmbakterien des Neugeborenen und Säuglings', *Fortshr. Med*, 3.5 (1885), 547–54.

Fleck, L., *Genesis and Development of a Scientific Fact* (Chicago: University of Chicago Press, 1979).

Fuentes, S., and others, 'From Rare to Dominant: A Fine-Tuned Soil Bacterial Bloom during Petroleum Hydrocarbon Bioremediation', *Applied & Environmental Microbiology*, 82.3 (2016), 888.

Gołofit-Szymczak, M., A. Stobnicka-Kupiec, and R. L. Górny, 'Impact of Air-Conditioning System Disinfection on Microbial Contamination of Passenger Cars', *Air Quality, Atmosphere & Health*, 12.9 (2019), 1127–35.

Hacking, I., *Historical Ontology* (Cambridge, MA: Harvard University Press, 2002).

Hamlin, C. A., *Science of Impurity: Water Analysis in Nineteenth Century Britain* (Berkeley: University of California Press, 1990).

Hesiod, *Theogony* and *Works and Days*, trans. and with introductions by Catherine M. Schlegel and Henry Weinfield (Ann Arbor: University of Michigan Press, 2006).

Hilt, E. E., K. McKinley, and M. M. Pearce, 'Urine is Not Sterile: Use of Enhanced Urine Culture Techniques to Detect Resident Bacterial Flora in the Adult Female Bladder', *Journal of Clinical Microbiology*, 52.3 (2014), 871–76.

Kass, E., 'Asymptomatic Infections of the Urinary Tract', *Journal of Urology*, 167 (1956), 106–20.

Knight, G. M., and others, 'Addressing the Unknowns of Antimicrobial Resistance: Quantifying and Mapping the Drivers of Burden', *Clinical Infectious Diseases*, 66.4 (2018), 612–6.

Landecker, H., 'Antibiotic Resistance and the Biology of History', *Body & Society*, 22.4 (2016), 19–52

Latour, B., *Aramis or the Love of Technology* (Cambridge, MA: Harvard University Press, 1996).

—— *Reassembling the Social: An Introduction to Actor-Network-Theory* (Oxford: Oxford University Press, 2005).

Liddell, H. G., *An Intermediate Greek-English Lexicon* (Oxford: Clarendon Press, 1889).

MacConkey, A. T., 'Bile Salt Media and Their Advantages in some Bacteriological Examinations', *The Journal of Hygiene*, 8.3 (1908), 322–34.

—— 'Further Observations on the Differentiation of Lactose-Fermenting Bacilli, With Special Reference to Those of Intestinal Origin', *Journal of Hygiene*, 9.1 (1909), 86–103, p 99.

Maskell R., L. Pead, and R. A. Sanderson, 'Fastidious Bacteria and the Urethral Syndrome: A 2-Year Clinical and Bacteriological Study of 51 Women', *Lancet*, 2 (1983), 1277–80.

Méric, G., and others, 'From Escherich to the *Escherichia coli* Genome', *The Lancet Infectious Diseases*, 16.6 (2016), 634–6.

Mol, A., *The Body Multiple: Ontology in Medical Practice* (Durham, NC and London: Duke University Press, 1999).

—— 'Not Quite Clean: Trailing Schoon and its Resonances', *The Sociological Review*, 68.2 (2020), 385–400.

Mulkay, M., *Sociology of Science: A Sociological Pilgrimage* (Milton Keynes: Open University Press, 1991).

Nomamiukor, B., and others, 'Living Conditions Are Associated With Increased Antibiotic Resistance in Community Isolates of Escherichia Coli', *Journal of Antimicrobial Chemotherapy*, 70 (2015), 3154–8.

Oudshoorn, N., *Beyond the Natural Body: An Archaeology of Sex Hormones* (London: Routledge, 1994).

Pouwels, K. B., and others, 'Selection and Co-Selection of Antibiotic Resistances Among *Escherichia Coli* by Antibiotic Use in Primary Care: An Ecological Analysis', *PLoS ONE*, 14.6 (2019).

Price, T. K., and others, 'The Clinical Urine Culture: Enhanced Techniques Improve Detection of Clinically Relevant Microorganisms', *Journal of Clinical Microbiology*, 54.5 (2016), 1216–22.

Rabbia, V., and others, 'Antibiotic Resistance in Escherichia Coli Strains Isolated From Antarctic Bird Feces, Water From Inside a Wastewater Treatment Plant, and Seawater Samples Collected in the Antarctic Treaty Area', *Polar Science*, 10.2 (2016), 123–31.

Sozzi, E., and others, 'Minimizing the Risk of Disease Transmission in Emergency Settings: Novel In Situ Physico-Chemical Disinfection of Pathogen-Laden Hospital Wastewaters', *PLoS Negl Trop Dis*, 9.6 (2015).

Stamm, W. E., 'Measurement of Pyuria and its Relation to Bacteriuria', *American Journal of Medicine*, 75 (1983), Supplement p. 53.

Tchobanoglous, G., and others, *Wastewater Engineering: Treatment and Resource Recovery* (New York: McGraw-Hill Education, 2014).

Theocritus, *The Idylls*, trans. by Robert Wells (Harmondsworth: Penguin, 1989).

Voswinckel, P., 'A Marvel of Colours and Ingredients', *Kidney International*, 47.4 (1994), S3–7.

Wall, R., *Bacteria in Britain, 1880–1939* (London: Pickering and Chatto, 2013).

Woolgar, S., and M. Ashmore, 'The Next Step: An Introduction to the Reflexive Project', in S. Woolgar, ed., *Knowledge and Reflexivity: New Frontiers in the Sociology of Knowledge* (London: Sage, 1991), pp. 1–11.

10

MICRO-GEOGRAPHIES OF KOMBUCHA AS METHODOLOGY: A CROSS-CULTURAL CONVERSATION

A.C. Davidson, Emma Ransom-Jones

THIS CHAPTER CHARTS A COLLABORATIVE EXPERIMENT BETWEEN EMMA (A microbiologist) and A.C. (a geographer) around how we understand kombucha, a drink which can be purchased commercially, or home brewed by fermenting tea with a starter microbial consortium, or SCOBY (Symbiotic Culture of Bacteria and Yeast).

Sales of kombucha have increased in the last decade as part of a growing market in 'functional drinks': non-alcoholic beverages with supposed performance or health benefits. Commercially produced kombucha has been described as a drink consumed by the more affluent (Spackman 2018) and in gentrifying neighbourhoods alongside artisanal products with local, sustainable and ethical credentials (Bond and Browder 2019). It is important, therefore, to consider Kombucha's geographical contexts and the social, material and economic circulations it is imbricated in. As Jasarevic (2015) highlights, in post-socialist Bosnia the 'mushroom in a jar' circulates within informal economies and traditional understandings of food and medicine, whereas in the North American context kombucha takes on both a highly commodified form within discourses of antibiosis (ibid.) and also a post-Pasteurian valorisation of artisanal and

DIY production within queer, anti-establishment economies and discourses (Maroney 2015; Katz 2012).

As the microbiome project (Rees, Bosch, and Douglas 2018) indicates, there is an increasing drive to bring disciplines together in the study of microbes. However, there is a risk within interdisciplinarity of re-discovering – and erasing – scholarship in other disciplines. In our collaboration, we wanted to avoid this, and instead of simply adding microbiological and ethnographic methods we wanted to engage in an 'experimental entanglement' (Callard and Fitzgerald 2015) to see what we might learn about kombucha and microbes together. In this chapter, to emphasise the dialogue between our different research approaches and paradigms we use the form of a conversation – an approach used in STS by Woolgar (1989), Hirschauer and Mol (1995) and Sariola et al. (2017).

Our collaboration raised more questions than it answered. Some are about the practices, insights and challenges of interdisciplinary work, while others are about kombucha itself. By moving ourselves, our research paradigms, methods, SCOBYs and kombucha samples between the lab, commercial production facilities and our own kitchens, we encountered different ways of producing, knowing and consuming kombucha. Below, we introduce our approach to inter-disciplinarity before discussing, in conversational form, what we found: there are micro-geographical variations to the kinds of kombuchas produced, consumed and analysed in the university lab, commercial production and home kitchen. These 'kombuchas multiple' (Mol 2002) differ in part because of the percep-tions, regulations and practices attached to where and how they were created. We could not, for example, drink anything created in the lab. Similarly, different kombucha producers held varying degrees of attachment to their kombuchas being 'alive', as opposed to more predictable and consistent. However, despite desires to affix a set of meanings or politics to kombuchas, the microbiology of the kombuchas was more complex and unruly. Standardised composition across batches and a complete verification of consistency would be difficult to confirm with certainty.

DISPLACING EXPERIMENTS

FIG. 10.1 A.C.'s home-brew kombucha in the kitchen (photograph by Dawn Woolley)

Kombucha offered us, as early career researchers, a low-cost way to experiment with human-microbe relations in distinctly different spaces. Our respective research methods differ, as do the disciplinary practices of writing (critically) about the research process. We settled on providing an outline of our approach below.

1. From November 2018, we held regular voice-recorded conversations around what an interdisciplinary ethnography of kombucha cultures might look like.

2. DNA extractions from ten commercially available SCOBYs were performed by Jess (a student in the microbiology lab at Huddersfield University) using the DNeasy PowerSoil Kit (Qiagen) and used for 16S rRNA gene amplification and sequencing by Novogene.

3. A.C. conducted in-depth interviews with four UK-based commercial kombucha manufacturers and two site visits to production facilities between

2018 and 2019, as well as online research and analysis of forums and marketing information.

4. Fermentation of kombucha in our kitchens was done in autumn and winter 2019 to observe our thoughts, feelings and practices around the brewing. The recipe/method is included here for readers who would like to replicate this method:

A medium-sized kombucha SCOBY was purchased online and placed in a clean two-litre glass jar with 750 ml black tea (boiled tap water with two organic black tea bags, brewed for 30 minutes and cooled) and 75 g of caster sugar. The jar was covered with kitchen roll kept in place with an elastic band. After an initial 14-day fermentation, this process was repeated with 650 ml of tea and 100 ml of liquid from the first fermentation.

5. A supervised visit to the lab during which Emma extracted DNA from one of our own SCOBYs (point 2) and A.C. observed.

Rather than writing about scientists or interdisciplinary collaboration from within an STS perspective (such as in Balmer et al. 2015), writing in conversation across disciplines was an important part of our experiment. As well as applying interdisciplinary approaches we wanted to break down some of the distinctions between the researcher and researched. Where possible, we wanted to avoid falling into the methodological and epistemological rules of either side of the interdisciplinary collaboration. Callard and Fitzgerald (2015: 4–7) suggest that very few experiments are conducted where scientists work alongside scholars in the social sciences or humanities.

This entangled method, and the conversations it enabled us to produce, were structured also by the expectations and practices within our disciplines (and the current volume). In our writing and editing, we wrangled with what constitutes appropriate structure and style and what counts as valid research for us, and our respective fields. In many respects, this volume and its form and scope was a more comfortable fit for A.C. than for Emma. Writing this as a conversation with ourselves placed within the text was a radical departure from the traditional structure and style of a scientific manuscript reporting the methods, 'facts' and outcomes of an experiment. We (en)countered a key disciplinary divide here in the lines we draw between 'fact' and 'opinion'. Emma reflected on how, within scientific paradigms, removal of bias and a distillation into a format of 'the results state this, therefore x' provides a solidity of 'fact' which is opposed to 'opinion'. For A.C., more accustomed to STS paradigms, the classification of 'fact' and 'opinion' is fraught (Stengers 2018) and itself political. This particular f(r)iction was reproduced also within what we came to understand about kombuchas: what kombucha can be verified to contain microbiologically, and the meanings it carries, are entangled but by no means predictably aligned.

THE METHODOLOGIES OF KOMBUCHA — BETWEEN THE LAB, WAREHOUSE AND KITCHEN

A.C.: I first encountered Kombucha in 2009 in the States, where one housemate brewed it in our kitchen, and another was buying it from a health food shop in small, expensive bottles. I was interested in how these two kombuchas were made within very different economies (DIY and gifting versus a food co-operative selling high-end foods). This is also why I was interested in understanding the ethos and practices of producers at different scales. Where did you first encounter kombucha?

EMMA: It was something one of our placement students was working on, and I was asking her what it was, what she was doing with it, why there was tea in the lab! In our lab, food or drink is banned for safety so I was wondering what she was doing with it. However, most of that work was focused on the actual SCOBY rather than the resulting drink, so it wasn't until you and I started working together that I tried kombucha.

A.C.: When I joined you in the lab to extract DNA from our SCOBY I was struck by how the *same* stuff we had been brewing at home, bought from the shop, and encountered in the lab, was something profoundly different because of the different spaces, practices and sets of knowledge it was being understood through (Mol 2002). For me kombucha is social, cultural, political and economic, and can't be understood outside the context and methods employed to study or produce it. For the producers I spoke to, it was a livelihood, a product, an experiment, a brand, and sometimes a calling or an embodiment of their personal philosophy and ethics.

EMMA: That's one of the things I hadn't even considered until we started working together. My research doesn't really involve interviewing the people behind the samples, unless it's to answer questions about dates, times and other metadata. It doesn't involve looking at their motivations or connection to the samples I'm working from, although I may be aware of it in an abstract sense.

A.C.: I guess for me it goes beyond the people behind the samples. Where possible, I preferred to speak to producers in their production facility, to photograph and experience the space itself. While there are some social scientists who might focus solely on what producers say about the kombucha, or how they say it, I'm especially interested in how this relates to the practices and to the 'stuff' of kombucha and the instruments and spaces involved.

I'm struck by how, in the lab as a microbiologist, the kombucha is a sample that needs to be separated from human variables like motivation or connection – unless they are human actions that directly affected composition. I'm curious about how the samples were labelled.

EMMA: They were actually just labelled with numbers one to ten, so although we had a record of what those numbers meant, we actually forgot it fairly quickly and it was only when we were analysing the data that I then started to put those labels back in. We often use more descriptive names for other samples, which might contain identifiers such as the place of origin or the date collected, but we keep them fairly simple.

A.C.: I'm interested also in how the methods we use to understand kombucha construct what it is. How do the methods you use in microbiology matter to how kombucha is known?

EMMA: They definitely matter, because depending on what methods you use you will potentially get very different results. For example, historically microbes were studied by isolating an individual species in the lab. The problem with this is that we can only grow an estimated 1% of these organisms, which means that the majority of species couldn't be studied and you would miss a huge amount of diversity. In addition, because you have to have a pure culture of a single organism to study it this way, you also miss out on both how the

microbes function in their environment (because it's difficult to exactly replicate these conditions) and how the whole community interacts. We now have
next generation sequencing where we can sequence members of a microbial
community without having to grow them first, and that has led to a rise in the
analysis of the whole community, rather than its individual members, but this
isn't without its own problems. We know that results can change due to using
different methods for the DNA extraction, PCR,[1] and sequencing analysis,
as well as the risk of introducing contamination into the samples.

A.C.: In a sense, next generation sequencing seems to bring microbiology out
of the lab and into the field, making it more like ethnography. You get the
chance to learn from interactions between different species in very specific,
'uncontrolled' environments. Except, you are not looking to interact with
the communities yourself, nor are you getting the live interactions. It's a
snapshot at 'death'/dispersal, right? I was struck by the energies – the speed
of the centrifuge – it took in the lab to extract the DNA.

EMMA: It's interesting that you mention moving into the field, as recently my
research has involved just that. I've taken the DNA extraction kit into the
field in places like Malawi and Patagonia to do DNA extractions as quickly
as possible after sample collection. With the invention and popularity of
the MinIon (a portable sequencing device), we are seeing more scientists
doing sequencing in the field, which is really exciting. In terms of getting
a snapshot, this is true of any sequencing, but if we continue projects over
time, we can build up a picture of what is going on and how things change
over time, particularly if we also collect other data that will influence changes
in the microbial community such as moisture content, temperature, pH and
so on. We can also use RNA rather than DNA for sequencing, which will
tell us which organisms are metabolically active (or alive) at that particular
moment in time and what they are doing.

A.C.: Was it necessary, then, to take multiple samples of kombucha from each
producer? It strikes me as difficult to pin kombucha down in time and place
when it's constantly fermenting and interacting with its environment. One
producer I spoke to said, 'This is why I talk about it [kombucha] less as a
single product and more as a methodology'.

EMMA: It was a single sample, so in and of itself we can't say every sample from x looks like this, but when we look at the samples together, we can build up a picture of the similarities and differences and compare different samples from similar environments. It's definitely worth bearing in mind that this is a limited sample, and more data is usually better, but that requires more time and money and is more complicated to analyse. Eventually we have to draw the line somewhere, but the good thing about this work is that it can be compared to work from other scientists doing similar things and together that adds to a much bigger picture.

A.C.: Given the variations between samples, is there a single definition, micro-biologically, of what kombucha is?

EMMA: Personally, I would define kombucha as tea fermented by the SCOBY, regardless of how it is brewed or the exact composition or flavour. This is a fairly simple definition, but I also recognise that there's a broad range of variables within the kombucha itself. For example, both a greyhound and a German shepherd are dogs, but they look and behave completely differently.

A.C.: To follow this species-based definition further: is there a particular com-munity of species that need to be present for something to be a SCOBY? Among producers there was some anxiety around what 'true' kombucha is. Being able to claim 'kombucha' can make the difference between gaining consumer recognition and being able to sell or failing to sell. Although one producer was told by Trading Standards initially that they couldn't call their product kombucha because nobody knows what that is! In microbiological terms, is a kombucha SCOBY unique or particularly different from any other symbiotic cultures of bacteria and yeast?

EMMA: There are core members of the community, yes. These are organisms that are found in every SCOBY, which in terms of bacteria are *Komagataeibacter* spp. and *Acetobacter* spp., and in terms of yeasts are *Zygosaccharomyces* spp. and *Brettanomyces* spp. (Marsh et al. 2014). But we also see that there are a huge number of other species present, and these can vary between fermenta-tions (Villarreal-Soto et al. 2018).

A.C.: There was some variation between producers about whether the final drink needs to contain live cultures at the point of sale to be called kombucha, or whether the acids produced by fermentation are what make it kombucha. I heard of producers using 'acid banks' to add 'the living cultures as a powder that's poured in' – is that still kombucha?

EMMA: While it's fermenting, the microbes are alive and it's the microbes that are living rather than the tea itself. In terms of what is actually in the kombucha itself afterwards, much of this depends on how the drink is processed, whether it's been sterilised or filtered to remove any living microorganisms, or whether it's just been bottled, at which point some microbes will remain. I'd say that as long as the tea has been fermented, it counts as kombucha. The composition of the drink can change during transport and storage, depending on the conditions – particularly the ethanol content, which can rise if there are live microorganisms present and fermentation continues. Also, the very nature of the SCOBY means that the microbes can change drastically from batch to batch and could potentially cause health issues.

A.C.: Kombucha producers I spoke to balanced 'keeping alive' and 'making die' differently. None of the producers I spoke to believed in pasteurisation, with most preferring forms of filtration. Yet they spoke with some awe and frustration about trying to 'control something uncontrollable'. Although I would have to speak to more producers, I found a tendency towards a kind of continuum of commodification, standardisation and 'livingness' based on scale of production. The smaller, more artisanal producers tended towards the side of 'aliveness', less standardisation and no or little filtration. To them, this is what distinguished kombucha from 'expensive pop'. Ostensibly due to the need for stability of the product over time and more stringent regulations in larger outlets such as supermarkets, producers with a wider geographical market tended to prioritise filtration, stability, 'safety' and shelf-life, arguing that the final product did not need to be living. Especially among larger producers, there was an adherence to only making claims about health that could be verified by 'science'. But, as we're seeing with COVID-19, 'science' isn't monolithic: are there microbiologists who consider there are benefits to consuming living microbial content?

EMMA: We've actually been consuming microbes for centuries, although we didn't know it, particularly in the form of fermented foods. Even today, approximately one third of the global human diet is fermented foods and beverages, so we absolutely do consume microbes. There are studies that demonstrate the benefits of this consumption, such as those seen due to the use of probiotics, which include improving the gut barrier and excluding pathogens from this environment, short-chain fatty acid production, and even neutralising potential carcinogens (Brodmann et al. 2017).

One of the important things to realise is that probiotics have been studied for a number of years, and we usually only need to look at one or two species and their interactions at any given time, which is relatively simple. With kombucha this is much more difficult as there are hundreds and sometimes thousands of species, so understanding all of those is much harder. You also have the additional problem that not all kombuchas are the same, adding another level of complexity. A number of studies have attributed potential health benefits to drinking kombucha, including diabetic patients having improved levels of blood glucose, the prevention of liver and cardiovascular diseases, and also the prevention of certain cancers such as renal and prostate cancer (Bhattacharya et al. 2013). I think that certainly it has potential for some people, but the issue with interventions such as this is that it's so difficult to determine that kombucha consumption is the only thing that has caused benefits. Not only that but kombucha itself is so variable, with the chemical composition varying from batch to batch (Jayabalan et al. 2014). To add even more complexity, no two individuals are the same and so even if they drink the same kombucha they may experience different effects.

A.C.: Is there any indication that there is a pattern in the variation? So, for example, did the lab research done on kombucha SCOBYs point towards any difference between the 'aliveness' of the kombuchas from smaller, artisanal producers or from the larger commercial producers?

EMMA: We don't yet have definitions for what we would consider smaller or larger producers, so we have split the samples simply into commercial and laboratory grown ones. In terms of 'aliveness', we couldn't actually say. First, because what would that definition be? A higher diversity of different species? More species isolated? Gas production during fermentation? And second, because depending on how we define it we don't necessarily have the data here to answer that question.

A.C.: There might be a difference here, too, when comparing SCOBY samples versus comparing the final drink, which has been filtered to varying extents. Going back to your points about potential health impacts, it's interesting to me how industry works with labs (like at our institution) and relies upon and is limited by what can be verified scientifically. The increased consumption of kombucha and its marketing and packaging is entangled in perceptions of health and wellbeing associated with probiotics, but also consuming less alcohol, fewer sweeteners, sugars and additives. As one producer put it, however, to avoid taking risks with making health claims, they end up: 'implying health, but not screaming it'.

There is speculation that growth of chronic diseases might be driving kombucha sales (Companies and Markets 2015). It's troubling when 'health' becomes interpreted as something provided by products sold to individuals. We are encouraged to be responsible citizens (Halse 2012 in Spackman 2018), judge what is healthy and curate our lifestyles accordingly. Wider determinants of health, like food systems, poverty, working and living conditions and structural violence (e.g. racism, sexism, ableism) are lost in this narrative. I am sometimes frustrated at lab-based sciences when industry-funded research appears to incentivise an individualised and product-based understanding of health (Stengers 2018). Doing 'science' properly seems to be about shielding it from wider social and political questions which are either seen as 'beyond the scope of the study', 'political', or 'biased' (Stengers 2018: 7). This avoids recognising how power is embedded in scientific practice and knowledge and holding sciences accountable to larger questions of how we define health, and why.

EMMA: In some respects, I actually agree, and I think we do need to have this dialogue. It does depend on where the research is coming from, as industrial and academic researchers will have different pressures, as well as who has funded it. Journals usually require authors to declare the source of funding and any potential conflicts of interest. One of the main issues I have with scientific publications is if the article is behind a paywall, then you automatically limit people's access to the research, which I don't agree with. You also have the issue that, even if a journal is open access, it is still written in a way that is not always accessible and understandable, particularly if the reader is not a specialist. There is a lot of good work being done with regards to making research more accessible and disseminating our findings to the general public, but I think we need to do more. I also think we need to teach more critical thinking so that even if people are presented with information, they have the ability to judge it for themselves rather than thinking that because a scientist states something it must be true.

MICRO-GEOGRAPHIES OF KOMBUCHA

A.C.: You mentioned how variable kombucha is. I'm particularly interested in geographical variation, and visited brewing sites where I could, and asked about their location. One producer said: 'our whole brew is unique to this geographical location'. Another mentioned their old water supply sometimes created a 'farty brew'. After switching to a new (non-local) water supply, the kombucha 'loved' the water and grew at a higher rate. A third producer described place-specificity in this way:

> ... they're starting with a similar culture growing in the same place. But as soon as they take that home, over a period of three days, it will have entirely changed. [...] Not entirely, there will be dominant strains, but very soon all the bacteria and yeast in the air from their kitchen, and [inaudible] will start to infiltrate it. So, it becomes a different drink.

One of the producers discussed how their SCOBY may be influenced by plant-based bacteria from the tea and from the green space nearby, as well as airborne yeasts from the neighbouring brewery. The yeast was considered a threat to the kombucha and while I was on site there was work going on to install a filtration system to help protect the brews. They were planning a brewery move and there was speculation that the brew and flavour would change. Do the different spaces and practices (possibly linked to different scales and ethos) of preparing kombucha show up in measurable differences in the microbiological make-up of the drink itself?

EMMA: Absolutely. The composition of the drink, both in terms of the microbial community and the chemical components is affected by the brewing process, from what tea is used, to how much liquid is added from the initial batch, how good the aseptic conditions are, how long it is brewed for and at what temperature (Jayabalan et al. 2014). The 'livingness' of kombucha is actually one of the things that makes it difficult to regulate and control. Kombuchas will vary in their composition, both from brewery to brewery but also between batches from the same company. The exact composition is affected by a number of factors, such as the water and tea used and the surrounding environment, as you found in the interviews, but also the vessel the fermentation takes place, in because the size and shape will affect the oxygen levels and therefore the microbes, the length and conditions of the fermentation process, and the different species of bacteria and yeast present, which will vary between SCOBYs.

A.C.: I'm fascinated that the geographies and climates at the scale of the vessel matter, too: a micro-geography! Although, some of the SCOBYs I saw in production facilities did not feel 'micro'... they seemed to expand to fill the surface area of the large vessel available.

Kombucha is literally shaped by what it's made to mean, how and where it is transported, advertised, made, bottled, sold and consumed. For some producers kombucha is an 'on trade' low-sugar non-alcoholic drink with a flavour profile reminiscent of alcohol, sold in dark brown bottles to minimise UV rays damaging the bacteria and yeast inside, and to provide the look of a premium spirit. It is introduced in a pop-up night club or a tap room as an alternative to alcohol. For others, shifting the packaging to cans or to a more gender-neutral or 'cleaner', minimalist style meant broadening the market from relatively-wealthy, female, health-conscious consumers. There's a wider geography of kombucha, too. There are politics and places deemed to suit kombucha better – urban cultures of London and Manchester, Bristol, Birmingham, Brighton, Berlin or Amsterdam. As one producer put it, 'Where people are a bit more liberal'. In our own geographical experimentation, too: No matter the actual composition of the home-, commercially-, or lab-brewed kombuchas, we treated each like fundamentally different things based on the places the drink was associated with.

EMMA: I remember saying to you before we started our home-brews that I'd brewed kombucha in the lab and there was absolutely no way I was drinking that. Which seemed strange to you at the time, but our lab is a Category 2 microbiology lab, which means that we have potentially pathogenic organisms in there and you would never take the risk. I think it probably made more sense when you came into the lab and I had to give you the health and safety induction about not even being allowed mobile phones.

A.C.: The lab visit made it sink in how this was different from our kitchens or the little corner lab in the warehouse, which a producer used to test different attributes of the brew. The process of putting on a lab coat, safety glasses and having your safety briefing emphasised the *difference* of this space. It didn't feel like the same kombucha. The SCOBY you were extracting DNA from, and the glass bottles in the lab filled with stages of kombucha ferment suddenly made it feel like a potentially dangerous substance. Even bringing the SCOBY from home and into the lab environment required a set of procedures to transform it into a thing fit for the lab: you had a sterile petri dish, we tried not to cross-contaminate it in various ways. 'Do I hold it with my hands to transfer it into this petri dish'?, I remember asking you, and yet, I'd held it in my hands at home without a second thought!

EMMA: For me, although they were using the same methods, brewing kombucha in a lab was very much part of an experiment, whereas at home the end goal was to be able to drink it. I think that is almost entirely due to the change in environment and my background. As a student, I was always taught to practise good aseptic technique, to ensure that samples were not contaminated, as well as the set of rules and behaviours that are required for good laboratory practice. Because I've been doing it for so long, the transition from 'outside' to the lab is almost second nature to me, despite it seeming completely foreign to other people. When I teach students, I have to write down the rules to remember to tell them everything, otherwise I run the risk of forgetting things simply because it seems obvious to me. However, there are things that, because of the work I do in the lab, I carry over to 'outside'. Things like the way in which I wash my hands (although due to recent events people are now doing this properly!), and recording 'experiments', particularly things such as cooking and baking recipes, the same way I would in my laboratory notebook.

When we were talking about trying different kombuchas I was also conflicted about my ideas regarding home-brewed versus commercial kombuchas. Part of this was born of the idea that my home-brewed one should be 'safe'. I know what I'm doing and was very careful about how I did things, but a part of me still felt the commercial brews would be safer, despite the fact that there isn't much regulation about the exact composition of commercial kombuchas. There are standards in terms of ethanol content, but in terms of the microbial composition I don't know of any, and as it's such a diverse community you could never be 100% certain of the contents without testing.

A.C.: We happily drank the commercial kombucha together, but it sounds like we both had mixed feelings about drinking our own. My relationship to my home brew shifted, and I no longer have my own SCOBY. There was a point where my awe, curiosity, sense of care and pride in the multiplying layers of SCOBY was outweighed by a wary disgust: what is this slimy, hungry thing proliferating in the jar?! It turned from a potentially health-inducing wonder to something more closely aligned in my mind with decay and danger: at one point I threw my SCOBY in the bin with very mixed feelings of regret, guilt and relief.

LEARNING WITH UNRULY SUBJECTS

Our interdisciplinary experiment has involved containing and editing unruly conversations into a language and content that is relevant in both our subject areas. Using the form of a conversation allowed us to maintain the differences and tensions between our epistemological frameworks. Within microbiology, the knowledge of what communities of kombucha microbes are and do, is uncovered through scientific methods (a 'naturalistic' approach). In contrast, within a more constructivist feminist STS tradition, the microbes emerge within social practices and the instruments and structures of scientific knowledge.

Our collaboration did not shift these respective epistemological positions fundamentally. This is unsurprising, as in some respects such a shift would have needed to undo our (early) careers' worth of training and knowledge. However, our experiments offered a significant opportunity to participate in, be exposed to, and troubled by concepts and methods outside our subject bubbles. Perhaps this serves as an apt metaphor for our interdisciplinary interactions: we have learned how kombucha's microbiological and social processes are interacting and inextricable at different scales. The kombucha that made its way into the university microbiology lab was there because of the ideas around health and wellbeing attached to probiotics, and because fermentation of sugars by the SCOBY produces something people have a taste for. The different contexts of the lab, our home kitchens and the commercial producers produced kombuchas that we perceived and dealt with in fundamentally different ways, despite their composition not necessarily showing large or predictable variation.

Yet, it is important not to overdetermine kombucha through its social construction. It can be tempting to see kombucha as a metaphor or harbinger for a new paradigm or radical social change – for a queerer or more symbiotic model of living with other beings. It has been suggested that SCOBYs might act as 'model systems' to address human social questions about competition and cooperation (May et al. 2019). However, our collaboration leaves us wary of imbuing kombucha with political meaning. Perhaps our geographical and microbiological lenses mean we insist on the particularities of relations in different contexts and at different scales. Despite playing with the word 'culture' in the title of this piece, communities cannot be studied at the microbiological level with conclusions scaled up to human societies. And despite microbes sometimes being anthropomorphised in the lab and production facilities, microbes cannot be read as if they were human.

From our work together, it is difficult to see kombucha fermentation as a revolution bubbling up from kitchen counters. This is not only a question of scale but of how kombucha becomes through wider social, political and economic configurations of production, consumption and social reproduction. The politics of kombucha needs to be understood through its conditions of production and the effects this hybridity of human-microbe and matter-meaning has in the world. Even if culturation and fermentation were to replace global energy systems and production based on extraction and combustion of fossil fuels (kombucha cellulose, for example, is already used to make plastic alternatives), would this simply be a new frontier – a new micro spatial fix – in a system that is built on, and requires, exploitation? On a less ambitious scale, our work indicates that kombucha operates through desires and markets for meaning, creativity, identity and health, rather than representing a systemic challenge to unhealthy environments and food systems. Those who have the microbial cultural capital (Paxson 2008) have a greater capacity to curate their exposures and to take risks with not knowing precisely what it is they are ingesting.

The microbial variation was part of the difficulty of 'fixing' kombucha in a definition, and in space and time. While there is a core community present in every SCOBY tested in our university lab, the amounts varied. Kombucha varies from SCOBY to SCOBY in terms of its initial microbial composition, the environment in which it is brewed, and the substrates used. The lab-grown and commercially produced kombuchas showed some variation in bacterial communities, but there was more significant variation in yeast communities. Our research was too limited to conclude that there is a significant difference in microbial communities between different sizes or types of kombucha producer. Confronted with its ever-changing nature, the attempt to pin down what kombucha *is* seems fraught. It may be more apt to say that multiple kombuchas become with the tools, practices, meanings and micro-geographies they are entangled with in hybrid human-microbial relations. This does not mean the slippery SCOBY and kombuchas can be made to mean and do whatever we want them to. The aliveness required to ferment – and to produce the purported health benefits of kombucha – is the same unruly process that brings risk and unpredictability, requiring work and care.

NOTES

1 For more information on PCR see: https://www.ncbi.nlm.nih.gov/probe/docs/
techpcr/.

REFERENCES

Balmer, A. S., and others, 'Taking Roles in Interdisciplinary Collaborations: Reflections on Working in Post-ELSI Spaces in the UK Synthetic Biology Community', *Science & Technology Studies*, 28.3 (2015), 3–25 <https://sciencetechnologystudies.journal.fi/article/view/55340/18172> [accessed 3 November 2020].

Bhattacharya, S., R. Gachhui, and P. C. Sil, 'Effect of Kombucha, a Fermented Black Tea in Attenuating Oxidative Stress Mediated Tissue Damage in Alloxan-Induced Diabetic Rats', *Food Chem Toxicol*, 60 (2013), 328–40.

Bond, P., and L. Browder, 'Deracialized Nostalgia, Reracialized Community, and Truncated Gentrification: Capital and Cultural Flows in Richmond, Virginia and Durban, South Africa', *Journal of Cultural Geography*, 36.2 (2019), 211–45.

Brodmann, T., and others, 'Safety of Novel Microbes for Human Consumption: Practical Examples of Assessment in the European Union', *Frontiers in Microbiology*, 8.1725 (2017).

Callard, F., and D. Fitzgerald, *Rethinking Interdisciplinarity Across the Social Sciences and Neurosciences* (London: Palgrave Macmillan, 2015).

Companies and Markets, 'Kombucha market sales forecast to total US$1.8Bn by 2020: Kombucha market by types - forecasts to 2020', <https://search-proquest-com.libaccess.hud.ac.uk/docview/1719914980?accountid=11526> [accessed 15 November 2020].

Hirschauer, S., and A. Mol, 'Shifting Sexes, Moving Stories: Feminist/Constructivist Dialogues', *Science, Technology, & Human Values*, 20.3 (1995), 368–85 <http://www.jstor.org/stable/690021> [accessed 30 October 2020].

Jasarevic, L., 'The Thing in a Jar: Mushrooms and Ontological Speculations in Post-Yugoslavia', *Cultural Anthropology*, 30.1 (2015), 36–64.

Jayabalan, R., and others, 'A Review on Kombucha Tea – Microbiology, Composition, Fermentation, Beneficial Effects, Toxicity, and Tea Fungus', *Comprehensive Reviews in Food Science and Food Safety*, 13.4 (2014), 538–50.

Katz, S. E., *The Art of Fermentation: An In-Depth Exploration of Essential Concepts and Processes From Around the World* (White River Junction, Vt: Chelsea Green Pub, 2012).

Maroney, S., 'Sandor Katz and the Possibilities of a Queer Fermentive Praxis', *Cuizine*, 9.2 (2018).

Marsh, J. A. A., and others, 'Sequence-Based Analysis of the Bacterial and Fungal Compositions of Multiple Kombucha Tea (Tea Fungus) Samples', *Food Microbiology*, 38 (2014), 171–8.

May, A., and others, 'Kombucha: A Novel Model System for Cooperation and Conflict in a Complex Multi-Species Microbial Ecosystem', *PeerJ- Life and Environment*, 7.e7565 (2019).

Mol, A., *The Body Multiple: Ontology in Medical Practice* (Durham, N.C. and London: Duke University Press, 2002).

Paxson, H., 'Post-Pasteurian Cultures: The Microbiopolitics of Raw-Milk Cheese in the United States', *Cultural Anthropology*, 23.1 (2008), 15–47.

Rees, T., T. Bosch, and A. E. Douglas, 'How the Microbiome Challenges Our Concept of Self', *PLoS Biology*, 16.2 (2018).

Sariola, S., and others, 'Coffee Time at the Conference: The Global Health Complex in Action to Tackle Antimicrobial Resistance', *Science & Technology Studies*, 30.4 (2017), 2–7.

Spackman, C. C. W., 'Formulating Citizenship: The Microbiopolitics of the Malfunctioning Functional Beverage', *Biosocieties*, 13.1 (2018), 41–63.

Stengers, I., *Another Science is Possible: A Manifesto for Slow Science* (Cambridge: Polity Press, 2018).

Villarreal-Soto, S. A., and others, 'Understanding Kombucha Tea Fermentation: A Review', *Journal of Food Science*, 83.3 (2018), 580–88.

Woolgar, S., 'A Coffeehouse Conversation on the Possibility of Mechanizing Discovery and Its Sociological Analysis', *Social Studies of Science*, 19.4 (1989), 658–68.

PLURIBIOSIS AND THE NEVER-ENDING MICROGEOHISTORIES

Charlotte Brives

VIRUSES ARE DEFINED BY SCIENTISTS AS STRICT PARASITES, ENTITIES WHICH cannot survive without a host organism. Generally speaking, viruses penetrate specific cells within a specific organism and use the metabolic machinery of those cells to power their own reproduction. For some virologists and philosophers of science, the dependency of viruses on their hosts means that they cannot truly be classified as living beings, since they are incapable of surviving alone, they exist 'on the fringes' of life. They are not living beings, but nor are they non-organic. The debate is unlikely to be concluded in the near future, since developments in our scientific understanding regularly offer new information which can be difficult to conceptualise. For example, the discovery of the existence of virophages, small viruses that infect larger ones, has put paid to the dogma that a virus can only be a parasite and never a host. It turns out that viruses are also vulnerable to infection.

Nevertheless, it is possible to conceptualise the problem in a different way: a strict parasite cannot be understood without reference to its host, since its very existence depends upon the relationship established between the two of them. In this respect, viruses require us to think beyond the old dichotomy of the living and non-living and instead to embrace a broader understanding of the fundamentally relational nature of biological entities. Although sequencing the DNA of viruses provides insight into their incredible genetic diversity,[1] the vast majority of viral characteristics, capacities and competences cannot be experimentally studied, understood or assimilated without reference to the interactions the virus forms with the living species (animal, plant, or bacterial) with which it co-evolves. Their very existence is therefore defined by relationality.

In this chapter, using the specific case of bacteriophage viruses (literally: bacteria-eating viruses) and their bacterial hosts, I explore how taking into account this relational dimension of biological entities can allow us to imagine new therapeutic assemblages. Since their discovery at the beginning of the twentieth century, phages have indeed been used to treat bacterial infections. Although they were neglected in the second half of the twentieth century, notably due to the discovery and then massive production of antibiotics in the 1940s, there has been growing interest in their use since the early 2000s, due to the rise in bacterial resistance to antibiotics.

This revival of phage therapy comes as a counterpoint to the multiple problems posed by the inattentions of production and massive consumption of antibiotics and calls for an examination of the way in which the relationships between humans, microbes and environments are conceived. Whether in bacterial infections or in viral epidemics, as the Covid-19 pandemic has shown and still shows, warlike metaphors predominate (Larson et al. 2005; Brives 2020).

But more generally, the different stories about microbes in social sciences and in biomedicine are often based on opposing duos: war/peace, probiosis/ antibiosis, Pasteurian/post-Pasteurian (Paxson 2008, 2011; Lorimer 2017, 2020; for further developments, see the introduction of this book). Even the term amphibiosis – coined by Theodore Roseberry in the 1960s and then used by the microbiologist Martin Blaser to recognise the possibility of a biological entity being friend or foe, depending on the context – does not extend beyond this binary view of relations between species (Blaser 2014). This is because these narratives are based on a relatively fixed conception of biological entities, and thus make it impossible to think about how their relationships, in one way or another, transform them.

Thus, the recognition of the variability of relations between humans and microorganisms, as this collective volume testifies, may be an important step but it is also a question of going beyond a fixist conception of both relations between species (by recognising that the relational status of 'friends' or 'enemies' is spatially and temporally located) and *of the species themselves* (by taking into account the transformative potential of interspecific encounters).

In this chapter, I describe the practices of isolation and collection of new bacteriophage viruses, which are essential to the development of phage therapy. In particular, I show how the collection constitutes the capture at a particular point in time, for reasons specific to the experimenter (and by extension to the functioning of phage therapy), of a constantly evolving relationship between a virus, a bacterium and a human. If not conducted carefully, however, this capture can lead to an essentialisation of the entities thus collected. It is then necessary to integrate this work of collection into a wider account of the relationships between humans, viruses and bacteria.

Observing and learning from viruses and bacteria gives us an opportunity to understand the term 'pluribiosis'. Pluribiosis is the recognition of the existence of multiple relational spectra between entities forever in the process of becoming, constantly shaped and transformed by their interactions with other living things, and by the context in which they occur.

In what way can this form of attention to the relations that pluribiosis represents help us develop alternative conceptions of health and ways of treating infections? Because it involves at least humans, viruses, bacteria and environments – according to temporalities specific to each biological entity – phage therapy offers us narratives that refuse fixity and recognise the situated knowledge (Haraway 1988) and situated biologies (Niewöhner and Lock 2018), and therefore the necessarily situated character, of their applications in biomedicine.

This chapter is informed by three years of fieldwork with agents in phage therapy (researchers, clinicians, patients, regulatory agencies) in France, Belgium, and Switzerland, as well as by my membership of bacteriophage virus research networks.

HOW TO PLAY WITH THE POTENTIALITIES OF PHAGES

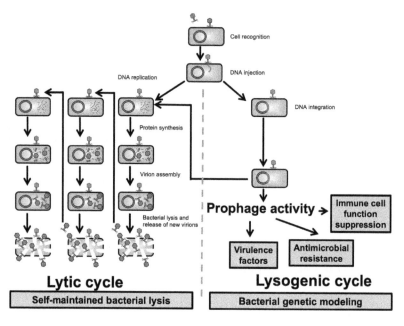

FIG. 11.1 Lytic and lysogenic cycles of bacteriophage viruses (credit: Tristan Ferry, Hospices Civils de Lyon, Phages In Lyon)

Phages and bacteria have been co-evolving in dynamic and complex ways from their origins. Phages are the most numerous forms of biological entity on earth. It is estimated that at any given time, 40% of bacteria on the planet are infected with a virus. However, the relationships between phages and bacteria are highly specific: a virus is generally only capable of infecting a single species of bacteria. Some are even specific to just one of the genetic variants of that species. Moreover, when a given bacteriophage comes into contact with a population of clonal bacteria (genetically identical bacteria), the consequences are not always the same (see Figure 11.1). Some of the bacteria will die, destroyed by the virus which has used them in order to self-multiply (lytic cycle). Others will learn to live with the virus, having acquired the ability to withstand infection either through mutation or selection. Others still will develop a profoundly intimate relationship with the virus: the latter will become integrated into the genetic material of its host, either temporarily or permanently (lysogenic cycle). If they do finally part ways, the virus may leave behind some of its genetic material and/or take away part of the bacteria's genome, leaving both entities transformed as a result (this is notably how viruses participate in the spread of antibiotic resistance genes in bacteria through transduction phenomena).

The bactericidal potential of phages has been used in therapy since their discovery in 1917 (d'Hérelle 2017). However, it was not until the second half of the twentieth century that the resources offered by phage therapy were understood.[2] Today, a consensus exists around the use of phages for therapeutic purposes, based on the use of strict 'virulent' phages (phages that perform lytic cycles and are unable to enter a lysogenic one when they encounter the bacteria of interest). Temperate phages could indeed give the bacterium new skills, including the impossibility of establishing any other relationship whatsoever with an identical phage.

The principle of the therapy is simple: isolate the bacterial strain responsible for the infection in a human, then find a strictly virulent phage active on this bacterium and administer it to the patient. Since phage therapy is still experimental, the process is generally split: hospital infectious diseases specialists isolate the bacterial strain, then send it to one or more research laboratories to determine whether they have phages active against the pathogen in their collections. Then, once one or more active phages have been isolated, characterised and produced according to standards ensuring their biological quality, they are sent to the hospital to treat the patient. This chapter is devoted to the isolation and collection of new phages. The availability of such collections is a *sine qua non* condition for the development of phage therapy. A collection may place a focus on the scientific and technical processes involved, but it also constitutes an ontological bifurcation, which can lead to different models of development.

The ethnographic part of this chapter is based on fieldwork carried out in a Swiss laboratory in November 2019. The team was led by Jim, a biologist who has been working on phages for over 20 years.[3] For several years now, Jim's team has been working on the creation of collections of virulent phages active on multidrug-resistant (MDR) bacterial species considered problematic in terms of public health by the WHO.[4] Jim almost never works in the lab. Most of his time is now spent filling out funding requests. I therefore spent most of my time with Julie, the team's technician, who does almost all the lab work, observing her manipulating phages and bacteria.

Shortly before I arrived in the laboratory, Jim received two strains of two different bacterial species responsible for the infection of a patient being treated at a university hospital in France. The patient was infected with a strain of *Klebsiella pneumoniae* (KP) as well as a strain of *Proteus miserabilis* (PM), both antibiotic-resistant. Faced with the failure of successive treatments, the doctors in charge of the patient turned to Jim to try phages. However, the laboratory did not have any phages active on Proteus, a bacterium with which it does not usually work, and the phages they had for Klebsiella were ineffective on the patient's strain. Jim and Julie decided to find phages active against these two bacteria to send to the university hospital.

There are different techniques for working with phages and bacteria. During my presence in the laboratory, Julie worked mainly in a solid environment, i.e. with petri dishes. In general, the techniques are relatively simple: Julie first pours a culture medium into large square petri dishes, to which she adds a bacterium of interest. The culture medium slowly hardens and forms a transparent agar. Normally, if this dish is then placed in an incubator at 37°C, the bacteria will reproduce. Thus, after a few hours, a bacterial mat can be observed. The agar then has an opaque appearance, proof of the presence of bacteria evenly distributed over the petri dish (see Figure 11.2). If, before placing this dish in the chamber, drops of solution containing phages are placed on the hardened agar, then we can observe plaque forming units (PFU): small transparent holes in the bacterial mat (see Figure 11.3). There are no more bacteria in these areas. They have been lysed.

Julie uses these techniques, which seem simple at first glance, to isolate new phages. But where to find them? As mentioned, phages, being strict parasites of bacteria, are found everywhere that bacteria live. The best place to find them is in so-called rich waters – sewage or treatment plants, for example. Over the past

FIG. 11.2 Petri dish containing a nutrient medium and a bacterial strain. After 24 hours in an incubator at 37°C, a uniform opacity can be observed due to the development of the strain, which forms a mat (photograph by Charlotte Brives, 2019).

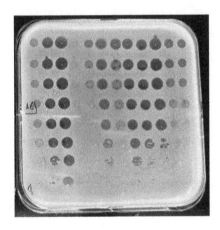

FIG. 11.3 Petri dish on which drops containing bacteriophage viruses have been placed before placement in the incubator. We can observe plaque- forming units (PFU): the bacteria have been destroyed, their absence indicating the presence and activity of the bacteriophage viruses (photograph by Charlotte Brives, 2019).

three years, I have learnt that not all waters are equal. A technician working in a start-up told me water withdrawals downstream of the chemical industries should be avoided. And Julie mentioned: 'hospital waters work well, much better than anything else. We're very happy only looking in hospital waters'. Hospitals are overflowing with bacteria, which are most often multidrug-resistant due to the high selection pressure exerted by repeated antibiotic treatments on patients.

To this must be added the relational dimension of phages, which Julie repeated several times during my fieldwork: a phage cannot be thought of alone. It is always a phage/bacteria pair. So, when I asked her if, because of the co-evolution between phages and bacteria, it was not more interesting to look for phages in waters near where the patient fell ill, Julie gave this answer:

> Yes, most of the time that's an easier option. Because the population around
> you potentially has the same bacteria. We know that generally speaking the
> bacteria we find in Europe will not be the same as in the United States, so the
> waters will not work in the same way and there is little chance that a phage
> from the United States will work as well on our collections.

This territorialisation of the relationships between phages and bacteria was exemplified by Julie in the case of a patient hospitalised in a city close to where Jim's team is located. Several laboratories in Europe were asked to find an active phage against the bacteria responsible for its infection. Jim's lab, near the city where the patient was hospitalised, was the only one with phages that showed positive results on the patient's bacteria. This example is often brought up by various actors I have met in recent years to highlight the ecosystemic dimension of phage therapy.

We are therefore witnessing a geographical discrimination of waters, which reflects the co-evolutionary relationship of these two biological entities; the best place to find an active phage on a pathogenic bacterium is near the origin of this pathogenic bacterium.

However, Julie went even further, mentioning that she had often observed that French waters generally work better than Swiss waters, and she had developed a hypothesis for this:

> In France, we find them more easily than in Switzerland so I wonder if they
> use certain water treatment processes. Or perhaps the Swiss are cleaner than
> the French, perhaps they have more hygiene regulations than in France. I
> did wonder that. I think they may be cleaner than the French.

For Julie, not all waters are equivalent, and the factors involved are very diverse. The therapies used, hygiene rules, public health policies and water treatment may influence the presence and therefore existence (or not) of phages and their diversity.

It was by pouring rich waters onto the dishes and making repeat observations that Julie developed explanations and arguments for the richness of waters and the continuum between the micro- and macro-biology of entities and multi-specific communities.

She poured a nutrient medium into several petri dishes, to which she also added her bacteria of interest, either KP or PM. She then poured water from different sources onto each of the dishes and placed them in an incubator at 37°C for 24 hours. The next day, she looked carefully at her dishes for PFU. Wherever there was a hole in the mat, and therefore probably a phage, Julie took a sample. She prepared a test tube in which she put a liquid nutrient medium, the bacteria of interest and the sample taken on the PFU. She then placed everything in the incubator for three hours during which the bacteria (and perhaps the phage) reproduced. Finally, she centrifuged the tube for ten minutes.

The heavy bacteria were then concentrated in a pellet, a small deposit at the bottom of the tube. She recovered the supernatant, which she filtered to remove bacterial debris. Part of this filtrate was placed back on a petri dish containing the nutrient medium and the bacteria of interest. If there were still PFU after another round of incubation, she would repeat the process: sampling, incubation, centrifugation, filtration. Julie carries out between three to eight cycles (sampling, incubation, centrifugation, filtration) in order to isolate a phage. According to her, performing these separate cycles means she can be sure that the sample contains just one phage and that it is active.[5]

During these different cycles, Julie learnt a lot about her phages and bacteria: the ideal moment to put them in contact, the length of this contact time and the optimal temperature. The methods used may have been standardised, but she learnt to take into account not simply the characteristics of a phage and a bacterium but also the characteristics of their encounter – another reminder that each encounter, each relationship, is unique.

Julie summed this up during our discussion in the lab:

You have to grope about! You grope about and you have to test different methods. You might play with the temperature a little bit. It's a lot of trial and error. Everyone says it's super easy [to produce phages], and overall, it is easy. But you might have to make small adjustments. If you want phages that all have certain characteristics, you've got to work with the phage.

'Work with the phage'. Each phage/bacteria pair is unique, and so is the relationship between the technician and a given pair. The skills and know-how Julie has acquired from being in contact with microorganisms are essential. Some bacteria, such as *Staphyloccocus aureus*, are described by the technician as 'capricious', others as 'permissive'. Some do not 'work properly', which can mean that 'your phages will not perform as well'. Thus, it is a question of taking into account the particularities of each relationship and the way in which historicity is embodied in the biology of each organism.

NAMING A PHAGE, OR THE SNAPSHOTS OF MICROGEOHISTORIES

After these various stages, Julie obtained three active phages against the patient's KP strain and two phages for the PM strain.

These phages would later be sequenced to know their genome, but she was already convinced that the three anti-Klebsiella phages were different. In addition to having been isolated in waters of different origins, she showed me the PFU: 'they don't have the same morphology at all. Typically, for KP95, I'll have three different phages. These are good ones. This one's very tiny, it's not very clear'.

What she could see with the naked eye, with disconcerting ease, required my close attention, even though she had told me what to look for: the size of the PFU, the regularity of their edges, their opacity. Julie had developed a level of intimacy with the lab's phages that even Jim envied.

Her statement, 'They do not have the same morphology at all', is simplistic because it is in fact the PFU, the holes in the bacterial mat, and not the phages, which do not have the same morphology. The phages cannot be observed with the naked eye. This is yet another reminder that what was being evaluated was in fact a relationship, not a biological entity as such, whose presence and skills were only visible through their effects on bacteria and deeply mediated by the technician's perspective.

This point is illustrated by the assignment of a name to each of the new phages Julie had isolated. One of the anti-Klebsiella phages was named 4035-KP95. All the phages in the laboratory starting with 4000 are Klebsiella phages. It was therefore the 35th Klebsiella phage in the collection. The segment 'KP95' corresponds to the name of the bacterial strain from which the phage has been isolated. This reinforces, if necessary, the strong relational dimension and the historicity of each entity. Since phages and bacteria co-evolve permanently, if this phage were to come into contact with another bacterium, say KP112, the resulting phage could be given the name 4035-KP112, to take into account its probable evolution. It would no longer be exactly the same phage, as Julie explains: 'it's a phage-bacterium pair. Change your bacteria or anything else, and your results will be different. Your phage will not react in the same way'.

This leads us to another conclusion concerning the phage's entry into a collection: the act of naming the phage is not only a scientific 'birth' act of the phage, but above all an act of fixation, crystallisation, essentialisation of a relationship. The technician decides, at a given time, after bringing phages and bacteria together, to put an end to a relationship that is destined to constantly evolve. At that precise moment, the technician considers that the phage she has in front of her perfectly expresses the potential she wanted to exploit in its relationship with the bacteria of interest: this phage is virulent, exhausting (almost) all the bacteria it encounters in order to reproduce. This phage and this bacterium will then join the laboratory's collection. Each will be placed in tubes and stored in two freezers, to which only the technician and the team leader have access, at -80°C.

Once in the collection, all this work of isolation and characterisation must not be in vain: nothing must change. Patients' bacteria, like the phages of sewage water, must remain alive but no longer evolve, whether on paper or in a test tube because what the technician knows is only valid for this particular pair, at this particular moment in their relationship.

During the experiments, everything is based on relationships and everything happens because there are co-evolutionary relationships, therefore entry into the collection sanctions the objectification of microorganisms. The assignment of a name implies a marked identity. Each new phage is then sequenced, and the sequence of nucleic acids sets this identity in stone.

In this context, the laboratory's collections can be seen as snapshots of microgeohistories. Each phage has a history: it is isolated from a water sample collected in a specific place and at a given time, on the bacterial strain of a patient who themselves has a complex history, sometimes in a nearby area, sometimes not. Other phages, such as the hypothetical 4035-KP112, will result from the encounter between one of the phages in the collection and a new bacterium, perhaps taken from a person suffering greatly from its presence in his or her body. Collections are therefore the fixation, at a given moment, of a tripartite human/bacterial/phage relationship.

The colossal level of work required to maintain these collections, and the precautions surrounding their handling, however, testify to their scientific and therapeutic value as well as their precarity. During a laboratory ethnography conducted on the relationship between humans and *Saccharomyces cerevisiae* yeasts, I showed how access to the -80°C freezer, which contained the laboratory's yeast collection, was strictly regulated. The comings and goings around the freezer, the organisation of the laboratory, its implicit and explicit norms, the evident rules of laboratory life ensured that what was in the freezer, the yeast strains, remained identical to themselves and could continue to constitute 'reliable witnesses' to the experiment, to use Isabelle Stengers' expression (Stengers 1993; Brives 2017). In the Swiss laboratory I worked in, it was much the same. Everything is rendered more complicated because of the particularities of phages and bacteria, and the relational nature of the collections. When a particular phage has been isolated from a particular bacterium, both must be preserved.

These collections are precious. They are set up in order to create the greatest possible diversity of phages available in order to be able to treat patients. But it is important to remain cautious and to take them for what they are: snapshots of never-ending microgeohistory, never-ending multispecific dances. And yet phages are still most often presented, in conferences or writings aimed at the general public, as 'professional killers' of bacteria, or as 'snipers'. These metaphors are far from insignificant and can, as we shall see, guide the development of phage therapy in one direction or another.

PLURIBIOSIS, OR THE CREATIVE POWERS OF THE LIVING

The relational capacities of phages and bacteria have been observed and utilised in laboratories for decades. They have powered the development of molecular biology (Kay 1993; Morange 1994), opening up vast new horizons for both fundamental and applied research (for example the ability to produce genetically modified organisms, therapeutic molecules, biofuels, etc.), as illustrated by the award of the 2020 Nobel Prize in Chemistry to Emmanuelle Charpentier and Jennifer Doudna for their work on the CRISPR-Cas9 system. Many scientists do not consider phages as life forms, but simply as tools in the service of human needs. The manipulation of 'life' as a soulless, disembodied force has been the stuff of countless science fiction stories and dystopian visions, more often than not used to castigate mankind's tendency to objectify and commodify nature, a force which remains exasperatingly external to humanity. For other thinkers, these capabilities are a constant source of new questions regarding the spectrum of life, cooperation, evolution and ecology. Studying viruses and bacteria reveals far more than just a spectrum of relational mechanisms. It lays bare the essential plasticity of these entities, their shared existence in and through the relationships they form. Thanks to the fusion of its genetic material during a lysogenic cycle, the mode of existence of the virus changes radically. It becomes an integral part of the host bacterium. Some papers sometimes describe these viruses as being 'dormant', which could give the impression that during this time the virus is not *doing* anything. Meanwhile, the bacterium in which the virus is 'dormant' develops new capacities. To whom do they belong? The bacterium or the virus? Do the two entities still exist independently of one another, or have they become a new entity entirely, a hybrid? These questions are rendered even more complex by the fact that the new entity thus formed may enjoy only a fleeting existence. In certain conditions, the viral genetic material may separate from that of the bacterium, replicate itself hundreds of times to form new viral particles and break free, killing the bacterium in the process. Can the resulting entities be considered the same virus, or the same bacterium?

Once again, metaphors play an important role here. It is difficult to express 'viro-bacterial' behaviour in words without having recourse to the familiar vocabulary of sexual reproduction and immunology – both highly gendered discourses, as anthropologist Emily Martin has demonstrated (Martin 1991, 1995). Scientists talk of phages 'injecting' their DNA, 'penetrating' the host cell, 'lurking' or 'concealing themselves'. They describe them as 'sleeper agents' in bacterial DNA, when they are not acting as 'professional killers' or 'snipers'. The vocabulary used is all about transgression, violation, insidious conflict and destruction, while phage behaviours could be framed very differently, sometimes by the same researchers, talking about their incredible potentialities and the way they engage in kinky sex, 'homologous and illegitimate recombination with related and completely alien genomes, orgies of hundreds of genes' (Rohwer et al. 2014). Some virologists, having become intimately familiar with the world of phages and bacteria, are reluctant to say that the phage even 'kills' its host. In many cases, the bacteria simply die because all of its resources have been used up by the virus. These reformulations reveal the possibility of an entirely different narrative: one in which the virus does not intentionally kill the bacterium but instead uses it as a matrix for a process of replication and creation which incorporates fragments of the bacterium itself. A process of creative forces breaking free of the dogmas of sexual reproduction and immunology, unfettered from notions of self and other, organic intimacies which reveal the porous nature of the categories upon which modern Western thought relies to understand and control the world. This hints at the possibility of a more subtle spectrum of relations between entities, which are increasingly difficult to essentialise. And in a further layer of complexity, we must bear in mind that these relationships also depend upon the broader milieus within which they exist, and which they help to shape and compose, sometimes with spectacular results.[6]

These modes of interaction are not specific to viruses and bacteria. Between 5% and 8% of the human genome is of viral origin, i.e. created by the fusion, at one time or another in the evolutionary history of this species, of the genetic material of a virus with that of an 'infected' host cell. The most well-known example in the animal kingdom is the existence of syncytins, proteins essential to placental development. This capacity is specific to mammals but was in fact – and this is only a paradox if one is committed at all costs to maintaining the distinction between the 'essence' of a living thing and its pollution by external elements – made possible by interactions with a virus in the distant past (Dupressoir et al. 2012). This DNA of viral origin, much of which is considered to be 'junk DNA' because of its apparent (read immediate, current) uselessness, can be seen as a sort of fossil record of relational experiences – a precious archive of the events which led mammals to their current state.

The essentialisation of entities and relations is only possible if you stop their movement or slow it down sufficiently (when you do not simply freeze it as we saw in the lab). In this respect the microbial world is precious. Without claiming to account for all of the differences which exist between these forms of life, we can at least point out that the time frames in which they operate are clearly distinct from our own. The span of one human life is time enough for thousands of generations of bacteria, billions of cells living and interacting with bacteriophages, engaging in mutual transformations and acting upon the milieus which they inhabit. In short, bacteria work *much faster* than humans do and, in doing so, they allow scientists to observe processes which require painstaking reconstruction and considerable guesswork in the animal and plant kingdoms.

The importance of movement and the realisation that it is impossible to think effectively without it is fundamental to understanding viruses and bacteria. It is only the distortion effect induced by the slowing down of time that causes us to imagine univocal relationships between entities whose essential identities remain fixed, imagining the milieus in which they exist (and which they in fact help to shape and transform) to be simple backdrops or static scenery, when they actively participate in their transformation.

The observation of viruses and bacteria does not lead to an essentialisation of entities, relationships and milieus; rather, it allows us to consider pluribiosis: the entanglement of multiple situated relational spectrums that involve entities and milieus that are always in the process of becoming, constantly formed or transformed by interactions.

If essentialisations are necessary for scientific activity (and, more generally, action), the notion of pluribiosis reminds us that they are situated and fixed instantiations, snapshots, of the fundamentally relational nature of life. Reporting/focusing/accounting for situations and relationships that the different actors – biologists, ecologists, physicians, regulators, patients – that I have met or read about describe and go through, then, makes it possible to grasp the diversity and becomings of entities.

Pluribiosis is a heuristic concept because it recognises the importance of relations and milieus and, thus, prevents us from assuming what is biological or social, natural or cultural. It maintains a close attention to what the entities become and the transformations that shape the situations described and what they contain. It is a prescriptive concept as well, insofar as it recognises the fundamentally multiple and situated nature of knowledge about life (pluri-biosis) but also the transformation potential of these knowledges. If evolution and relation are constitutive of life, then the knowledge that claims to account for it, as well as its uses, must be included in the configurations in which it is produced. As the ethnography of our collection of bacteriophages has shown, this is an element that should not be overlooked in the development of phage therapy.

TOWARDS A PLURIBIOTIC MEDICINE

Paying attention to the forms of interaction between phages and bacteria, and observing laboratory practices that allow the isolation and selection of phages for their capacity to develop one form of interaction to the detriment of others, encourages thoughts of another conception of medicine and care. This is a medicine that I have chosen to describe as pluribiotic, considerate of the never-ending histories of multispecific assemblages which are always in the process of becoming.

Because they never lose sight of the evolutionary and creative capacities of the living, researchers and physicians condition therapeutic success on the use of not one but several phages for a given bacterium. Although a phage can be selected and 'trained' for its lytic abilities, the creative powers of living things cannot be controlled and mastered. Once brought into contact at the time of patient treatment, phages and bacteria will continue to explore a spectrum of relationships that can never be completely reduced to what humans want to do with them. The disappearance of the pathogenic bacterium can be ensured by the joint action of a single phage and the human immune system. The former will drastically reduce the bacterial population, the latter will then be able to effectively treat the infection. Although different phages chosen by humans because of their virulence on the pathogenic bacteria are administered, each one will start its own dance with the latter, each one will use it as a fertile matrix to reproduce, reinvent itself, metamorphose. The bacterium will then no longer be able to interact with the phages long enough to find new assemblages, new becoming-with (Haraway 2003). It will disappear.

For these reasons, the availability and the success of phage therapy depends on the constitution of phage collections. The practices that enable these collections are therefore fundamental and at the heart of the development of this alternative/complement to antibiotics, as are the issues they raise. For those who are not attentive, for those who do not grasp the resources offered by pluribiosis and the patient adjustments made between phages, bacteria, humans and the environment, collections can appear as a manna: reified, controllable, standardisable, exploitable and mass usable entities. If neglected, collecting appears to be an end, not a necessary detour. The microgeohistories at work are then frozen in History, that of Human control over Nature.[7] The collecting of phages becomes a tipping point, a possible bifurcation between radically different projects and conceptions of infection, care and the production of new therapies.

This is precisely where the possibilities of phage therapy come into play: in the choices we make in the way we approach and use these collections.

Currently, there is some form of consensus on the possibility of developing two models of therapy, which can easily be linked to a differential use of collections and to opposing conceptions of the living: the 'sur-mesure' and the 'prêt-à-porter' models (Pirnay et al. 2011). The first involves the selection, within collections, of highly virulent phages on the bacterial strain responsible for the infection. It may also involve adjusting these phages to the bacterial strain, by 'training' the phages to increase their virulence. In this model, the assemblages between phages, pathogenic bacteria and humans come first. The second model decontextualises the infection. Favoured in particular by start-ups, it is based on the development of cocktails containing a few phages that show activity on a wide variety of strains of a given bacterial species. The collections can help to identify such phages. These phages could then be produced, marketed and administered en masse. In this 'prêt-à-porter' conception of treatment, which can also be described as a 'one-size-fits-all' approach, the living, co-evolutive dimension is unthinkable. The objectified phage becomes an umpteenth antibiotic and is used as a chemical molecule (Brives and Pourraz 2020). The phages of this type of cocktail could then be only partially active and, for example, infer the selection of resistant bacteria.

The sometimes deregulated and often unquestioned use of antibiotics in human and animal health has, however, largely led to the rise of antimicrobial resistance (AMR). What has been forgotten is precisely the dynamic, relational and adaptive nature of living things, the creative power of the living. Science historian Hannah Landecker (2016: 21) has shown how the antibiotics industry has completely changed the biology of bacteria:

> The bacteria of today are not the bacteria of yesterday, whether that change is registered culturally, genetically, physiologically, ecologically or medically. Bacteria today have different plasmids and traits and interrelations and capacities and distributions and temporalities than bacteria before modern antibiotics. It is not even clear that 'bacteria' remains the only or the most salient category with which to think about antibiotic resistance. This biological matter, chewing away its own ontology, is historically and culturally – and materially – specific to late industrialism, produced in and by previous modes of knowledge.

AMR, to which phages participate when developing lysogenic relations to bacteria, can be seen as the manifestation of pluribiosis, of the creative power of the living. These creative powers are not in themselves good or bad. They simply create new assemblages. The living acts and reacts. Faced with chemical molecules, bacteria have evolved very quickly towards new and cumulative forms of resistance. What if, instead of chemical molecules or in addition to chemical molecules, bacteria were massively exposed to standardised phage cocktails, biological entities that also have tremendous evolutionary capacities?

The deeply relational nature of living things is a forgotten element in antibiotic therapy. Phages, by their particularities, help us to remember this dimension and to develop, as many agents in phage therapy hope, a medicine that actively takes pluribiosis into account.

It is therefore a matter of making a choice to be attentive to pluribiosis; to contextualise within never-ending microgeohistories; and to renounce both 'one-size-fits-all' solutions, which will imply creating new models of development (Brives and Pourraz 2020). Also to be renounced is the perpetuation of the story of Human control over Nature, the possible consequences of which humans can no longer ignore.

NOTES

1 See the phylogenetic map available at: http://virusmap.univ-lyon1.fr/.

2 For more details on a historical approach to bacteriophages and phage therapy, see the special issue edited by Neeraja Sankaran (2020).

3 For reasons of confidentiality, Jim's identity, his laboratory and the city in which it is located have been removed.

4 These bacterial species are known under the acronym ESKAPE, for *Escherichia coli*, *Staphylococcus aureus*, *Klebsiella pneumoniae*, *Acinetobacter baumannii*, *Pseudomonas aeruginosa* and *Enterobacter sp.*

5 Confirmation of the purity of the phage will come with sequencing and a more complete characterisation of the isolated phage, a stage in the process that I do not cover in this article.

6 For an example of the involvement of bacteriophage viruses in trophic chains, see Peduzzi et al. (2014).

7 In *Facing Gaïa, Eight lectures on the new climatic regime* (2017), Bruno Latour uses the term gaïahistoire, which he contrasts with History. Donna Haraway takes up this distinction between geohistory and the History of Man's control of Nature in *Staying with the Trouble* (2017).

ACKNOWLEDGEMENTS

I thank the Kilpisjärvi Collective, Alexis Zimmer and Bruno Latour for comments on earlier drafts of this text. I acknowledge the support of the Agence Nationale de la Recherche (grant no ANR-18-CE36-0001) and the Région Nouvelle-Aquitaine (grant no 2018-1R40218).

REFERENCES

Blaser, M., *Missing Microbes* (New York: Picador, 2014).

Brives, C., 'Que font les scientifiques lorsqu'ils ne sont pas naturalistes ? Le cas des levuristes', *L'Homme*, 222 (2017): 35–56.

—— 'The Politics of Amphibiosis: The War against Viruses Will Not Take Place', *Somatosphere* (2020) <http://somatosphere.net/2020/the-politics-of-amphibiosis.html/> [accessed 6 November 2020].

Brives, C., and J. Pourraz, 'Phage Therapy as a Potential Solution in the Fight against AMR: Obstacles and Possible Futures', *Palgrave Communications*, 6.100 (2020).

Dupressoir, A., C. Lavialle, and T. Heidmann, 'From Ancestral Infectious Retroviruses to Bona Fide Cellular Genes: Role of the Captured Syncytins in Placentation', *Placenta* 33.9 (2012), 663–71.

Haraway, D., 'Situated Knowledges: The Science Question in Feminism and the Privilege of Partial Perspective', *Feminist Studies*, 14.3 (1988), 575–99.

—— *The Companion Species Manifesto: Dogs, People, and Significant Otherness* (Chicago: Prickly Paradigm Press, 2003).

—— *Staying with the Trouble, Making Kin in the Chthulucene* (Durham, NC: Duke University Press, 2016).

d'Hérelle, F., 'Sur un microbe invisible antagoniste des bacilles dysentériques. Compte-rendu de l'Académie des Sciences' 165.11 (1917), 373–5.

Kay, L., *The Molecular Vision of Life* (Oxford: Oxford University Press, 1993).

Landecker, H., 'Antibiotic Resistance and the Biology of History', *Body & Society*, 22.4 (2016), 19–52.

Larson, B. M. H., B. Nerlich, and P. Wallis, 'Metaphors and Biorisks: The War on Infectious Diseases and Invasive Species', *Science Communication*, 26.3 (2005), 243–68.

Latour, B., *Facing Gaïa: Eight lectures on the New Climatic Regime* (Polity Press, 2017).

Lorimer, J., 'Probiotic Environmentalities: Rewilding with Wolves and Worms', *Theory, Culture & Society*, 34 (2017), 27–48.

—— *The Probiotic Planet: Using Life to Manage Life* (Minneapolis: University of Minnesota Press, 2020).

Martin, E., 'The Egg and the Sperm: How Science Has Constructed a Romance Based on Stereotypical Male-Female Roles', *Journal of Women in Culture and Society*, 16.3 (1991), 485–501.

—— *Flexible Bodies* (Boston: Beacon Press 1995).

Morange, M., *Histoire de la biologie moléculaire* (Paris: La Découverte, 1994).

Niewöhner, J., and M. Lock, 'Situating Local Biologies: Anthropological Perspectives on Environment/Human Entanglements', *Biosocieties*, 13 (2018), 681–97.

Paxson, H., 'Post-Pasteurian Cultures: The Microbiopolitics of Raw-Milk Cheese in the United States', *Cultural Anthropology*, 23 (2008), 15–47.

—— *The Life of Cheese: Crafting Food and Value in America* (Berkeley: University of California Press, 2012).

Peduzzi, P., and others, 'The Virus's Tooth: Cyanophages Affect an African Flamingo Population in a Bottom-Up Cascade', *ISME*, 8.6 (2014), 1346–51.

Pirnay, J. P., and others, 'The Phage Therapy Paradigm: prêt-à-porter ou sur-mesure?', *Pharmaceutical Research*, 28 (2011), 934–7.

Rohwer, F., and others, *Life in Our Phage Wordl: A Centennial Field Guide to the Earth's Most Diverse Inhabitants* (San Diego: Wholon, 2014).

Sankaran, N., ed., *Diversifying the Historiography of Bacteriophages*, Notes and Records: Special Issue, 74.4 (London: The Royal Society, 2020).

12

OLD ANTHROPOLOGY'S ACQUAINTANCE WITH HUMAN-MICROBIAL ENCOUNTERS: INTERPRETATIONS AND METHODS

Andrea Butcher

EARLY ANTHROPOLOGY CONVENTIONALLY DEALT IN ACCOUNTS OF HOW human-material relations configure 'being human', developing theories to explain cultural organisation, social practices, symbolic systems and collective meaning-making. In this chapter, I ask whether early anthropology tells us anything about 'being microbial'. Do the ethnographies of yesteryear provide insights into how microbes have shaped social worlds and lives across time and space? As we explore the different ways that ethnography can give space and voice to our microscopic companions, I revisit ethnographies underpinned by classical anthropological approaches and search for evidence of how microbes are imagined, defined, explained and encountered cross-culturally.

I had initially planned to examine this question by revisiting classic structural anthropology texts dealing in notions of purity and pollution to search for hidden microbial transcripts (descriptions of microbial agency on the one hand, and the social, ritual and magical practices that determine the appropriate place for microbial matter on the other) lurking in these accounts. My chosen texts were Mary Douglas' *Purity and Danger* (1966) and Louis Dumont's *Homo Hierarchicus* (1972), given the emphasis on notions of purity, impurity and pollution within them. These texts deal with concepts of 'matter out of place', and being key in any anthropological training programme, I thought they were bound to yield hidden microbial transcripts. But after an initial review of the material, this didn't seem to be the case. Rather, they appeared to approach these questions via abstract, immaterial elements of cultural systems, with substance being incidental to rules governing social order and the maintenance of social boundaries.

Instead, I decided to look again at ethnographic texts that influenced my own enquiry during my doctoral research, in which I examined social transformation at the nexus of development, environment and Buddhist religious practice in Ladakh, the Indian Himalaya. These texts were authored by Sophie Day (1989), Martin Mills (2003), Stan Royal Mumford (1989) and Maria Phylactou (1989). With the exception of Mumford (1989), these ethnographies were conducted in Ladakhi villages during the 1980s and 1990s, prior to road connectivity to the urban centres of Leh and Kargil.[1] The site of Mumford's ethnography (1989) was the mountain valleys of Manang district in Nepal. Because these texts shared remarkably similar descriptions of the social and ritual landscape, they shaped my analysis of how democracy, global governance and planned development are conceptualised and performed in Himalayan Buddhist regions. My analysis was further influenced by a destructive cloudburst during the fieldwork phase in 2010, the causes of which were explained using concepts of purity and pollution defined by multiple climate perspectives: scientific, ethical (more specifically karmic) and autochthonous. Now that the direction of my own intellectual enquiry has turned towards knowing microbes, I consider here the ways my Ladakhi respondents might sense, and make sense of, these microscopic entities. If it is possible to discern autochthonous, ethical and scientific explanations in local descriptions of climate (Butcher 2017a), then why not an autochthonous and ethical microbiology?

Proponents of multispecies ethnographic and new materialist approaches pose new questions of matter, agency, ontology and relationality, making it possible to place microbes in more prominent ethnographic positions (Giraldo Herrera 2018; Gilbert, Sapp, and Tauber 2012; Haraway 2015; Hird 2009; Tsing et al. 2017). Where previously, microbes were treated as 'bare life' – without sentience and thus not capable of intentionality – these microscopic others are now permitted their own biographies and political lives (Giraldo Herrera 2018; Kirksey and Helmreich 2010). Inspired by these new ontological possibilities, I use this chapter to practice a microbial queering – or bacterialising – of old ethnography, re-evaluating my previous interpretations of cultural data by returning to earlier Himalayan Buddhist ethnographies to ask how things could be otherwise. I approach them with fresh eyes, searching for multispecies assemblages in my interpretation of landscape history in the Himalayan region of Ladakh, while retaining the binary categories of purity and pollution as optics for seeking out microbial transcripts in the descriptions of human and other-than-human nurturing or polluting behaviours, and their subsequent outcomes.

I begin by briefly examining the texts of Douglas (1966) and Dumont (1972), attending to some of the criticisms. I argue that their approach lacks a material and sensorial aspect, which I attempt to provide in the subsequent sections as I search for microbial transcripts lurking in ethnographic detail that indicate how human-microbial relations were (and continue to be) perceived and enacted. I then compare the ethnographic descriptions and the concepts used with new theories of human and microbial personhood being advanced by multispecies ethnographers and biology philosophers. I move on to ask if it is possible to 'bacterialise' old ethnography; whether by reinterpreting the symbolic underpinnings of discriminatory behaviours described, and representations of social order analysed, binaries can provide insights into the different ways human societies conceptualise and identify microscopic companions. I conclude by arguing that such an approach can elucidate perceptions of, and responses to, medical and ecological vulnerabilities in the Anthropocene.

STRUCTURAL ANTHROPOLOGY

Pink et al. (2015: 3) have asserted that in order '[t]o engage in a particular approach to ethnography, we need to have a theory of the world that we live in'. For structural anthropologists, that theory was rational, systematic, psychological and human. Structural anthropology rose to prominence in the post-war era of the twentieth century, departing from previous anthropological theory by privileging pattern over substance. Its principal protagonist, Claude Lévi-Strauss, wished to establish anthropology's credentials as a rational discipline of scientific repute. For Lévi-Strauss, anthropology's primary task was to reveal the underlying patterns of human thought, the characteristics of which he argued were universal, and which produced the cultural categories that carry social meaning and organise social relations. Influenced by Saussurean linguistics, Lévi-Strauss sought to understand the relationship between opposing ideas and their resolution via rules of marriage and kinship, mythology and ritual. He undertook this task through an analysis of ethnographic data in existing texts, rather than by conducting his own empirical research. What resulted was an elegant but highly abstract method for analysing cultural systems, built on rational rather than empirical foundations (Barnard 2000: 127).

This resolution of opposites set the tone for other structural anthropological enquiries. Douglas and Dumont both drew upon Lévi-Strauss' method for their own theorising. Like Lévi-Strauss, they compared ethnographic accounts, searching for patterns that (they argued) were shared cross-culturally (or in Dumont's case across the Hindu subcontinent). Both interpreted social relations as structured according to rules of inclusion and exclusion, boundary maintenance and a resolution of ambiguities. While both writers were interested in classifications of purity and pollution, both rejected the possibility that these structures had any foundation in pre-scientific conceptions of hygiene and public health. For example, in *Purity and Danger* (1966: 30), Douglas denied the existence of medical materialism as the cause of disease in the nineteenth century, arguing that prior to the establishment of germ theory any association with contemporary public health and hygiene codes was coincidental.[2] Instead, her analysis of dirt and order rested on observable patterns evidenced in the symbolic action of any given culture, 'primitive' or modern, which (she argued) had no hygienic basis for discrimination. In *Homo Hierarchicus* (1972: 60), Dumont similarly critiqued the reification of concepts of pure and impure with European epistemologies of hygiene, instead seeking out universal elements of the Hindu caste system and arguing that the notions and categories of purity and impurity evident in social hierarchies had an ideological rather than material or hygienic basis.

Contributors to this volume similarly trouble such hygienist reductionism, although where we diverge from Douglas and Dumont is over the question of whether a rejection of hygienist reductionism leads to the *a priori* assertion of an inability to perceive microbes. And if microbes can only be understood with reference to germ theory and public hygiene codes, does this render all relations with them essentially negative? Giraldo Herrera (2018: 89) suggests otherwise with his assertion that '[…] our relations with microbes are complex and not restricted to dealing with filth, disease, or contagion'. In his historical enquiry into the biosemiotics of Amerindian shamanism, Giraldo Herrera explored the possibility that microbes develop their own processes of interpretation, communication and meaning-making (ibid.). Critical of early anthropology's religious-symbolic reductionism (a hangover, he argues, of Judeo-Christian theology), Giraldo Herrera instead looks for continuities between animistic practices and modern scientific epistemologies (or what he calls syncretic ontologies), seeking out contact points between the knowledge of Amerindian shamans and scientific theories of contagion.[3] He argues that, rather than being *discovered* by the scientific revolution, microbes were instead observed and interpreted in *novel ways* by the scientific revolution and thus assigned *different characteristics* by it.

Giraldo Herrera's propositions resonate with my own re-evaluation of the way I had been interpreting Himalayan Buddhist social worlds, and I keep them in mind during my search for hidden microbial transcripts in the chosen ethnographies. In their work, each writer attends to different aspects of village life. For example, Day (1989) examines the phenomenon of the oracle (the possession of human bodies by territorial divinities) and the liminal position of village oracles between diagnoses of demonic affliction on the one hand, and the reverence offered to monastic oracles on the other. Phylactou (1989) examines both the familial and architectural structures of household organisation and marriage as ritual exchange. Her analysis focuses on how the symbolism observable in social and architectural structures mirrors representations of local cosmology and the different planes of activity therein. Mumford (1989) analyses Buddhist monasticism in a Nepalese village and its ongoing dialogue with an older shamanic practice of a neighbouring village. His ethnography produced insights into how Buddhist authority in Tibetan communities rests on the ability of monastic incumbents to control terrestrial – or chthonic – divinities. Mills expands upon this with his examination of the nature of authority in Tibetan Buddhist monasticism, the foundations of which, he argues, rest on a concept of personhood in which people are embedded within and constituted by 'a matrix of chthonic forces and sources of symbolic power' (2003: 243).

In their own way, each of these ethnographies demonstrated the historical and intimate connection between human activity and the demeanour of these other-than-human entities who are instrumental in determining the fortunes of worldly endeavours (a theme that I extended to practices of the local development institutions, see Butcher 2015). The authors analysed their data religio-symbolically for the most part, examining concepts of order and disorder, boundaries, and social and ritual practices, like Douglas and Dumont. Despite their distinct focuses, their descriptions of cosmology and numinal entities were almost identical. I therefore practise a reinterpretation of the ethnographic data in relation to descriptions of environments where microbes reside, and the relationships Himalayan Buddhist persons have with them. It is also possible (and presumably more plausible) to search for microbial transcripts in practices of Sowa Rigpa (the Tibetan Buddhist system of medicine) or in the geomantic rituals that are influenced by the Chinese astrological system. For reasons of space, I concentrate on social relations and ritual practices relating to my doctoral research – managing climates and environments in challenging times. These include environments and elements whose microbiomes are the subject of scientific scrutiny, for example soils and water (e.g. Bass et al. 2019). They also include atmospheres through the concept of bioprecipitation, or rainmaking bacteria (Morris et al. 2014), whereby bacteria living on plant surfaces are disturbed (whether by winds or human-related activities such as harvesting) and carried into the atmosphere where they provoke precipitation in the form of rain, snow or hail (Giraldo Herrera 2018; Schnell and Tan-Schnell 1982). Similarly, earth systems and Gaian theory demonstrates how atmospheric regulation is a multispecies biotic endeavour that bacteria participate in (Hird 2009: 120; Tsing 2015: 22). As we shall see in the ethnographies, local weather conditions are also the subject of blessing and pollution concerns, and relations with chthonic divinities.

THE FIELD

Ladakh is a high-altitude desert in India's Western Himalaya. The region was an independent Buddhist kingdom with monastic links to Tibet until 1846, when it was annexed by the Dogra rulers of Jammu during the British Imperial period. The territory was absorbed into the Indian Union in 1947; it formed part of the State of Jammu and Kashmir until 2019, when it was granted Union Territory status and separated from the rest of the State. Ladakh's Buddhist demographic has the majority but only just; there is also a sizeable Muslim population, a small Christian population and a strong military presence due to its position on disputed border territories with Pakistan and China. Prior to 1947, the mainstay of Ladakh's economy was agriculture, with some modest trade links towards China in the East and Central Asia to the West. Agriculture was fed by glacial melt waters, with households cultivating the few grains and vegetables hardy enough to withstand the harsh growing conditions. Once part of the Indian Union, Ladakh became the recipient of state-led development interventions, and the economy has since diversified to include military, administrative and NGO occupations, with further employment opportunities offered by its formidable tourist sector. Until recently, Ladakh's climate was characterised by long, frozen winters (with night-time temperatures plummeting to -20°C or below) and warm, dry summers. Over the past 15 years, however, the region has experienced warmer, more humid winters and the intrusion of the Indian monsoon in summertime months.

Once open to foreign visitors in 1973, Ladakh began attracting Tibetologists along with other academic and independent researchers, lured by the ease of access compared to the now restricted Tibetan plateau, and the opportunities for researching Tibetan monasticism – and the village life attached to it – *in situ*. As a result, a wealth of literature exists on social life in the region, ranging from village ethnographies to contemporary studies of climate and the environment, religion and cultural heritage, and the implications of political change and development. My research straddled each of these themes, building upon previous ethnographic work that explicitly connected the practices of Tibetan monasticism to the formation and maintenance of relationships in an autochthonous social world (Day 1989; Mills 2003; Mumford 1987; Phylactou 1989). I was interested in how these relationships were being reshaped as part of the experience of Indian statehood and planned development (Butcher 2015, 2017a, 2017b). As stated already, as my research progressed, I began questioning whether it was accurate to apprehend autochthonous entities in purely religious terms, noting instead epistemological confluence in descriptions of what 'made' weather (Butcher 2017a). The shift occurred following the 2010 cloudburst and subsequent flash flooding, which claimed 300 human lives,[4] unknown animal and livestock lives, and devastated property and farmland. Following the disaster, I kept hearing how the *lha-lu* – the mountain deities and autochthonous inhabitants of the region – had sent the flood, a retributive act protesting at the ritual, moral and material pollution caused by human activities.

Now, I am interested in whether divine retributive explanations can also take on a biological form, for example in accounts of ecological damage and infectious diseases sent by chthonic entities with guardianship over rocks, trees, soils, water, foodstuffs and medicinal plants. In the following section, I invite the reader to conceptualise a social world in which the descriptions of these entities can be interpreted as more than symbolic (even as they are mediated symbolically), and that despite being institutionalised in household, village, and monastic ritual practices, microbes are indeed lurking in the detail.

HIDDEN MICROBIAL TRANSCRIPTS

A principal theme running through all descriptions of Tibetan Buddhist social and cultural life is the ritual relationship that individuals, lay households and temple households (monasteries, in other words) have with the chthonic inhabitants with whom they share their domain – the mountain deities, soil owners and water spirits. While there is much variation in classification and nomenclature of deity cults across the Himalaya, a ubiquitous feature is the partition of physical space into a three-tiered cosmology of a heavenly realm (*stenglha*), a middle realm (*barsam*), and a watery underworld (*yoklu*). These are distinct realms with distinct inhabitants. Nevertheless, they are interconnected, and activities in the middle realm, where humans and animals reside, have consequences for the upper and lower realms. Conversely, inhabitants of these realms can determine the conditions of the middle realm such as health, wealth, fertility and climate. In Ladakh, for example, the mountain divinities residing in the heavenly realm, the *yullha*, are guardians of the physical domain. They control weather and water, sending snow in the winter and sun in the spring to melt the snow and irrigate the crops. They have authority over minor spirits in the lower realms, so it is important not to offend them. The lower realms, the *yoklu*, are home to the landlords of the soil or 'foundation owners' (*sadag* and *zhidag*), and the water spirits (*lu*). Represented as fish, snakes or lizards, these entities inhabit soils, plants and water, and are associated with fertility, abundance and nourishment. Also, as Day (1989: 62) points out, they belong to the annual cycle of renewal, growth, depletion and death. Further divinities of note are the household gods, or *p'alha*. The *p'alha* are sensitive to the breaching of household boundaries, for example during liminal states of birth, marriage and death. Their shrines, located at the apex of the house, contain a vase filled with grain and pierced by an arrow, symbolising the fertility and wealth of the household. During the annual renewal of the vase's contents, swollen grain is a sign of successful harvest, while dehydrated and rotten grains indicate problems for the household (Day 1989: 159; Mills 2003: 158; Phylactou 1989: 76).

Boundaries of the realms are regularly crossed, for example *yullha* are brought down and housed in shrines on mountain passes or at the peak of the village.

Many are pressed into service as defenders of the Buddhist doctrine, with some appearing as oracles to assist monastic rulers in their daily ministrations (Day 1989; Mills 2003; Mumford 1989). Others form part of the healthcare system, offering diagnoses for bodily afflictions, remedies for the removal of poisons and so forth (Day 1989; Mills 2003). The boundaries can be crossed in the opposite direction as well; in Ladakh some *yullha* are believed to be Buddhist monks and nuns (Mills 2003: 249), while in other parts of the Himalaya they are local ancestors (Yeh and Coggins 2014). Purification of demonic entities signifies another cosmological boundary shift (Day 1989). Similarly, the *lu* follow families into their homes, where they watch over grain stores and the kitchen hearth where the stove is placed (ibid.: 63). Thus, the success of agriculture, preservation of food, and the health and wealth of the household are reliant on maintaining friendly relations with the chthonic inhabitants with whom villagers share the realm. However, these entities are highly sensitive to offensive pollution of various kinds, and the ritual removal of pollution is a continuous activity in the middle realm.

Blessing and pollution

Matter in and out of place is either sanctified or afflicted by invisible sources of blessing and misfortune: *chinlab* and *dip*. Both essences are made manifest by human activities occurring in the middle realm, for example embodied practices of devotion, or polluting practices associated with agriculture, foodstuffs, animal husbandry and construction (including of temples and shrines). Yet bodies and matter associated with all three realms – humans, non-human animals, soils, water and weather – are sensitive to their effects. Mumford's ethnography (1989: 97) describes *chinlab* as an essence from a primal era of blessing, traces of which are found in the present. Sources of *chinlab* include sacred valleys, mountains or lakes, and caves where incarnate masters are said to have meditated (ibid.: 97). Buddhist stupas, statues and enlightened masters (for example the Dalai Lamas, and other high masters or reincarnated yogins) are containers for *chinlab*. *Chinlab* can be planted; for example, when water, soil or herbal medicines gathered from sacred sites are 'brought back to the village to empower the health of the family or to be put into the fields to make them more fertile' (Mumford 1989: 77). Ethnographic accounts describe *chinlab* as falling like rain, or flowing like a stream from above, cleansing and purifying the territory and its inhabitants and creating the proper conditions for agriculture (Day 1989: 57; Mills 2003: 160; Mumford 1989: 97; Phylactou 1989: 62).

Conversely, health afflictions and unfortunate events are attributed to *chinlab's* opposite, *dip*, a polluting essence that accumulates in individual bodies, households and territories. *Dip* results from activities that are ritually polluting, for example when social hierarchies are undermined or household and cosmological boundaries are crossed (Day 1989; Phylactou 1989). Morally or karmically polluting character traits include selfishness and failure to respect the Buddhist teachings. However, *dip* also manifests when certain activities are performed without due concern for the welfare of chthonic entities, thus causing offence. Mumford (1989: 101–02) describes offences and harm towards them that require human action to repair the damage: poisoning lakes and digging the earth, or urinating, defecating and washing too close to their homes. One must seek permission from the foundation owners (*sadag* and *zhidag*) before digging the land for agriculture or construction. These concerns remain today, with development personnel expressing concern that people were no longer seeking chthonic permission ahead of activities such as implementing novel agricultural interventions (Butcher 2015). Furthermore, people were concerned that new kinds of economic activity were creating new forms of pollution that offended their chthonic neighbours, for example poor sanitation infrastructures and solid waste disposal, or exhausts emitted by motor vehicles and aeroplanes due to unregulated urbanisation and an expanding tourist sector (Butcher 2017b). Increasing numbers of tourists and military personnel caused further unease; as visitors, these groups do not understand how to behave in places where the chthonic entities reside, defiling their homes by throwing rubbish or urinating and defecating close to streams, lakes, shrines or on high passes.

Such pollution invites dangerous retribution from the various guardians of weather, water and soils. Individual cases of *dip* are experienced as skin diseases such as such as boils, leprosy and so forth, inflicted upon them by capricious *sadag* and *lu* (Mumford 1989: 101–2; Mills 2003: 289). When *dip* contaminates the territorial homes of mountain deities, they become offended and dangerously retributive, sending afflictions in the form of pestilence or disasters such as earthquakes, avalanches, hailstorms and floods, for example the 2010 cloudburst (Butcher 2013; Mills 2003: 206; Mumford 1989: 135–7). Many of my own respondents were concerned that new forms of pollution produced by economic activities and social practices associated with Indian state development were stimulating greater concentrations and widespread distribution of *dip*. They were afraid that the *lha-lu* were becoming increasingly offended by changes in physical, ritual (and karmic!) pollution, and this was making them dangerously retributive, sending warmer winters, less snowmelt for irrigation, and devastating rainfall (Butcher 2013, 2017a). They complained of deteriorating water quality or new illnesses that local practitioners of the Tibetan medicine system did not recognise and thus could not diagnose or treat (2009, personal communication). Without the support of these invisible entities, productive and reproductive life was not possible. Indian state development now forms part of productive and reproductive life.

Restoring order

Restoring normal relations with chthonic village folk requires ritual remediation to eliminate or neutralise pollution and restore blessing. This is managed either with immediate or daily removal (for example purification of households and temples with juniper smoke or offerings of water for bathing the divinities), purification ceremonies (following a ritually determined period of confinement) or activities to restore blessing (such as prostration, circumambulation, or similar performances of veneration). However, it can also take the form of offerings made as apologies, which can include foods known for their beneficial microbial communities, such as barley dough, fermented foods such as beer (Day 1989: 137, 145; Mumford 1989: 128; Phylactou 1989: 137) or white sweet foods such as milk and yoghurt (Day 1989: 63; Mumford 1989: 101–2;

Phylactou 1989: 56). More recently, the response to stronger, more destructive concentrations of *dip* has been to increase the frequency and intensity of ceremonies and performances for replenishing *chinlab*. These mainly take the conventional form of financial sponsorship of new statues, stupas, or participation in mass prayer festivals. However, novel activities associated with climatic and environmental protection are also increasingly in evidence, such as the record-breaking tree-planting events organised by international social movement 'Live to Love' in 2010 and 2012, when the movement's founder, exiled Tibetan religious leader the Gyalwang Drukpa, simultaneously performed religious empowerments (Butcher 2017a). Local residents associated both the establishment of these immature woodlands and the attendant empowerment ceremonies with the cleansing and purification of atmosphere where the *yullha* have their homes, thus restoring their friendship and preventing a recurrence of the terrible cloudburst that occurred in 2010 (ibid.).

CHTHONIC PERSONS

Regional anthropologists (myself included) have translated the entities inhabiting this lively autochthonous domain as kinds of numina. Relationships with them continue to be mediated using symbolic sources of power in a ritualised environment conditioned by concepts of blessing and pollution. Humans are conceived as chthonic persons (Mills 2003), intimately bound to the other-than-humans with whom they share residence in the tripartite cosmology, and who can nurture *chinlab*, generate pollution or invite retributive action. Put another way, people's behaviours either nurture health and abundance or produce dangerous situations of dearth and dysbiosis, while these invisible chthonic entities are associated with elements whose microbiomes are the subject of scientific scrutiny. This hints at some kind of microbial relationship – for better or for worse.

Here, I briefly compare the ethnographic details presented above to alternative concepts of both microbial *and* human personhood being posited by multispecies ethnographers and science philosophers, to seek out resonance and fresh interpretive possibilities. Giraldo Herrera (2018: 69–71) invites us to perceive the 'cellular souls and microbial spirits' inhabiting and participating in an environment that includes human and non-human animals, plants, soils, water sources, atmospheres and so forth. These cellular souls and microbial spirits attack, appease, communicate, take advantage of and compete for resources (ibid.: 71). They reproduce and proliferate under favourable conditions, sleep when resources are scarce, direct currents of air and determine precipitation (ibid.). Giraldo Herrera's explanations are analogous to the descriptions found in the ethnographies examined above, in which the writers illustrate the different ways that Ladakh's chthonic persons interact to influence the conditions and dynamics of the elements. *Yullha* send snowmelt and rain to fall onto the ground below, rendering it fertile; the *sadag*, *zhidag*, and *lu* nourish the soils, nurture agriculture and watch over stored foods, preventing them from spoiling. The ethnographies go as far as describing their winter hibernation when the ground is frozen and resources are low (Day 1989: 62; Mumford 1989: 104; Phylactou 1989: 56). They are sensitive to environmental pollution, leading to dangerously retributive action that includes meteorological events such as cloudbursts and hailstorms (Butcher 2013, 2015, 2017b). Failure to make appropriate reparations results in skin diseases, failed harvests and ecological ruin (Day 1989: 470; Mills 2003: 289; Mumford 1989: 101–2; Phylactou 1989: 57). These beings have intention, social hierarchies, processes of interpretation and ways of making sense of the world, qualities that Giraldo Herrera claims microbes also possess (2018: viii, 41).

Mills' (2003) concept of chthonic personhood resonates with novel theories of immunity and identity. Mills examined chthonic personhood in the context of Buddhist ritual practice and monastic authority, although I suggest one can also read this concept microbially. He described Lingshed's villagers as belonging to a 'fertile chthonic territory' (ibid.: 249), embedded in ritual relations with a variety of divinities and numina – a situated and distributed chthonic agency, where absolute separation between humans and territorial divinities cannot be assumed. This latter point is explained using the anthropological theory of gift exchange whereby, during ritual offerings, some essence of the giver is also transferred:

> In the Himalayan context, the complex and life supporting relations of exchange between man and landscape [...] means that both the concerns and the identity of the supernatural and the human become intertwined (ibid.: 258).

This ecological representation of chthonic agency, encapsulating human and other-than-human actors and their capacities, chimes with new philosophical and biological insights into human-microbial relations that challenge normative definitions of identity and the discrete individual. For example, new theories of immunology posit mammalian organisms to be heterogeneous ecosystems, comprising microbial as well as mammalian cells and genes (Giraldo Herrera 2018: 69; Lorimer 2016; Pradeu 2012). These organisms are constantly interacting with, open to, and partially constituted by their environments via openings in the digestive, reproductive, excretory and respiratory systems (Pradeu 2012). Bioscientists David Bass et al. (2019), philosophers of biology Méthot and Alizon (2014) and more-than-human geographer Jamie Lorimer (2016) each examine the role environmental and human microbiomes play in regulating health and metabolic processes. These writers use *ecological* models for human-animal-microbe relations, in which health or disease are a consequence of the dynamic interaction of multiple symbionts, host and environment. Gilbert, Sapp and Tauber (2012) use their holobiont (multicellular eukaryotes plus their microbial symbionts) concept to challenge normative biological categorisations of living entities. I suggest the holobiont also challenges anthropological categorisations of other-than-human behaviour as numinal, for example where diagnostic practice, disease causality and cure are interpreted as supernatural presence. Nor would it be possible to discuss chthonic persons without reference to science feminist Donna Haraway's proposal to engage in a process of re-worlding in the chthulucene, an epoch of sympoetic (becoming with) collaborations between humans and multiple chthonic companions for overcoming the diverse planetary systems crises wrought by the Anthropocene (2015: 160). Through these examples, the concept of chthonic personhood resonates with Lorimer's (2016: 58) statement that 'being human is a multi-species achievement'.

I am aware of the dangers of reifying evidence to suit an argument. For reasons of space, I have made highly discriminative decisions about which practices to foreground, and as a result I have inevitably simplified descriptions and sidestepped nuances, which readers familiar with the Buddhist Himalaya will find frustrating. Many blessing and pollution manifestations cannot be attributed to microbial activity, and in these cases numinal explanations may more accurately reflect local concepts of world-making. Nevertheless, I hope also to have demonstrated that by analysing chthonic persons using religious concepts we similarly make assumptions about their numinal nature, and that reinterpretations foregrounding the possibility of microbial sensing can produce what Giraldo Herrera (2018: 81) describes as 'alternative sources that bring additional perspectives through which we can address the reality and history of microorganisms'. I suggest that a microbial sensing of conditions is discernible in the ethnographies; soils, water, plants, food and even atmospheres all are places where microbes reside, interact, share information and evolve. *Sadag, lu,* microbes: all are invisible but lively social entities that can pollute, are affected by pollution and can respond in dysbiotic ways. They spoil food, cause disease and generate dangerous cloudbursts. They also grant fertility, nourish bodies and nurture earthly abundance. Analysing ethnographies from the perspective that people *can* sense microbes, *can* perceive their activities in particular environments, and that people become *with* microbes opens up possibilities for a more microbial understanding. It enables us to ask new questions of data and provides situated knowledge and explanations in circumstances of bodily and ecological dysbiosis, and the new human-microbial collaborations being forged therein.

BACTERIALISING OLD ETHNOGRAPHY

If engaging in a particular approach to ethnography requires a theory of the world that we live in (Pink et al. 2015: 3), then in a dynamic and ever-changing world our theories need to be malleable and accommodating. Historically in anthropology, concepts of purity and pollution – and the matters and practices associated with them – have been analysed as religio-symbolic systems, which anthropologists utilised to draw inferences about structure and order in human societies. As shown above, new ways of thinking offered by new theories of immunology, biological identity and multispecies approaches are changing the way we think about microbes as lively entities, and our relationships with them. Therefore, if we are moving to more ecological and relational interpretations of human-microbe relations, is there any value in 'bacterialising' binaries in ethnographic data? Do concepts of purity and pollution still retain theoretical and methodological purpose?

I would say yes, depending on what the researcher wants to achieve. Douglas and Dumont approached social organisation from the concept of purity and impurity, which they applied to their search for patterns of behaviour and order in kinship rules, hierarchy, classification of matter and so forth. By retaining purity and pollution as symbolic concepts (as I have done here), we can find patches of data that shed light on how microbes have shaped social worlds and social lives across time and space; how they have been imagined, defined, explained and encountered cross-culturally, and their value for interpreting human-microbial experiences and relationships in the Anthropocene. In their collection of essays examining different *Arts of Living on a Damaged Planet,* Tsing et al. (2017) request that we pay attention to the multiple living arrangements of the human and more-than-human, using them to develop tools and methods for collaborative survival in a 'more-than-human Anthropocene'. Using binaries such as pure and impure, or blessing and decay when searching for transcripts of human-microbial entanglements in previous ethnographic records helps us understand how different human societies conceptualise their worlds and relationships with the microscopic, and the multiple ways that humans and microbes experience and respond to crises of climate, ecology, medicine and health (either collaboratively or in tension). We can use binaries to follow how narratives, practices and explanations persist, shift or become entangled with other epistemologies of the Anthropocene found in the life and political sciences. In the Himalayas, are current health controversies such as antimicrobial resistance or viral pandemics being explained according to the presence of *chinlab* and *dip*? Are microbial transcripts apparent in the creation of storms being classified as forms of localised chthonic retributive action? When anthropologist Nils

Bubandt states how '[i]n the Anthropocene, both climate science and biology seem to bring spirits, once thought to have been killed by secular thought, back to life [...]' (2017: 125), can a microbial interpretation turn those numina into *cellular* souls and *microbial* spirits?

Mary Douglas' denial of medical materialism in premodern societies rested on the assumption that if microbes were the product of nineteenth century scientific discovery, they could not also be ontologically prior. How could her subjects possess the ability to sense microbes if they had not yet been 'discovered' and subsequently cultured in nineteenth century French laboratories? I have explored the possibility that the capacity to sense microbial practices is discernible in ethnographic descriptions of daily activities, ritual cycles, explanations of fortune and misfortune and descriptions of agricultural abundance. I have suggested retaining the binary concepts of purity and pollution where they attend to embodied practices and interactions, modes of relations, methods of discrimination, situated theories, cosmological representations and so forth. I hope to have demonstrated how, by returning to old anthropological accounts and recycling older concepts, ethnographers can produce fresh insights into how human-microbial relations were (and continue to be) perceived and enacted.

TRANSCRIPTION NOTE

There are wide variations in pronunciation across the region. I have transcribed local terms according to Western Ladakhi pronunciation.

NOTES

1 The village of Lingshed, where Mills (2003) conducted his ethnography, still lacks road connectivity.

2 Bruno Latour made a similar argument in his examination of how germ theory was established as the basis for hygiene practices and public health legislation, stating that microbes did not exist before 'Pasteur made them up' (1999: 147). In this ontological reasoning, microbes were brought into existence via the tools and the purpose of scientific

discovery: the microscopes, scientific experiments, and the subsequent legislation governing microbial management in the public sphere.

3 Giraldo Herrera also criticises the radical alterity proposed by proponents of the ontological turn for its comparable separation of different modes of thought and being, which he argues removes the possibility for circulation and cross-fertilisation of ideas (2018: 3–8).

4 According to official figures at least, the true number will never be known.

REFERENCES

Barnard, A., *History and Theory in Anthropology* (Cambridge: Cambridge University Press, 2000).

Bass, D., and others, 'The Pathobiome in Animal and Plant Diseases', *Trends in Ecology and Evolution,* 34 (2019), 996–1008.

Bubandt, N., 'Haunted Geologies: Spirits, Stones and the Necropolitics of the Anthropocene', in Tsing, A. L. and others, eds, *Arts of Living on a Damaged Planet* (Minneapolis: University of Minnesota Press, 2017), pp. 121–141.

Butcher, A., 'Keeping the Faith: Divine Protection and Flood Prevention in Modern Buddhist Ladakh', *Worldviews,* 17 (2013), 103–14.

——— 'Ceremonial Activities in Secular Development: The Spiritual "Problems" for Ladakh's Secular Encounter', *The Tibet Journal,* 40 (2015), 197–220.

——— 'Networks of Weather and Climate Interventions in the Western Himalaya', *European Bulletin for Himalayan Research,* 49 (2017a), 5–35.

——— 'Development, Wellbeing and Perceptions of the "Expert" in Ladakh, North-West India', *Anthropology in Action,* 24 (2017b), 22–31.

Day, S., 'Embodying Spirits: Village Oracles and Possession Ritual in Ladakh, North India' (PhD Thesis, London School of Economics, 1989) <https://ethos.bl.uk/OrderDetails.do?did=1&uin=uk.bl.ethos.318353> [accessed 30 March 2011].

Douglas, M., *Purity and Danger: An Analysis of the Concepts of Pollution and Taboo* (New York: Routledge, 1966).

Dumont, L., *Homo Hierarchicus: The Caste System and its Implications* (Oxford and New York: Oxford University Press, 1972).

Gilbert, S. F., J. Sapp, and A. I. Tauber, 'A Symbiotic View of Life: We Have Never Been Individuals', *The Quarterly Review of Biology,* 87 (2012), 325–41.

Giraldo Herrera, C. E., *Microbes and Other Shamanic Beings* (Basingstoke: Palgrave Macmillan, 2018).

Haraway, D. J., 'Anthropocene, Capitalocene, Plantationocene, Chthulucene: Making Kin', *Environmental Humanities,* 6 (2015), 159–65.

Hird, M. J., *The Origins of Sociable Life: Evolution After Science Studies* (Basingstoke, New York: Palgrave MacMillan, 2009).

Latour, B., *Pandora's Hope: Essays on the Reality of Science Studies* (Cambridge, MA: Harvard University Press, 1999).

Kirksey, S. E., and S. Helmreich, 'The Emergence of Multispecies Ethnography', *Cultural Anthropology*, 25 (2010), 545–76.

Lorimer, J., 'Gut Buddies: Multispecies Studies and the Microbiome', *Environmental Humanities*, 8 (2016), 57–76.

Méthot, P.-O., and S. Alizon, 'What is a Pathogen? Towards a Process View of Host-Parasite Interactions', *Virulence*, 5 (2014), 775–85.

Mills, M. A., *Identity, Ritual and State in Tibetan Buddhism: The Foundations of Authority in Gelukpa Monasticism* (Abingdon: Routledge Curzon, 2003).

Morris, C. E., and others, 'Bioprecipitation: A Feedback Cycle Linking Earth History, Ecosystem Dynamics and Land Use Through Biological Ice Nucleators in the Atmosphere', *Global Change Biology*, 20 (2014), 341–51.

Mumford, S. R., *Himalayan Dialogue: Tibetan Lamas and Gurung Shamans in Nepal* (Madison: University of Wisconsin Press, 1989).

Phylactou, M., 'Household Organisation and Marriage in Ladakh, Indian Himalaya' (PhD Thesis, University of London, 1989) <https://ethos.bl.uk/OrderDetails.do?did=1&uin=uk.bl.ethos.261706E> [accessed 11 August 2011].

Pink, S., and others, eds, *Digital Ethnography: Principles and Practice* (Los Angeles: Sage Publishing Limited, 2015).

Pradeu, T., trans. by E. Vintanza, *The Limits of the Self: Immunology and Biological Identity* (Oxford and New York: Oxford University Press, 2012).

Schnell, R. C., and S. N. Tan-Schnell, 'Kenya Tea Litter: A Source of Ice Nuclei', *Tellus*, 34 (1982), 92–5.

Tsing, A. L., and others, eds, *Arts of Living on a Damaged Planet* (Minneapolis: University of Minnesota Press, 2017).

Tsing, A. L., *The Mushroom at the End of the World: On the Possibility of Life in Capitalist Ruins* (Princeton, Oxford: Princeton University Press, 2015).

Yeh, E. T., and C. Coggins, eds, *Mapping Shangri La: Contested Landscapes in the Sino-Tibetan Borderlands* (Seattle: University of Washington Press, 2014).

MATTERING PRESS TITLES

CPSIA information can be obtained
at www.ICGtesting.com
Printed in the USA
LVHW042350291221
707460LV00008B/978

9 781912 729180